50 FACTS EVERYONE SHOULD KNOW ABOUT CRIME AND PUNISHMENT IN BRITAIN

James Treadwell and Adam Lynes

First published in Great Britain in 2019 by

Policy Press
University of Bristol
1-9 Old Park Hill
Bristol
BS2 8BB
UK
t: +44 (0)117 954 5940
pp-info@bristol.ac.uk
www.policypress.co.uk

North America office:
Policy Press
c/o The University of Chicago Press
1427 East 60th Street
Chicago, IL 60637, USA
t: +1 773 702 7700
f: +1 773 702 9756
sales@press.uchicago.edu
www.press.uchicago.edu

British Library Cataloguing in Publication Data
A catalogue record for this book is available from the British Library.

Library of Congress Cataloging-in-Publication Data
A catalog record for this book has been requested.

ISBN 978-1-4473-4381-3 paperback
ISBN 978-1-4473-4383-7 ePub
ISBN 978-1-4473-4384-4 Mobi
ISBN 978-1-4473-4382-0 ePdf

The right of Adam Lynes and James Treadwell to be identified as editors of this work has been asserted by them in accordance with the Copyright, Designs and Patents Act 1988.

Cover design by Lyn Davies
Printed and bound in Great Britain by Clays Ltd, Elcograf S.p.A
Policy Press uses environmentally responsible print partners

Contents

Part One: Historical context

Part Two: Crime in Britain today

Part Three: International comparisons

Part Four: The police

Part Five: Prison realities

Part Six: Criminal justice

Part Seven: Black market Britain

Part Eight: Violent Britain

can in the boxing ring

Part Nine: Victims

Part Ten: Crime and technology

Notes on the editors

Dr Adam Lynes is a Senior Lecturer in Criminology at Birmingham City University, where he has taught since 2012, covering topics from criminological theory to organised and violent crime. He has published research focusing on violent crimes such as serial murder, family annihilation and organised crime. He is also the lead for the Crime, Culture and Contemporary Media research cluster for the Centre for Applied Criminology.

James Treadwell is Professor in Criminology at Staffordshire University since 2017, having started his career as a Lecturer in Criminology in 2003 at the University of Central England. He has recently been researching prison and criminal drugs markets, examining the cultivation of cannabis in economically deprived areas and prison-based drug supply as part of a larger project on bullying, violence and victimisation in prison. He is also a member of the executive with the British Society of Criminology, and was Academic Advisor on the Howard League Commission into Ex-Military Personnel in Prison.

Introduction

Upon embarking on this journey of compiling facts about crime-related matters from contemporary issues in prisons to crime and its victims, a quote from one of the earliest pioneers in academic populism, Carl Sagan came to mind:

> We wish to find the truth, no matter where it lies. But to find the truth we need imagination and skepticism both. We will not be afraid to speculate, but we will be careful to distinguish speculation from fact. (Carl Sagan (1980) *Cosmos: a Personal Voyage*, Episode 1)

Clearly, Sagan was framing this eloquent statement around the scientific pursuit for knowledge about the Universe and our place within it, and not about crime per se. This book is indeed focused on the topic of crime and criminal justice, yet Sagan's words provide an important reminder that this assortment of 'facts' consists of countless voices – each trying to influence and shape how we perceive crime, criminals and its victims, while attempting not to drown and be silenced by all the others.

'Facts' can be myth busting or truth revealing. The term 'fact' can, of course, have different meanings in different contexts: a fact may sometimes have been presented as an absolute fact (a truth that is uncontested) or as a relative fact, and yet, what constitutes the parameters of truth or fact can be contested in all realms. The language of criminology and academia necessarily often deals in caveats, where estimates, approximates, averages and suggestions are cautiously preferred to grand and sweeping claims that might be proven falsehoods.

Crime is also an emotive subject, where values, morals, ethics, beliefs, views and opinions sit alongside fact. What constitutes a fact in criminology is rightly often contested. Hence we have used the term 'facts' here not to introduce the readers to absolute or uncontested topics, but rather to attempt to frame a broad discussion that involves 50 academics, some well established, some earlier in their careers, writing accessibly on issues on which they are knowledgeable.

The text is in many ways a provocation. It was conceived as an attempt to give readers an accessible introduction to the topics of crime and punishment in Britain today. What appears here are several discussions around crime and the criminal justice system, where the term 'fact' is broadly used to take accepted wisdom and then discuss that critically in a bid to get readers to think more deeply about issues. Yet how to structure this is, in and of itself, not unproblematic.

The Ministry of Justice is a ministerial department of the British government, and while historically people may have asserted that 'British justice is the finest in the world', the organisation of England and Wales, Scotland and Northern Ireland into separate legal systems already means that to talk of crime in Britain is problematic. That does not stop the term being used. For example, Former Lord Chancellor Charles Falconer lamented in February 2018 in the *Guardian* that 'British justice is in flames. The MoJ's fiddling is criminal' (Falconer, 2018).

Yet perhaps our first fact ought to be that British justice is problematic. While clearly it is acceptable to talk of crime and punishment in Britain (and that is what we have attempted to do, and we have tried to make it clear when details relate to England and Wales and the criminal justice system in that context), the legal system in Britain is not structured so as to unite England, Wales, Scotland and Northern Ireland, which in actuality have separate legal systems.

We have attempted to be accurate, presenting material so as to be clear, but the spirit of this text is one that encourages critical engagement, and to encourage the reader not to simply accept at face value what is claimed as fact. In particular, the social sciences are often presented as dealing with facts, when in reality they are a framework for interpreting, systemising and predicting future outcomes based on empirical observations.

This of course brings us to a vital question: what is a fact?

In simple terms, a fact is a statement of knowledge that is true or can be proved with evidence. The usual test for a statement of fact is verifiability – that is, whether it can be demonstrated to correspond to experience. But what is useful in some ways, in establishing facts, is to consider them as opposed to opinion, rooted in speculation and conjecture, for the facts at least are produced in conjunction with research and study, rather than intuition alone.

This book was driven by two connected aims. First, it was intended to give those new to criminology, or interested in it, an accessible introduction to some the issues and topics encountered in academic criminology that captured something of the diversity of the core subject matter, while also highlighting the variation in debates that are encountered within it. Second, we aspire to help to create a better general knowledge and wider debate about some of the core issues in relation to crime and punishment in Britain.

A 'fact' can, on occasion, get lost to hyperbole, feeling, conjecture, speculation and so-called 'common sense'. With this in mind, we will occasionally have to resort to estimates or arguments that are controversial and contested. We ask our readers, therefore, to approach the text here with a critical mind, undertaking an objective evaluation of what is presented in order to form their own views and judgements, because we would suggest that this is the very essence of studying crime, criminal justice and criminology as an academic subject.

Yet when it comes to debates on crime and punishment, it is important that we do not simply descend into populist and common sense arguments, built solely on emotion or gut feeling. That is not to deny the place of emotion or common sense, but rather to suggest that sometimes in the social sciences, the evidence and reality might be counter-intuitive – what at first appears to be the case may not be, when we look at empirical evidence. Yet the desire to do that seems to be under attack.

Recently, on both sides of the Atlantic, political arenas have been transformed into hotbeds of misinformation. What better term to capture this than the contemporary mantra of 'alternative facts', a phrase used by US Counselor to President Trump, Kellyanne Conway, in a press interview on 22 January 2017, in which she defended White House Press Secretary Sean Spicer's false statement about the attendance numbers at inauguration (Swaine, 2017). Debate rages in academic settings such as the university campus as a place of contentious and controversial ideas, not least those involving crime and criminal justice. Take, for instance, debates about 'no platforming' against the freedom to give what some might regard as offensive views airing in university settings – for example, the scientific basis of gender and transgender identity, or the links between ideological or religious doctrines and violent extremism, which have become increasingly debated public issues.

We do not want to dwell on our view of the damage caused to the social sciences by liberal postmodernism, and the extreme ends of the denial of truth. Yet it seems that social science remains locked in a constructivist mode, and taken to its extreme end, any 'fact' can simply be merely a social construction. Even gravity can be regarded as a social construction rather than a fact (unless you jump from the top of a skyscraper). Ultimately, the business of academic criminology is not one that claims to be unscientific, so dealing in facts becomes something of a necessity. We must start somewhere, and we would hope that those drawn to social science like criminology can see the merits of basing evidence on empirical data rather than raw appeals to emotion.

While it is right to debate facts, there is a strong imperative, in this epoch of growing anti-intellectualism, to stick fast to high ethical and intellectual standards and to encourage debate that is rooted in empirical evidence. That is what we hope the facts in this book do.

Today, we face an array, an overload of information and misinformation. How do we separate myth from reality, fact from speculation, conjecture and opinion? For such a sensitive issue as 'crime' – a topic that requires careful data gathering and objective deliberation – the threat of the calm academic's voice being ignored in a 'post-truth' age is a very serious and real one. While all information can be regarded as socially constructed, some arguments are better linked to fact than others. It is an assertion (or opinion, often originating from right-wing tabloid newspapers) that prison is used too little in the UK. On the contrary, it is a fact that in comparison to much of the rest of Europe, England and Wales have a very high prison population. Again, the reasons for this might be debated, and it has been variously posited that there has been a notable upsurge in the rates of violent interpersonal and sex-related crimes, along with a growth in drug offences. But we at least ought to start with a recognition that discussion of criminal justice matters need to be based, to some extent, on the facts, while similarly arming ourselves with a scepticism about where the facts come from and how robust and reliable they are.

This book, then, is a starting attempt to strip away some of the prevailing myths and misconceptions surrounding crime and criminality. In the coming pages, the contributors will explore crime in England and Wales, Britain and beyond. Yet we also ought to say what this book is not. It is not comprehensive coverage of the state of crime in Britain; rather, we asked 50 criminologists to contribute what they thought was an interesting and useful 'fact' that people ought to know about crime and its control. Taking inspiration from a short guide used as promotional material at Birmingham City University by one of the authors, and one of the author's rather novel induction exercises previously used at the University of Leicester (where academics were asked to present 'facts' and falsehoods to an incoming cohort of first-year undergraduate criminology students), we decided to try and produce an innovative text containing 50 facts that people ought to know about crime and punishment.

With this understanding, the reader can then consider the facts. We do not expect the reader to accept them nor to take them at face value necessarily, but to use them to frame and ask further critical questions. In an age in which more and more politicians and agencies are utilising and exploiting notions of 'fake news' and 'post-truth', the need for well-informed, well-researched, accessible, objective and nuanced voices has never been greater. With this aim, and taking to heart Sagan's warning of distinguishing speculation from fact, this book intends to offer a more critical perspective on some of society's most topical issues.

This book offers 50 compiled facts, each written by criminologists who are experts in their field, who work in academic settings and who responded to our appeals to assist. The 50 facts are arranged as separate chapters within 10 themed parts. We hope to provide an interesting foundational knowledge for those coming to criminology anew, or simply looking for more information about the topics and subjects that field covers.

What we do know is that, in basing the contributions here on research and data, the 50 contributing authors present facts that will give the reader a better knowledge of the contemporary place of crime and control in Britain. It will better equip you reader with imagination and scepticism, and a basic knowledge that will aid you to appraise and critically evaluate the claims you hear being made about crime. We hope you enjoy it.

Part One
Historical context

FACT 1

The Crime Survey for England and Wales in 2017 states that there were 10.8 million incidents of crime in the previous year

Simon Winlow

The number of crimes in England and Wales is very difficult to establish and estimates vary between data sources, but the Crime Survey for England and Wales in 2017 (Office for National Statistics, 2017a) estimated there were 10.8 million incidents of crime. The fluctuation of crime statistics has become a staple feature of our postmodern mediascape. Newspapers and news broadcasters cover in detail the publication of police crime statistics and the Crime Survey for England and Wales. Occasionally, genuine experts are invited to comment on the rise and fall of recorded crime. However, these news stories are, for the most part, accompanied only by the most meagre contextual discussion. Our police forces are usually singled out for attention. Either crime has risen, and the police are to blame, or crime has fallen, and the police are to be congratulated. Many commentators appear to assume that there exists a stable population of committed criminals, who are either enabled or dissuaded by the actions of the police. However, in reality, the activities, policies and strategies adopted by the police do not play a key role in determining the sum total of crime in Britain. Issues associated with policing – for example, police funding and fluctuations in the number of serving police officers – are occasionally acknowledged in the broadsheet press, and some serious broadcasters may occasionally touch upon government policy and the form and function of our broader criminal justice system. However, the fundamental issues that give shape to the reality of crime – the actual crime that takes place out there in the real world – are rarely held up for critical consideration.

One of the first things that criminology students learn at university is to be suspicious of crime statistics. There are almost 70 million people living in Britain today. Only around 50,000 households take part in the Crime Survey for England and Wales. This crime survey is by far the most comprehensive and methodologically robust attempt to produce statistics that represent the reality of crime and victimisation in Britain, but it leaves huge gaps and provides only a very basic guide to the diverse crime problems that afflict our nation.

While attempts have been made to plug these gaps, many crime forms remain hidden from view. For example, many forms of violence are underreported and underrecorded. A huge amount of non-lethal violence is missing from crime statistics. There are many reasons for this. We may not remember being the victim of a minor act of violence, especially if violence is a routine feature of our everyday life. We may not interpret a violent incident as a violent crime. Instead, we may interpret such events as a legitimate fight separate from the world of law and order. The sentiments that accompany violence, and the emotions triggered by recalling violent incidents, are often difficult to deal with. Many prefer not to think or talk about their experiences of victimisation and would rather keep such troubling events private. All these things, and much else besides, mean that it is very difficult to construct a reasonably accurate statistical measure of violent crime. We should also note that there are some groups of people who are subject to repeat victimisation. A victim of domestic abuse, for example, may be repeatedly subject to violent assault, and may also be subject to verbal, sexual and psychological abuse.

Even in a large survey like the Crime Survey for England and Wales, it is very difficult to fully integrate those marginalised and hidden populations who are most likely to experience violence regularly, and so the global figure we see in our newspapers is inevitably a poor reflection of the overall reality of violent crime. These problems become even more acute when we turn our attention to those forms of crime that, in the popular imagination, do not produce an identifiable victim. We are all, in fact, victims of crimes committed by financial elites, and yet we are unlikely to consciously recognise our own victimhood. We do not immediately feel ourselves to have been directly damaged by such crimes, so we do not report our victimhood to the police, or to the interviewers who gather data for the Crime Survey for England and Wales.

There are many other crimes that remain hidden from view. Underreported, unacknowledged and poorly understood, especially by government, these crimes form part of what criminologists refer to as the 'dark figure of crime': the great mass of crimes that simply do not appear on the public record, and yet whirr away constantly in the background of everyday life. When crime statistics are covered in news broadcasts, viewers are usually given the headline global figures. 'Violent crime is up 10%.' 'Rape has fallen 27%.' Of course, statistics such as this cover over the complexity of everyday life and the diversity of social experience with crass generalisation. The reality of violence, and the reality of rape, or indeed any other crime form, is tricky, uneven and simply not suited to this kind of generalised measurement. If we are to draw closer to the truth of such crimes, we must develop a more nuanced approach. For example, in Britain today, it is possible to visit many neighbourhoods strewn with crime problems; it is also possible to visit many neighbourhoods that, at least on the surface of things, experience almost no crime whatsoever. Crime is an everyday reality for some people. For them, crime is simply there, a regrettable reality, an unavoidable fact of life. For others, crime intrudes hardly at all. They remain untouched by the drudgery of low-level violence and abuse, and separated from the manifold risks and pitfalls that lie scattered around our most impoverished areas. They are exposed only to the dramatisation of crime and violence in movies, books and on television. They know it exists, but they remain at a safe distance from it.

Dorling's (2004) careful demographic analysis has revealed that in some of our most impoverished locales the murder rate is six times higher than the national average. It should be perfectly obvious that beneath a headline like 'violent crime is up 10%' lies a reality in which some people experience violence with regrettable regularity, while others can live a full life without ever having to encounter it. The sum total of violent crime can rise enormously in one locale and fall away sharply in another. It can remain obdurately high in some neighbourhoods, while others are almost entirely free from it. Yet still we tend to be exposed only to a global figure that amalgamates these two extremes and everything in between.

So, we must acknowledge the inherent limitations of survey methods, and we must note that crime is not evenly dispersed throughout the country and the population. We must also acknowledge a more fundamental limitation. Crime statistics address crime – acts that break laws – but they tell us nothing about broader forms of harm and suffering. Those acts that breach criminal laws are by no means the only acts that cause harm to individuals, societies or the natural environment. There are some activities that are powerfully corrosive to our collective and individual safety, welfare and interests, and yet these activities remain entirely legal. Tax avoidance, for example, tends to result in governments allocating less money to schools, roads, hospitals, prisons, universities, and so on. It also inspires anger, enmity and a simmering sense of injustice among those groups who believe themselves to be contributing proportionally more to the nation's finances. It is perfectly clear that failure to adequately provision the welfare state produces a broad range of deleterious social effects. Yet tax avoidance is not a crime. There are many other non-criminalised activities that produce a panoply of harmful outcomes. The diversity and undeniable importance of these harmful activities has prompted some social scientists to suggest that the academic discipline of criminology should abandon its traditional focus on crime and legality and commit itself to the detailed investigation of harm, in all its forms (see Hall and Winlow, 2015).

My intention is not to portray crime statistics as inherently useless. Rather, my suggestion is that criminologists need to treat crime statistics with care. We should never assume that they are an accurate reflection of reality. The correct approach is to remain sceptical, mindful of the limitations of statistical methods, alert to the complexity of everyday life, and aware that the results of even the most robust and expansive crime surveys are there to be interpreted, contextualised and explained, rather than simply accepted as social facts. Some crime forms are clearly amenable to statistical measurement, while many others are not. For example, homicide statistics are quite reliable. It is very difficult to dispose of a dead body, and medical science can now quite accurately identify the cause of death.

But how can we, in an age in which internet-connected handheld devices are ubiquitous, produce a reasonably reliable statistical measure of hate crime, or bullying and harassment? How can we accurately measure insider share dealing, violent assault, stock manipulation, illegal drug transactions, soliciting, domestic violence or kerb-crawling? How can we truly come to know the reality of the low-level crime that afflicts so many low-income neighbourhoods? How can we capture the reality of what appears to be routine illegality in the City of London's financial district?

The answer is perfectly straightforward: we must dispense with surveys and head out into the real world, to observe and speak to the perpetrators and victims of such crimes. We must ask them about their lives, ambitions, motivations and feelings. We must ask them about the pressures they face, their interactions with the criminal justice system, and the emotions that grip them when they find themselves embroiled in a criminal event. We must look at the world with unflinching honesty and boundless curiosity and ask ourselves: what's really going on here? And when all of that is done, we must interpret our data and use it to produce new and insightful accounts of human beings and the complex world we live in.

Professor Simon Winlow, Northumbria University

FACT 2

Capital punishment in the UK was abolished in 1965, but the Death Penalty was a legally defined punishment until 1998

Duncan Frankis

The British criminal justice system in the 18th and 19th centuries has become infamous for being extensive and retributive. While murder was the most common crime punished by death, there was a multitude of lesser offences that led to execution. In 1688, there were 50 crimes for which a person could be put to death, but by 1765 this had risen to about 160 and to 222 by 1810 (Glyn-Jones, 2000).

It is important to note here that many of these crimes punishable by death were associated with theft of some kind. For example, an individual could be sentenced to death for the stealing of goods worth more than five shillings (today worth around 25p), taking goods from a shipwreck, and pilfering from a naval dockyard. While it should be noted that only around 20% of crimes normally resulted in execution, the act of public executions, including even small children (King and Ward, 2015), was clearly designed to act as an individual and general deterrent. Given Britain's industrial and economic growth during this 'bloody' period, most of the new laws introduced during that period were concerned with the defence of property, which some academics have argued was as a method of class domination and suppression of the poor by the rich and ruling class (Devereaux, 2013).

The period referred to as the 'bloody code' came to an end as the 19th century drew to a close, with law makers seeking new and less severe forms of punishments that would still provide the necessary deterrence so highly sought after. With the use of transportation to the then English colonies including Australia and Tasmania for a considerable number of convicts, the Judgement of Death Act 1823 was passed, which made the Death Penalty discretionary for all crimes except treason and murder. Gradually, during the middle of the 19th century, the number of capital offences was reduced, and any hangings that took place were held in relative privacy behind the walls of prisons (McGowen, 1994). There was also the growing awareness that the argument of deterrence was weakening, especially when considering how other countries, such as Iceland, Italy and Sweden, experienced no significant rise of violent crime in the wake of removing the Death Penalty altogether.

Historically, capital punishment was often made into a public spectacle, with members of the public being able to witness the executions. The primary reason for such public displays of punishment was the reason that it would act as an effective deterrent to others. On 26 May 1868, Michael Barrett was executed at Newgate Prison. His execution was the last public hanging in the UK, yet executions behind the prison walls in the United Kingdom took place until 1964.

The culture of capital punishment in Britain in the 18th and 19th centuries prompted Sir Samuel Romilly, a legal reformer, to urge the House of Commons in 1810 to make changes to judicial practices, claiming that there was 'no country on the face of the earth in which there have been so many different offences according to law to be punished with death as in England' (House of Commons, 1810). Despite an increasing level of pressure to reform attitudes towards crime, the Tory government of the early 19th century was reluctant to introduce reforms: the end of the 18th century had seen the beginning of violent social revolutions in America, France, Haiti, Dutch and Belgian territories, as well as in Ireland, and the socio-political elite of Britain was becoming increasingly paranoid about changing power dynamics and the social structure. Punishments for lesser crimes were regarded as a deterrent to non-conformist or radical social thought, and as a way of maintaining the elitist status quo.

While the argument in support of the Death Penalty deteriorated over time, it was a series of high-profile wrongful executions that played a major part in the abolition of capital punishment in the United Kingdom in 1965. One of these high-profile wrongful convictions was that of Welshman Timothy John Evans, who was charged and convicted of murdering his wife and infant daughter in 1949. With the police sure that Evans killed his family, they proceeded to interrogate him; and when asked if he had killed his wife and child, he replied that he did murder them (Potas and Walker, 1987). It was later revealed that much of his confession was actually dictated to Evans by police investigators, and there was an almost total absence of forensic evidence. His trial lasted three days and the jury took only 40 minutes to return a guilty verdict – Evans was hanged on 9 March 1950. Three years later, police uncovered a number of bodies at 10 Rillington Place, the location where Evans and his family had stayed when their murders took place. It transpired that Evans's wife and child, along with at least six other women, were the victims of serial murderer John Christie. Christie was a wartime constable, who also fraudulently let out rooms in 10 Rillington Place – including to Timothy and his family (Jenkins, 1988). While Christie would also be hanged for his crimes, the case of Timothy Evans was one of several that eventually contributed to the abolition of capital punishment in Britain.

Although unused, the Death Penalty remained a legally defined punishment for certain offences such as treason. No executions were carried out in the United Kingdom for any such offence after the abolition of the Death Penalty for murder. Despite this, though, there remained working gallows at HMP Wandsworth, London, until 1994, which was tested every six months until 1992. On 20 May 1998, the House of Commons voted to ratify the 6th Protocol of the European Convention on Human Rights prohibiting capital punishment except: 'In time of war or imminent threat of war'. The last remaining provisions for the Death Penalty under military jurisdiction (including in wartime) were removed when section 21 of the Human Rights Act 1998 came into force on 9 November 1998.

From February 2004, the UK complied with the 13th Protocol, which prohibits the Death Penalty in all circumstances. However, there has been, and continues to be, public and media calls for its reintroduction, particularly prompted by high-profile murder cases, such as those involving the murder of police officers. The government has repeatedly refused to reinstate capital punishment; in June 2013, a new bill for capital punishment in England and Wales was introduced, but was withdrawn that same year.

Dr Duncan Frankis, University of Birmingham

FACT 3

Homosexual male (gay) sex was only decriminalised in England some 50 years ago

Em Temple-Malt

Lesbian and gay relationships are increasingly becoming part of the 'wallpaper' of our everyday lives and visible within popular and everyday culture. Turn on the telly or tune into the radio, chances are that the programmes are being presented by people who happen to be gay or lesbian. Popular soaps have story-lines that feature people in same-sex relationships facing ordinary issues, rather than narrow, sensationalist issues centring on their sexuality. Pop songs and music videos are equally inclusive. Take, for example, the track *Symphony* by Clean Bandit featuring Zara Larsson (2017), depicting one man's grief following the loss of his male lover who was killed in a bike accident. Gay male relationships are also visible in TV adverts, such as McCain's (2017) *We Are Family*, which portrays two gay dads. In addition, the Lloyds TSB (2017) *Taking that Next Step* advert features a gay man proposing to his male partner, suggesting Lloyds TSB are there to support the key phases of their customers' everyday lives. These are remarkable transformations that have taken place in a relatively short space of time. With the ubiquity of gay male relationships in popular culture, it may seem hard to believe that homosexual male relationships were once punishable by law and that homosexual male sex was only decriminalised just over 50 years ago, in 1967.

Sociology and criminology give us a series of tools that help us to understand why society labels certain groups as criminal and punishes their behaviour. We can, for instance, look at legislation that has labelled specific behaviours as a criminal offence because it leaves a permanent lasting record, and allows us to infer how society once perceived homosexual (gay male) relationships. It also equips us to understand the varied ways that people respond and behave, when their behaviour is labelled 'criminal'.

The Criminal Law Amendment Act was introduced in 1885 and specifically criminalised sexual acts between men as 'gross acts of indecency'. The punishment meted out to those convicted of such offences was two years' hard labour. The Act was introduced in the Victorian era, when two significant developments were in motion. First, greater attention was paid to policing inappropriate and 'unnatural' sexual acts – such as masturbation and any sexual acts that were unlikely to contribute to the reproduction of the next generation of the workforce. Second, this was the era of the rise of medical experts, sex scientists, and sexologists – with the power to shape knowledge shifting from the clergy to these medical experts. The early sexologists began cataloguing, labelling and creating categories of sexual tastes and persons. It was now that the categories of 'homosexual' (and later 'heterosexual') were developed.

The Irish literary figure and playwright Oscar Wilde, seemingly conforming to societal expectations (married with a wife and children), was famously prosecuted under this Act. Wilde's prosecution and revelation of his sexual acts with a man attracted a lot of public attention. His biggest crime was likely the societal scandal caused by his prosecution, because the trial publicly disclosed all the details of his relationship that were supposed to remain hidden discreetly in the shadows and invisible. Weeks (1989: 103) explained how Wilde's trial acted as a terrifying moral tale of the dangers of criminal behaviour. He was sentenced to hard labour and sent to Reading Gaol from 1895 to 1897.

Just over 80 years later, in 1967, the Sexual Offences Act decriminalised homosexual acts between men, but only under very specific circumstances. The act legalised sex between two consenting male adults aged 21-plus. Sex was restricted to two participants at any one time and was to take place in a private dwelling (that is, the couple should own the property and not be lodging or renting) and no other person should be present in the house.

This change in law did not come without its detractors. Mary McIntosh, observing the way society approached gay men in the late 1960s, claimed that criminalising homosexual men's relationships had a particular role or societal function to play. McIntosh (1968) pointed out that criminalising gay men, and associated punishments, created a very visible boundary around behaviour deemed normative, permissible and acceptable, and behaviour that was taboo, dangerous and to be avoided. She also suggested that making homosexual behaviour criminal and punishing offenders helped to keep the majority of society pure and ensured that the remainder of society was law abiding.

While decriminalisation was progress, it still created significant difficulties. The most obvious was how men who desired other men were to meet each other.

Similarly to the UK, homosexuality was also illegal in America in the mid-1960s. Laud Humphreys, an academic in the Chicago School of Sociology that specialised in studies of deviance, undertook an ethnographic study (involving covert participant observation, interviews and a social health survey) to explore the impact that the criminalisation of homosexuality was having on gay men. Contrary to McIntosh's (1968) observations that criminalising homosexuality would ensure that men refrained from such activities and would remain law abiding, Humphreys' study revealed that it placed men in precarious and vulnerable situations, and so they often engaged in clandestine and risky behaviours in order to fulfil their (illegal) sexual needs. Humphreys work, published as *The Tearoom Trade*, suggested that many men who were engaging in homosexual sex in public restrooms were heterosexually married with children but engaged in casual sexual encounters with other married men in the same situation to minimise the adverse consequences of their illegal homosexual activities being revealed to the wider community. Exposure meant men risked earning a criminal record, acquiring a discredited identity (Goffman, 1990 [1963]), which could end careers, bring shame on one's immediate and extended family, and lead to a loss of respect and standing in the community.

Humphreys' seminal study is perhaps now more famous for the highly unethical and questionable research practices he used in his pursuit of knowledge. Key problems were the use of deception and the risks his research posed to himself and his participants. Such measures are unlikely to be tolerated in current research projects. Yet at the time, he justified the deception as necessary, suggesting that if he had disclosed he was a researcher, then he would never have been able to observe the 'highly discreditable behaviour' of his participants (Humphreys, 1975: 25). His research also posed extraordinary risks to himself and his participants, because his fieldwork contained detailed and incriminating evidence about the places where those men were engaging in criminal acts, which could have led to the prosecution of his participants, had this information been seized by law enforcement.

However, employing these methods meant Humphreys was able to debunk powerful myths about the 'dangers and threats' of homosexuality. At the time, there was a lot of secrecy and ignorance around homosexuals and homosexuality, which allowed misunderstandings to circulate about the dangers that homosexual men posed to others. The most common perception was that homosexual men were paedophiles and preyed on young people (Weeks, 1989). Humphreys' close documentation of intricate and complex interactions involved in tearoom trade and health survey data meant that he could say with confidence that the public using the public restrooms would not be in any danger. The kinds of participants using tearooms for illegal sexual gratification prioritised their safety and reputation over the desire to receive sexual pleasure, and would cease any interactions if there were even a slight risk to their safety.

In contrast, lesbians' sexual acts were never subjected to the same intense legal regulation that men's behaviour was (Weeks, 1989: 99). This was because of prevailing assumptions that women did not have a sexuality and were not plagued by sexual urges in the same way men were and would therefore certainly never experience physical attraction and desire for other women (Weeks, 1989: 105).

In the UK, the Sexual Offences Act 1967 decriminalised homosexual acts in private between two men, both of whom had to have attained the age of 21. It drew heavily on the Wolfenden committee, which had been set up to investigate homosexuality and prostitution in 1954, and included on its panel a judge, a psychiatrist, an academic and theologians. They formed the view (with one dissenter) that criminal law could not credibly intervene in the private sexual affairs of consenting adults in the privacy of their homes. However, the 1967 Act applied only to England and Wales and did not cover the Merchant Navy nor the Armed Forces. Homosexual acts were decriminalised in Scotland by the Criminal Justice (Scotland) Act 1980, which took effect on 1 February 1981, and in Northern Ireland by the Homosexual Offences (Northern Ireland) Order 1982.

However, it should be remembered that it was only in 2003 that the Sexual Offences Act (which only came into force in May 2004) removed any legal distinction in the criminal law between heterosexual and homosexual activity, and in 31 January 2017, the Policing and Crime Act 2017 came into effect, after being given Royal Assent. A section of the 2017 Act, known as 'the Alan Turing law' (Turing was prosecuted in 1952 for homosexual acts and accepted chemical castration treatment as an alternative to prison), officially gave posthumous pardons to the thousands of homosexual men from England and Wales who had been convicted under old sodomy laws, and gave those still living the opportunity to apply to have a conviction erased.

These recent developments provide a useful reminder that while the story of Britain in recent years is one of growing social acceptance, we ought not to lose sight of the long-lasting legacy of previous criminalisation of homosexuality.

Dr Em Temple-Malt, Staffordshire University

FACT 4

The Royal Society for the Prevention of Cruelty to Animals (RSPCA) was set up 60 years before the National Society for the Prevention of Cruelty to Children (NSPCC)

Jo Turner

Contemporary society is peppered with state regulation – regulation of housing, driving, communication and education, to name but a few. Even without taking into account the mass of health and safety regulation that has increased over the 20th century, state regulation controls virtually all activity that people engage in varying degrees. We live very much in a 'regulatory-state', where there are rules, regulations and laws that govern everyday life (Braithwaite, 2011). But life was not always like this.

Godfrey et al (2007) argue that it was in the second half of the 19th century that Britain saw the beginning of this regulatory state, which then grew exponentially over the 20th century. They argue that private and local authority agencies, backed by central government, turned to social regulation to alleviate the poverty and deprivation caused by industrial, economic and urban changes that took place during the previous decades of the 19th century. Thus began a time of social responsibility aimed at addressing the challenges brought on by the enormous changes of the Industrial Revolution. It was during this period, over the 19th century, in this atmosphere, that the conditions under which children and animals were kept – and how they were treated – became pressing issues. It seemed that their life experiences could be improved through regulation. However, it was the welfare of animals that took precedence.

The Royal Society for the Prevention of Cruelty to Animals (RSPCA) originated in the early 19th century (Rivito, 1987). It was the first animal charity in the world, although many other European countries and America followed suit shortly afterwards. The Society for the Prevention of Cruelty to Animals was founded in a London coffee shop in 1824, but became the RSPCA in 1840, when Queen Victoria bestowed her patronage on the Society. At a time when animals were used for food, chattels or sport rather than as pets, the RSPCA's focus in those early days was the welfare of animals in dangerous occupations, such as 'pit ponies' and horses and ponies used to pull traps, for example. As well as bringing prosecutions for the mistreatment of animals, the RSPCA also campaigned to influence the law regarding animal welfare. It was instrumental in prohibiting cruelty to cattle, then domestic animals such as dogs, and in the passing of the 1835 Pease Act, which forbade bear baiting and cock fighting – popular but cruel 'sports'. More recent 20th-century successes have been the RSPCA's influence on legislation on the use of animals in laboratories, fur farming, and the banning of fox hunting with dogs.

During the 19th century, child cruelty and neglect were considered tragic consequences of life among the poor. Child labour exploitation was tolerated, as it was cheap. Children were also able to carry out many tasks that adults could not, for example crawling into confined spaces such as chimneys. Furthermore, much child cruelty was deemed necessary to discipline the child. Much of this cruelty took place within families, schools and factories. However, similar to animal protection, work to protect child welfare also started in the early 19th century. The 1834 Poor Law Amendment Act set up workhouses for destitute people in England and Wales; and for children who had been deserted or neglected by their parents, the workhouse became a refuge (Hulonce, 2017). Campaigning to alleviate the horrors of 19th-century child labour culminated in: the 1833 Factory Act, which prohibited the employment of children younger than 9 years of age and limited the hours that children between the ages of 9 and 13 could work; and the 1842 Mines Act, which raised the starting age of colliery workers to 10 years.

However, formal means to regulate the welfare of children came 40 years later than the setting up of the RSPCA, with the establishment of the London Society for the Prevention of Cruelty to Children in 1884. In 1889, it became the National Society for the Prevention of Cruelty to Children (NSPCC) and set up a number a regional aid committees to deal with business outside London (Behlmer, 1982). Hence, the NSPCC, in setting up a nationwide body of professional inspectors following a set of clear policy guidelines and answerable to a central head office, established throughout England a systematic programme of welfare intervention that was based on modern notions of family surveillance: regular visits, advice and warning (Hendrick, 1994). In 1892, Asquith, as Home Secretary, said the NSPCC offered an essential and complementary role to the police, primarily because its main concern was not to punish the wrongdoer but to prevent crime. In this vein, the bulk of NSPCC business increasingly took the form of neglect cases, where offending parents would be advised, warned and kept under the regular surveillance of inspectors.

The NSPCC, working with the police, paid particular attention to specific families, keeping them under surveillance for quite lengthy periods, although the NSPCC emphasised its reluctance to remove children from their parental home. Behlmer (1982: 175) has estimated that between 1870 and 1908 (when the Children's Act came into force) less than 1% of all children involved in NSPCC cases were removed from the parents. During this time, both parents (or guardians) were considered to have equal but different responsibility for the children under their care – the man provided financially and the woman took responsibility for nurturing the children. These gender assumptions fundamentally affected the way the law functioned in relation to cases of alleged neglect (despite the recognition by the 1870 Married Women's Property Act that married women were as liable as men for the support of their children). So, as long as a man could show in court that he had worked and provided financially for the family, it was women who bore the brunt of prosecutions for neglect (Turner, 2012). Cases of child sexual abuse were few, but fewer still were those where a woman appeared as defendant. This is not to say that the offence did not take place, rather that few were reported or detected. Jackson (2000: 108), in her study of the way in which sexual abuse was debated and dealt with in the Victorian and Edwardian period, found that in 99% of her sample the defendant was male.

So, why was the RSPCA set up before the NSPCC? As previously stated, during the 19th century, both animal mistreatment and child cruelty and neglect were considered tragic consequences of life among the poor. Furthermore, much child cruelty was deemed necessary to discipline the child. The well-known principle of 'spare the rod and spoil the child' indicated that corporal punishment of children was considered an appropriate measure in child rearing (Taylor and Powell, 2017). There was a longstanding tradition that private or state agencies did not interfere with family affairs – men, as head of the household, were expected to keep their wives and children under control, to discipline them. They were his property.

Hence, even when other areas of life were being increasingly regulated, family affairs, including the welfare of children, were deemed to be out of the reach of the state; there was a reluctance to 'interfere'. The family was deemed to be a private and sacred enclave, into which the law had no place to venture (Morley, 2017). During the

19th century, parental rights to discipline and punish their children were paramount; inch by inch, the NSPCC has developed and extended its reach to protect more and more children. However, even now, parents in England and Wales still retain the right to smack their child, if it can be deemed 'reasonable punishment'.

Dr Jo Turner, Staffordshire University

Part Two
Crime in Britain today

FACT 5

Vehicle crime in England and Wales has fallen by 80% since 1993

Liam Brolan

For many people, cars are an integral part of everyday life. They provide us with a means of travelling to and from work, allow us to visit friends and relatives, and create a sense of independence unrivalled by public transport. The initial cost of purchasing a car, combined with the additional, ongoing expenses of fuel, road tax, MOTs, general maintenance and, of course, insurance, mean that cars are often one of the most expensive purchases people make. Owning a vehicle requires a substantial investment in terms of both time and money. It is therefore unsurprising that we begin to form attachments to them. Some take great pride in them, clean them regularly and take precautions to ensure that they are protected against damage, accidents and perhaps most importantly, theft.

Since 1993, vehicle-related theft in the United Kingdom has fallen by 80%. This stark decrease can be attributed in part to the ongoing developments in vehicle security. What is more, the falling case of car crime provides an interesting counter-narrative to that which people are often exposed to, about how crime is increasing. Indeed, the falling rate of vehicle-related theft might suggest that, in some instances at least, it may be possible to 'design out' crime.

By definition, vehicle-related theft includes stealing or attempting to steal a motor vehicle, parts or accessories from a motor vehicle or anything from inside a vehicle (ONS, 2017). Figures from the 1981 British Crime Survey showed that there were 1,757,000 incidents of vehicle-related theft in the 12-month period leading up to December of that year. This figure rose steadily over the next 12 years, peaking in

1993, when 4,293,000 incidents of vehicle-related theft were recorded. Police recorded data presents a similar upwards trend. However, since the early 1990s, the number of vehicle-related thefts has been on the decline. In 2016, the Crime Survey for England and Wales reported just 878,000 incidents – a decrease of almost 80% when compared to the figures produced in 1993. So, to what can we attribute this dramatic fall in the incidence of vehicle-related theft and what does this teach us about the prevention of crime more generally?

Situational crime prevention, as described by Clarke (1997: 2) focuses on the circumstances in which crime takes place. It seeks to introduce 'discrete managerial and environmental change' which reduces the opportunity for crime to occur. Unlike other areas of criminology, situational crime prevention is less concerned with the causes of criminal behaviour and instead, endeavours to make criminal action 'less attractive to potential offenders' (Clarke, 1997: 2). One such way of achieving this is through a process known as 'target hardening'. As a crime prevention strategy, 'target hardening' aims: 'to impede access to the target by strengthening its defences ... the intent is to make targets more resistant and time-consuming to overcome, and thus to entail more risk, effort and energy for would-be attackers' (Kitchen and Schneider, 2007: 34).

It can be said that over the course of the last 50 years, the vehicles we use daily have undergone a considerable amount of 'target hardening', particularly in relation to the addition of a range of security features. The first major change to vehicle security came in 1971, when all new British cars were fitted with steering column locks. The steering column lock causes the vehicle's steering system to lock into place if there is an attempt to steer the vehicle without first inserting the key into the ignition. According to Home Office research, in 1973, new cars were three times less likely to be stolen than they were in 1969 – prior to the introduction of the steering column lock (Mayhew et al, 1976). This therefore suggests a degree of preventative success. Interestingly, however, the risk posed to older cars – those without a steering column lock – almost doubled over the same period, indicating that criminals had begun to shift their attention to vehicles with less security, and those which therefore made easier targets.

Over the next two decades, the level of vehicle-related theft continued to rise steadily. A 'second wave' of security was witnessed throughout the 1980s and 1990s, with manufacturers fitting both central locking and alarm systems to their vehicles (Morgan et al, 2016). It was not, however, until the mandatory implementation of the electronic immobiliser in 1998, that levels of vehicle-related theft began to fall significantly. Once installed, the immobiliser works by blocking a vehicle's electrical circuits when a key is not present in the ignition. A transponder, which is fitted into the key or key fob, contains a microcircuit with a code. It therefore prevents the vehicle from starting unless the code present matches that of the vehicle (van Ours and Vollaard, 2016: 1267). Interestingly, Morgan and colleagues suggest that the speed in which a new security measure spreads is almost as important as the effectiveness of the device itself (Morgan et al, 2016: 6). They suggest that the most significant reductions in vehicle-related crime occurred several years after the introduction of the new technology, once more than half of the vehicles on the road had been fitted with them. In an international review of the impact of the device, Brown (2016b) found that there was a reduction in the incidence of vehicle-related theft in 15 out of the 16 countries examined after its introduction.

As was the case following the introduction of the steering column lock in 1971, the inclusion of the electronic immobiliser on all new vehicles in 1998 resulted, again, in a shift in the modus operandi of those offenders engaging in vehicle-related theft. Brown and Thomas (2003) suggest that some vehicle-related theft was displaced because of offenders turning their attention to older vehicles, which did not benefit from the added protection of the technology. However, as the research discussed earlier has shown, the efficacy of the technology in reducing vehicle-related theft should not be downplayed. Indeed, Brown and Thomas (2003) acknowledge that although some displacement does occur, it is outweighed by the overall gains in terms of reducing the rate of theft.

The electronic immobiliser subsequently proved to be an effective anti-theft device that could stand the test of time, and the level of vehicle-related theft would continue to fall for the best part of the next 20 years (Morgan et al, 2016). However, in contrast to the previous two decades, data published by the Office for National Statistics, suggests that the level of vehicle-related theft in England and Wales rose by approximately 30% between 2014 and 2016. This sharp increase is being attributed to the fact that 'thieves are now becoming more and more well equipped with technology capable of defeating car manufacturers' anti-theft systems' (Evans, 2017). The use of so-called 'immobiliser bypass technology' has seen a rise in cases, where criminals can create duplicate keys for the vehicles they are targeting. According to the Metropolitan Police (2015):

> Thieves use a device which bypasses the vehicle's electronic information as the owner locks it, or they break into the vehicle and connect a device to the OBD port, downloading the vehicle's information onto a blank key in a matter of seconds. The new key is then compatible with the vehicle, so it disables the alarm and the vehicle can simply be driven away. (Brown, 2016b)

The decrease in the level of vehicle-related theft since 1993 does indeed indicate that the preventative efforts of vehicle manufacturers have been effective in reducing this type of crime. The introduction of steering column locks, central locking and alarm systems has helped to bolster vehicle security, making them less attractive targets to potential offenders. It was the introduction of the immobiliser technology, however, that triggered a major decline in the incidence of vehicle-related theft. Despite this, it would be misleading to suggest that it is possible – at least in the case of vehicle-related theft – to completely 'design out' crime. Displacement, for example, has been a recurring issue throughout the history of developments in vehicle security. Statistics collated in the years following the introduction of both the steering column lock and the electronic immobiliser indicate that, as newer vehicles became increasingly harder to steal, older vehicles subsequently became increasingly more vulnerable to theft. So too, recent statistics published by the Office for National Statistics suggest that vehicle-related theft is far from being eradicated in the United Kingdom, as a result of the introduction of immobiliser bypass technology and changes in the modus operandi of offenders.

Despite a steady decline in the recorded level of vehicle-related theft since 1993, it has been suggested that vehicle manufacturers are engaged in what Brown (2016b) describes as a 'co-evolutionary arms race', whereby developments in vehicular security are overcome by increasing levels of ingenuity on the part of the criminals, which subsequently leads to further developments in security. Therefore, to safeguard effectively against this type of crime, vehicle manufacturers should continue to employ 'target hardening' techniques that seek to deter the would-be offender, by increasing the overall amount of time, effort and risk associated with the theft of a motor vehicle.

Liam Brolan, Birmingham City University

FACT 6

Businesses face higher rates of victimisation than households or individuals

Matt Hopkins

In criminology, the topic of commercial victimisation (or crimes against business) has received relatively little attention. That said, some scholars have argued that commercial victimisation is worthy of criminological enquiry as the very existence of some businesses can be jeopardised by the financial impacts of victimisation, and many staff who work within businesses can be exposed to crime, for example through violence and abuse from customers (see, for example, Hopkins and Gill, 2017).

Globally, research on commercial victimisation is very patchy. While business crime surveys have been completed in China, Australia, Mexico and Nigeria (for a review, see Mugellini, 2013), the United Kingdom is the only known nation where survey data is collected annually through the English/Welsh commercial victimisation survey. Generally, national (and some ad hoc localised) surveys have pointed to higher risks of victimisation for businesses than households or individuals. Businesses tend to experience higher average numbers of crimes than individuals or households. For example, the average number of burglaries per 1,000 business premises is 215, compared to 27 as recorded against 1,000 households.

Some research has noted that business 'lifestyles' or routine activity patterns shape exposure to victimisation, and has illustrated how differing products and services offered, opening hours, business size, and methods of service (that is, self-service scanners versus staff-operated till systems) can all shape exposure to victimisation (Beck and Hopkins,

2016; Hopkins and Gill, 2017). There is also inter-sector variation. For example:

- The highest rates of burglary are recorded in the arts/ entertainment sector (633 per 1,000).
- The highest rates of fraud are recorded in the retail sector (881 per 1,000).
- The highest rates of assaults/threats are recorded in the accommodation/food sector (2,158 per 1,000).
- The highest rates of online crime are recorded in the admin/support sector (3,631 per 1,000). (Office for National Statistics, 2017a)

Hopkins (2016a) also asserts that business exposure to victimisation is also associated with being situated in more economically deprived areas. Businesses located in areas with an index of 1 or 2 (the most deprived) have the highest incidence rates. Previous research has highlighted that residents located in the poorest areas of cities have higher risks of victimisation than those in more affluent areas (Bottoms, 2012), and these patterns appear to be replicated for businesses. It has also been identified that there are disproportionate financial effects of crime, with Hopkins (2016a) reaffirming that smaller businesses are least able to withstand the effects of crime. When financial costs of crime and security for those businesses with a turnover of over £200,000 per annum are compared to those with a lower turnover (turnover is defined as the total revenue that a business generates over the course of a year before expenses are considered), the larger turnover businesses experience higher prevalence and higher incidence rates of crime. These translate into greater average financial losses to crime, with these businesses losing, on average, over £11,000 to crime each year.

When expressed as a proportion of turnover, crime loss for these businesses is 3.4% – significantly higher than that of the higher turnover businesses (0.18%) and expenditure on crime prevention/security is also significantly higher for the smaller businesses (as a proportion of turnover) – at 0.4% as compared to 0.07% for the higher turnover businesses. This indicates that larger businesses may be at greatest risk of experiencing crime, but that they can possibly absorb crime costs and preventative expenditures much better than smaller businesses.

Although the study of commercial victimisation remains at the periphery of mainstream criminology, the high concentration of crime in some sectors makes it a potentially fruitful avenue for further exploration. While some research has suggested there has been a 'crime drop' in the commercial sector, with falls in both the prevalence and incidence of crime in recent years (Hopkins, 2016b), high crime rates are still observed when compared to households and individuals. As evidenced in this discussion, crime also disproportionately concentrates against businesses in the most deprived locations, and smaller business are the most financially vulnerable to crime.

While a greater number of systematic reviews of security efficacy (such as the review of tagging conducted by Sidebottom et al, 2017) would be welcome, scholars have even raised concerns about how seriously some businesses take crime prevention at all. For example, Beck and Hopkins (2016) outline how the development of technological developments in retailing – such as fixed and mobile scanning pay systems – are driven by the pressures in large corporations to achieve profits, but at the same time generate crime opportunity. They argue that larger corporations have a social responsibility to be mindful of the criminogenic impact of their business practices, but suggest that many corporations only take crime risks seriously when they impact upon profit margins (Hopkins and Gill, 2017). While such corporations may often view crime as an irritation, previous research has pointed to the more serious effects of crime, such as emotional impacts on staff and even business closure.

Dr Matt Hopkins, University of Leicester

FACT 7

From 2007 to 2017, there were around 2.3 million deliberate fires in the UK, resulting in over 25,000 injuries and over 900 deaths

Tammy Ayres

In the year ending December 2017, there were 321 fire-related fatalities (including 71 from the Grenfell Tower fire) compared with 278 in the previous year (an increase of 15%). While of course not all of these are deliberate, the level of harm caused by fires is worthy of attention for those studying crime.

Arson, also known as deliberate fire-setting and pyromania, falls under the remit of criminal law or mental (ill) health. There is a difference between arson, which is defined by the criminal law and involves intent, and deliberate fire-setting that does not always involve intent. In fact, 'arson will always be a deliberate fire, but not all deliberate fires are arson' (APF, 2014: 5). Arson is an under-researched topic, particularly in criminology, and 'appears to be one of the least understood criminal behaviours' (Gannon and Barrowcliffe, 2010: 2), despite its devastating consequences, which include destruction of property, life-changing injuries and loss of human life. It is estimated that arson costs England approximately £1.7 billion per year (Department for Communities and Local Government, 2011).

Arson exists in law as Criminal Damage by Fire, Criminal Damage Act 1971, s.1(3), which makes it an offence to destroy or damage property intending thereby to endanger the life of another or being reckless as to whether the life of another would thereby be endangered. For offences involving simple arson the property of another must be damaged. For the aggravated offence in s.1(2), it can be any property, including the defendant's own.

The legal definitions differ from the mental health definition. Pyromania is a pattern of deliberate fire-setting for pleasure, satisfaction or arousal derived from the relief of tension experienced before setting fires. It is a mental disorder classified under the Diagnostic and Statistical Manual of Mental Disorders (DSM IV)/ International Classification of Diseases and Related Health Problems (ICD 10) as an impulse control disorder, where individuals repeatedly fail to resist impulses to deliberately start fires to relieve tension or for instant gratification. 'Fire-setting' is a more inclusive term than arson or pyromania, and 'describes any problematic act of setting fire to property, including the natural environment, outside accepted social and cultural boundaries' (Doley et al, 2016: 1).

Just under a third (30%) of all primary fires attended by the Fire Service in 2016/17 were deliberately started (Home Office, 2017b), although accurately measuring the prevalence of deliberate fire-setting is problematic due to difficulties with detection, apprehension and conviction (Doley et al, 2016). There is a large attrition rate between the two sets of data collected on deliberate fire-setting in the UK, which is undertaken by the fire service (recorded as deliberate fires) and the police (recorded as arson) (Palmer et al, 2010). It is estimated that the police record just over half of deliberately set fires attended by the fire service; from 2015 to 2016, estimates show that 14% of criminal damage and arson offences that should have been recorded as a crime by the police were not, resulting in its under-recording (Palmer et al, 2010).

According to the fire service, in 2016/17 there were 76,106 deliberate fires in England (an increase of 3.4% since 2015/16), resulting in 47 fatalities and 1,027 non-fatal casualties, with 46% requiring hospital treatment. The fire and rescue service in Wales attended 7,128 deliberate fires in 2015/16 (an increase of 11% since 2014/15), of which 19% (1,371) were primary fires and 81% (5,757) were secondary fires. The 7,128 deliberate fires in 2015/16 resulted in two fatalities and 62 non-fatal casualties, and 'over the last decade around 1 in 5 fatalities and 1 in 8 non-fatal casualties in fires occurred in deliberate fires' (Welsh Government, 2017: 22).

In contrast, the police recorded data showed 26,246 incidents of arson in 2016/17, with the minority (14%) endangering life. In 2017, there were 3,904 convictions for criminal damage and arson in England and Wales: 27% received a caution and 29% received a custodial sentence, with the average custodial length for criminal damage and arson being 29 months (Ministry of Justice, 2017a).

For some, arson is just one of numerous offences they commit among a more generalised pattern of offending, making it difficult to distinguish them from other types of offenders. These individuals are commonly known as the *generalist offenders* in the research literature. Other academics have suggested fire-setters to be a unique category of offender with very specific treatment and rehabilitation needs, in a model known as the *specialist hypothesis* (see Gannon et al, 2013). Arsonists also have high rates of reconviction (Hollin et al, 2013), although research estimates that recidivism rates range from 4% to 60% depending on the sample (Brett, 2004).

The prevalence of deliberate fire-setting is underestimated – particularly among the general population, where estimates vary from a lifetime prevalence rate of 1% through to 11% (Doley et al, 2016) – as most research focuses on clinical and criminal samples (for example, Noblett and Nelson, 2001; Hollin et al, 2013). One in ten people admitted to psychiatric services have a history of fire-setting (Hollin et al, 2013). In fact, some research has recommended that a 'comparison of arsonists in prison, hospital and community settings' be undertaken, to obtain a more accurate picture (Jayaraman and Frazer, 2006: 300). Rates of pyromania are also very low and only a minority of convicted arsonists satisfy the diagnostic criteria for pyromania (Rice and Harris, 1991; Lindberg et al, 2005). Although pyromania is a psychiatric condition related to pathological fire-setting, arson has also been associated with several other psychiatric conditions, including depression, personality disorders, schizophrenia, substance use (drugs and alcohol) and childhood disorders. However, the relationship between fire-setting and other mental disorders is complex and multifaceted, requiring further investigation.

As already stated, there is a dearth of research on deliberate fire-setting and thus a dearth of theory underpinning it. What there is has traditionally focused on applying criminological risk factors (Brett, 2004) or generic theories to explain fire-setting (for example, social learning theory); or has created typologies based on motivation, demographics (for example, age and gender), offence characteristics, clinical and legal distinctions, which have been heavily criticised. There have, however, been several advancements in the development of fire-setting theories, particularly in the field of psychology. A good example is the Multi-Trajectory Theory of Adult Firesetting, which outlines five subtypes of fire-setter irrespective of gender (anti-social, fire-interest, grievance, multifaceted and emotionally expressive/need for recognition), and aims to provide a comprehensive theory of fire-setting (see Gannon et al, 2012).

While most of the research focuses on juvenile fire-setters, less is known about adults, although the motivations for deliberate fire-setting vary across and within each group, particularly between males and females. Both juvenile and adult fire-setters are more likely to be male, but there has been an increase in the number of females (Soothill et al, 2004), and research has indicated that numerous gender differences exist across and within the groups (see Palmer et al, 2010). However, it is unclear, due to contradictory research, whether the psychiatric disorder pyromania is more frequently diagnosed in men or women (Doley et al, 2016).

What is clear is that interventions and treatment for deliberate fire-setting are also influenced by age, with interventions for juvenile fire-setters utilising family therapy, psychosocial and educational approaches, as well as cognitive behavioural therapy and pharmacological interventions, which are also used with adult arsonists (Palmer et al, 2010). However, the number of standardised psychological treatments available are severely limited, as is the research evaluating their efficacy (Lambie and Randell, 2011). There are only two standardised interventions currently available for incarcerated arsonists in the UK and no community programmes have been empirically validated, making it difficult to determine 'What Works' as effective intervention with fire-setters (Doley et al, 2016), particularly female fire-setters. Yet 'Research concerning best practice for fire-setting offenders is under developed' (Doley et al, 2016: 228), indicating the lack of evidence base underpinning fire-setting both in terms of explaining it, and also the interventions aimed at rehabilitating juvenile fire-setters and adult arsonists.

In fact, there is a dearth of knowledge about arson in general, particularly in comparison to other criminal behaviours, and it has been described as 'one of the least understood criminal behaviours' (Gannon and Barrowcliffe, 2010: 2). The fire-setting literature has also ignored the issue of culture (Lambie and Randell, 2011) and political economy, thus failing to understand fire-setting in its wider context. Consequently, further research is needed, to address the gaps in knowledge and our understanding of arson, and its prevention and treatment.

Dr Tammy Ayres, University of Leicester

FACT 8

Between 2016 and 2017, 80,393 hate crimes were committed in England and Wales

Stevie-Jade Hardy

As part of everyday life in England and Wales, people are targeted on the basis of their identity, perceived 'difference' or vulnerability. Research into this form of crime – which is more commonly known as 'hate crime' – has shown that victims tend to suffer repeat experiences. These can include physical acts of violence as well as other forms of targeted hostility, such as being spat at, being called abusive names, receiving offensive messages, experiencing criminal damage and encountering harassment, humiliation and other types of intimidatory behaviour (Williams and Tregidga, 2013; Chakraborti et al, 2014; Awan and Zempi, 2016). This growing body of research evidence also demonstrates that hate crime causes considerable damage to the emotional and physical wellbeing of victims and their families, and spreads fear and mistrust within wider communities (Williams and Tregidga, 2014; Iganski and Lagou, 2015; Brown et al, 2017).

In recognition of these harms, the UK government has taken steps to develop policy and legislation that treats hate crime differently to 'ordinary' forms of crime. The College of Policing, who are the professional body responsible for setting standards in professional development across English and Welsh police forces, produced operational guidance which defined hate crime as: 'Any hate incident, which constitutes a criminal offence, perceived by the victim or any other person, as being motivated by hostility or prejudice' (College of Policing, 2014: 3).

The College of Policing guidance stipulates that the police are obliged to record an offence as a 'hate crime' if the incident was motivated by hostility on the grounds of any one of five monitored strands of identity: namely, disability, race, religion, sexual orientation and transgender status (College of Policing, 2014). However, there is a degree of flexibility in the policy, which enables police forces to record other forms of targeted hostility as hate crime in addition to the five monitored strands. This has resulted in a number of police forces amending their policies to include other categories such as 'alternative subcultures', 'misogyny' and 'sex workers'.

The need for this more inclusive framework has been highlighted by recent research, which has sought to document the experiences of victim groups, who have tended to be overlooked by policy. In the biggest study ever conducted in the UK on hate crime victimisation, Chakraborti et al (2014) heard from significant numbers of victims who belonged to 'hidden', less familiar communities and groups, including asylum seekers and refugees, people with learning difficulties and/or mental ill-health, trans people, homeless people, and people victimised because of their 'different' modes of dress, appearance or lifestyle. These participants were found to experience similar forms of victimisation and suffer the same level of physical and emotional impact as the more familiar, more established victim groups (Chakraborti et al, 2014).

Another strength of the way in which hate crime policy has been conceptualised in the UK is that it adopts a victim-based approach. The College of Policing guidance states that the defining factor in recording an incident as a hate crime is the perception of the victim or any other person (such as a witness, a family member or support worker) and not the discretion of the investigating police officer (College of Policing, 2014). This means that if a victim, or any other person, walks into a police station and states to the duty officer that they have been attacked on the basis of one of the five strands of identity listed earlier, the officer should record the offence as a hate crime and investigate it as such. The policy has been designed in this way in an attempt to redress the imbalance of power that has historically characterised the relationship between the police and marginalised communities within society (Hardy and Chakraborti, 2017b).

Despite the implementation of this victim-centred policy – and new laws which provide the courts with the power to increase the sentence for any offence proven to be motivated by hostility or prejudice – the UK's approach to dealing with hate crime is hampered by a number of issues. One of the biggest challenges facing criminal justice agencies is that hate crime is significantly under-reported, with the official police recorded figure of hate crime thought to be a considerable underestimate of the actual number of hate crimes taking place in the UK. For instance, the Crime Survey for England and Wales, which provides an alternative measure of hate crime victimisation, estimated that 222,000 hate crimes took place in 2015/16, which is significantly higher than the police recorded figure of 62,518 (Corcoran and Smith, 2016). Research has highlighted that there are a range of factors which affect a decision to report to the police, including the perception that incidents will not be taken seriously, that reporting will make the situation worse, and that the process of reporting is too time-consuming and emotionally draining (Christmann and Wong, 2010; Antjoule, 2016; Hardy and Chakraborti, 2017a).

Victim dissatisfaction with how the police handle hate crime cases has also been identified as a key issue in official sources of data and research findings. The Crime Survey for England and Wales suggests that compared to general crime victims, hate crime victims are less likely to be satisfied with the police response both in terms of effectiveness and fairness of the service provided (Corcoran and Smith, 2016). Based on combined 2012/13 to 2014/15 surveys, just 52% of hate crime victims were found to be very or fairly satisfied with the handling of their case, compared to 73% of general crime victims (Corcoran and Smith, 2016). More worrying still is that research suggests that many hate crime victims are unaware of, or do not have access to, support services to assist them as they progress through what is often perceived to be a slow and intimidating criminal justice system (Hardy and Chakraborti, 2016, 2017a). These factors can exacerbate the harms associated with the original hate crime and can cause added distress to victims and their families.

Finally, there is mounting concern that the current approach to dealing with hate crime perpetrators – often described as punitive – is not an effective way to address offending behaviour (Walters and Brown, 2016). Hall, for instance, has been critical of the overreliance on prison as a way of dealing with hate crime perpetrators. He observes that this form of punishment has limited deterrent value to many offenders, and that the overcrowded and constrained conditions in many prisons make it difficult to undertake the level of rehabilitation required to truly address prejudicial attitudes (Hall, 2013). Furthermore, research has demonstrated that even those who have been affected by hate crime are keen to see greater use of alternative approaches that tackle offending behaviour and repair the harms caused, including educational programmes and restorative interventions (Walters, 2014; Hardy and Chakraborti, 2017a).

In short, the UK has developed one of the most robust frameworks for dealing with hate crime. These developments are significant, because they embody the UK's values of appreciating and respecting diversity, demonstrate an understanding of how impactful hate crime can be, and send a clear message of condemnation of prejudice. However, this discussion has highlighted a number of barriers that hinder the effectiveness of this progress. The government, criminal justice agencies and other relevant public sector organisations need to work together to overcome them. More broadly, and in the context of heightened tensions and escalating levels of hate crime within society (National Police Chiefs' Council, 2017), it is imperative that we all embrace our collective responsibility to challenge prejudice and hostility in all its forms.

Dr Stevie-Jade Hardy, University of Leicester

FACT 9

The cost of waste crime in the UK exceeded £1 billion for the first time in 2016

Haydn Davies

Regulatory crime is often seen as the 'poor relation' of violent crime and it certainly receives less publicity. Yet the costs in financial, enforcement and amenity terms have been growing every year, since the criminalisation of most waste offences in the Environmental Protection Act in 1990. Waste crime is attractive to organised criminals, as the profits are high, the enforcement authorities underfunded, the overheads small and the chances of detention slight.

Though there is no universally agreed classification of waste crime, but it can be categorised into:

- the setting up and operating of illegal waste sites (which may operate for a short or long period);
- the illegal burning of waste;
- fly-tipping;
- misclassification and fraud;
- serious breaches of permit conditions, including the abandonment of waste;
- illegal exports of waste. (Environmental Services Association Education Trust, 2017)

All of these carry criminal penalties or fixed regulatory penalties and, in the case of the illegal disposal of hazardous waste, can attract an unlimited fine and up to five years' imprisonment (s.33(8),(9) Environmental Protection Act 1990) – some of the most draconian penalties in environmental law.

The operation of illegal waste sites has the potential to cause severe and widespread damage to the environment and human health. Lawfully operated waste sites are tightly regulated under the Environmental Permitting Regulations 2010 (and for hazardous waste the Hazardous Waste Regulations 2005) and are subject to mandatory conditions of operation covering emissions to air, land and water. Needless to say, illegally operated sites observe none of these regulations, with the result that vast quantities of waste are often stockpiled on land, without any segregation of waste, or any means of preventing water contamination, soil contamination or air pollution. The extent of this contamination can be staggering. In 2011, Carl David Steele was jailed for 15 months for illegally dumping 1 million tyres across the UK (Guardian, 2011).

On 15 July 2016, the longest-ever jail sentence for waste crime – 7.5 years – was imposed on Terence Solomon Dugbo. Dugbo fraudulently claimed to be recycling electrical waste goods on a massive scale, but in the process deprived the legitimate waste recycling industry of £2.2 million. This case is an excellent example of the lucrative and organised nature of waste crime. It also highlights the fact that many waste criminals are serial offenders. Dugbo had previously been convicted of illegally exporting electrical waste goods to Nigeria, which is not only a domestic crime but also a breach of international law, since the Basel Convention (1989) forbids the 'dumping' of waste from an Organisation for Economic Co-operation and Development (OECD) country in a country outside the OECD (see Environment Agency, 2016).

Fly-tipping has seen a serious resurgence in the past five years or so (Environment Agency, 2017), despite the enhanced penalties for illegal disposal of waste (see previous paragraph) and the power of local authorities to issue fixed-penalty notices (DEFRA, 2016a). Historically, fly-tipping was a largely uncontrolled and unregulated activity (strictly it was not completely unregulated, but regulation was not uniform across England and Wales) until the advent of the Control of Pollution Act 1974 and the creation of specific offences related to the illegal disposal of waste, which were later consolidated and incorporated into the Environmental Protection Act 1990. This resulted in a considerable decline in fly-tipping in the 1980s. However, the onset of consumerism and the 'disposable' nature of contemporary consumer goods, fuelled by globalisation, resulted in a massive per capita increase in both household (an 11% increase occurred between 1997 and 2007 – see ONS, 2009: 64) and commercial waste in the UK, which has now stabilised at around a total of 25,000,000 tonnes created per annum (DEFRA, 2016b).

Fly-tipping has been exacerbated by two further developments. First, the effects of the EU Landfill Directive (1999/31/EC), which requires a progressive reduction in disposal to landfill across all EU states and subjects all such disposal to taxation which increases every year; and second the requirements for increased recycling of waste under the terms of the EU Waste Framework Directive (2008/98/EC). Together these have resulted in an increase in the costs of disposing of waste and a decrease in the convenience of disposal of waste. The results are evident to anyone who drives through the margins of cities and into the countryside. Statistics for 2017 (DEFRA, 2017) indicate a 7% increase in fly-tipping compared to the previous year, which represents a total illegal disposal tonnage of more than 1 million tonnes. Fly-tipping has been on the increase again for the past four years (despite a decline in the previous six). The estimated cost to local authorities (and hence the taxpayer) of clearing this waste was an estimated £57.7 million in 2016/17, and that does not include the secondary effects on the environment in terms of pollution of air, land and water.

In summary, waste crime, along with other types of environmental crime, does not have a very high profile in the public mind. People tend not to walk the streets in fear of waste crime in the same way as they might in fear, for example, of terrorism. However, the effects on public health, public amenity and environmental quality are far more widespread and affect vastly more people than acts of terrorism. With the cost of waste crime in the UK exceeding £1 billion for the first time in 2016, perhaps it is time to take such behaviour and actions more seriously?

Professor Haydn Davies, Birmingham City University

Part Three
International comparisons

FACT 10

There is a 0.9 per 100,000 people murder rate in the UK; in Lithuania, it is 5.9 per 100,000

Dan Rusu

Homicide is one of the most serious crimes of all and, due to its grave and irreparable consequences, it has been widely researched in a global context. When such research takes place, it can sometimes throw out some very odd lessons. One that has received lengthy attention is the seemingly huge variation in levels of recorded homicide between the UK and Lithuania, because in the case of the latter it is a country that for several years has recorded what is a seemingly staggeringly high murder rate.

Available data is provided by international institutions and organisations such as the United Nations, Interpol, European Sourcebook on Crime and Criminal Justice Statistics, Eurostat, and the World Health Organization. Analyses are directed at a global level, between continents, but also in a more directed and focused manner, between countries. Discrepancies between nations have been widely acknowledged, with the Americas having had homicides rates almost eight times higher than Europe and Asia since the 1950s (UNODC, 2013). However, despite a general consistency of low murder rates in the European continent, analyses have found that clusters of states differ very significantly (Marshall and Summers, 2012), with the Baltic States making the top of the list (Marshall and Summers, 2012; UNODC, 2013).

One of the leading examples is the calculated rates per 100,000 inhabitants between Western Europe and Central and Eastern European states. Notably, the difference between the United Kingdom and Lithuania is an interesting comparison. According to the UNODC *Homicide Statistics* (2015), the murder rate per 100,000 people is 0.92 in the UK, while in Lithuania it is 5.98. The latter has a significantly higher homicide rate than any other European country, and even makes the top in a global context, having seven times the average homicide rate in the EU (Andresen, 2012). Such a peculiarity (considering that regional proximity denotes cultural, legal and political homogeneity to a certain extent) attracted the attention of researchers across the globe, and represented an opportunity for criminologists to test their theories.

In a report on crime trends over recent years, Lithuania saw an average 8.76 murders per 100,000 heads of population every year during the period 2002-08, making Lithuania the EU's murder capital by some margin. Yet Lithuania is probably not a country that you would consider a hotbed of violence. It declared independence from the Soviet Union in March 1990, rapidly starting its transition from a planned economy to a market economy. The neoliberal character of the system that followed the Lithuanian anti-communist revolutions created a sharp ideological shift from a philosophy of egalitarianism and social welfare system inherent in the communist republic to a society based on capitalist values; this is considered to have led to a strong sense of injustice among the population in the years that followed the revolution (McCall et al, 2012). Significantly, it was this political and social reality that captured the attention of criminologists, who now had the chance to test their already established theories of crime. Such work has been undertaken by Pridemore and colleagues in Russia, who paved the way for similar research in different countries; one such example is Lithuania.

In fact, statistical rigour, although paramount in most research, poses several challenges that are not lessened when the research is comparative and cross-national. According to the UNODC (2013: 102), homicide is defined as the 'unlawful death purposefully inflicted on a person by another person'. The definition provided by Eurostat (European Commission, 2010) is 'intentional killing of a person'. Despite the apparent clarity of the definitions, in practice, states have difficulties in unifying their definitions of what constitutes homicide. In England, homicide covers a range of situations where a person is killed. For example, it includes premeditated and intentional killing, but also non-intentional killing, whereas not every country has such a comprehensive word in their lexicon. In other words, in some European countries the English term 'homicide' and 'murder' are translated into the same word, although very much different concepts in English (Smit et al, 2012). It is for this reason that researchers have warranted in favour of using the term 'intentional killing', a narrower definition, which excludes killing in self-defence, killings in legal interventions, or those who kill as a consequence of negligence (UNODC, 2013).

Let us take euthanasia as an example. Although legally possible in some countries, such as the Netherlands, Belgium and Luxembourg, in countries where euthanasia is considered unlawful, it matches the term homicide, that of 'intentional killing of a person by another' (Smit et al, 2012). This ultimately affects what countries report as data to the United Nations. In 2014, Eurostat and the United Nations Office on Drugs and Crime (UNODC) launched a joint data collection on criminal justice statistics; although using the United Nations crime questionnaire, coupled with the relevant Eurostat questionnaire, the responsibility to provide the necessary data was still placed on each country's relevant authorities. Although registration systems have been upgraded throughout the European Union in recent years, the need for further improvement has been widely acknowledged.

Crime statistics are essentially numerical details recorded by criminal justice and public health sources, and subject to all the complexities that can come with human judgement, manipulation and error. In countries with an accurate registration system, both information provided by criminal justice data and public health data should provide similar results; however, discrepancies emerge where administrative records are poor (UNODC, 2013). Also, it is a reality that not all crime is reported to the police, and there are cases when the police do not record, or do not accurately record, all reported crimes (Rogers and Pridemore, 2017). Further questions relate to what is actually reported, as counting unites by each member state. For example, does a nation count one homicide as one victim, despite the number of offenders, or are there situations where multiple offenders are counted separately despite the victim (Rogers and Pridemore, 2017). Data provided by the World Health Organization through its homicide victimisation data is generally used to avoid definitional problems and problematic statistics; this is due to the uniform definition proposed by the International Classification of Diseases coding system. However, little has been done to control for classification errors and missing observations. A further limitation is posed as deaths might be recorded incorrectly, when the exact cause of death is unidentified (Rogers and Pridemore, 2017).

Homicide data carries significance only when considered in a comparative context. In other words, knowing the fact that (according to the UNODC) Lithuania has a homicide of 5.9 per 100,000 people is not significant, unless we know that surrounding countries have a higher or lower rate, as elaborated in the present fact of crime. This comparative context attracted the attention of scholars across the globe, who, although they have made important progress in understanding the underlying mechanisms behind homicide rate differences, are still at the beginning of an early research journey. So we might ask, what do we take from this? Is Lituania really almost six times more violent and murderous than English cities? If it is, what factors underscore this? One factor is likely to be found in the fact that, according to World Health Organization data published in 2018, Lithuanians are among the world's heaviest drinkers, and the country's addiction to alcohol has shown little sign of abating.

In 2016, Lithuanians drank, on average, the equivalent of 18.2 litres of pure alcohol per person, up from 14.9 litres more than a decade ago, and we know well that alcohol consumption can be a significant factor in criminal violence. Moreover, in Lithuania, homicides are most often shown to be committed by relatively young adult males (on male victims) at a residence in an urban environment (Andresen, 2012). Indeed, in 2018 Lithuania's coalition government passed legislation banning alcohol advertising entirely from TV, radio or newspapers, cutting the hours at which alcohol could be sold in shops and – potentially most controversially – increasing the legal drinking age from 18 to 20.

The lessons are that while cross-cultural comparisons are useful, we need to be cautious about making sweeping claims about different geographical and cultural contexts where crime is concerned. Furthermore, care must be taken when comparing crime rates across different countries, because there are significant variations not only in social and economic conditions, but also in criminal justice systems and the definitions of criminal offences that these different systems use.

Dan Rusu, Birmingham City University

FACT 11

The age of criminal responsibility in England and Wales is the lowest in Europe at just 10 years old

Emma Kelly

The age of criminal responsibility refers to the age at which a person can have criminal proceedings brought against them for crimes they have committed. Unsurprisingly, the debate around when exactly an individual is of the 'right age' to have criminal proceedings brought against them is a complex, often political, and an emotionally charged one. In Britain, there is perhaps no better example of this debate than the murder of James Bulger.

On Sunday, 14 February 1993, authorities in Liverpool discovered the remains of two-year-old James Bulger at the railway line near the disused Walton and Anfield train station. Bulger, who was last seen on a grainy CCTV image leaving the Bootle Strand shopping centre, where he had momentarily been lured away from his mother, was seen in the company of two older boys, but was found cut in half and with 42 injuries across his body. Upon the identification and arrest of the killers, there was a shock as to just how young the perpetrators were. Robert Thompson and Jon Venables were both just 10 years old at the time of the murder – making them some of the youngest murderers in the country. At their trial, which was continually under the watchful glare of the media and thus the public, the boys were sentenced to custody until they reached adulthood. While arguments were made regarding the troubled environment in which these two boys grew up, there was very little consideration given to such factors, with Mr Justice Morland telling Thompson and Venables that they had committed a crime of "unparalleled evil and barbarity ... In my judgment, your conduct was both cunning and very wicked" (House of Lords, 1997).

The media coverage of the case fundamentally branded the boys as evil, products of moral decay, and that the murder of a two-year-old little boy was 'an indication of a deeper moral malaise afflicting the whole of British society' (Green, 2008: 202). The neoclassical perspective that individuals rationally calculate the benefits and costs of criminal behaviour had now permeated into the realm of how the criminal justice system viewed children. In light of this now high-profile murder, Grewcock (1996) suggests that our legal system 'is a system which fails the accused. It places a child as young as 10 in an adversarial framework designed for adults and judges that child essentially by the same standards' (Grewcock, 1996: 55).

While the UK's criminal justice system fundamentally views criminals – be they young or old – as agents of free will and rationality, this is not the case in other countries. In Norway, for example, the age of criminal responsibility is 15. 'Norwegians seem culturally incapable of accepting that children under 15 should be prosecuted as adults' (Green, 2008: 209). Silje Redergard was a five-year-old girl who, on 15 October 1994, just 20 months after the murder of James Bulger in the UK, was beaten and left to freeze to death by three six-year-old boys in Trondheim, Norway (Cornwall, 2016). According to Aftenposten (1994; in Green, 2008: 199), the boys were not punished in anyway, but were instead offered places at kindergarten, in part so that teachers and psychologists could monitor them and assist them in coming to terms with what they had done. There was also minimal press coverage and it never extended beyond the realms of being viewed as a tragic incident (Green, 2008).

This is in stark comparison to such headlines such as 'James Bulger: The death of innocence' (*The Independent*, 1993) and 'Freaks of Nature' (*Daily Mirror*, 1993) in Britain. In contrast, the Redergard case was kept out of the glare of publicity and, within a month, the boys went back to school and were able to remain with their families (Cornwall, 2016). The press coverage of the Norwegian case lasted for approximately two weeks and the perpetrators' identities and names were never disclosed; even now their anonymity is protected (Barry and Leonardsen, 2012). However, in relation to the Bulger murder, 'the trial judge ruled that criminals' identities should be revealed, and so their names and hauntingly vulnerable mug shots were slashed across every newspaper' (Goldhill, 2010). Moreover, the coverage of the case lasted for over 18 months. Still to this day, it is referred to in Parliament and around the world when incidents of children killing other children occur. Indeed, as David Green has noted: 'many Norwegians need little prompting to recall the horrible details of the Bulger case, but most have much more difficulty recalling those of the Silje case' (Green, 2008).

The mainstream media in Britain are encouraged to make a scandal of an issue in order to sell newspapers and, as the competition is so great, it is deemed that the one with the most sensational headlines will sell the most. In Norway, there are only two national dailies and many others are on subscription. This makes the task of reporting easier for the press, as regardless of how provocative a headline might be, there is no guarantee it would sell more newspapers, as many are already subscribed (Green, 2008). As Green suggests, 'The killing of Silje was constructed in the [Norwegian] press as a tragic accident, a terrible aberration, a non-criminal act in every sense, perpetrated by innocents on the innocent' (Green, 2008: 7). Hence, Norwegian society adopted a compassionate, calm approach, and the press coverage, although minimal, focused on how Silje's mother had forgiven the boys who killed her daughter, and how she has offered consolation to other bereaved families. In Britain, however, the coverage on the Bulger case induced widespread fear and presented a 'bleak vision of a nation in the midst of a rapid and degenerative descent into moral chaos' (Green, 2008: 202).

Unlike the Bulger case, in Norway 'there was no mass pouring of outrage from the family, the community or the press, no cries for vigilante justice, and no political manoeuvring by any party's politician to politicize the incident' (Green, 2008: 7). According to Lijphart (1999), the Norwegian political culture is a consensus model, which is based on inclusiveness, bargaining and compromise, meaning that power is shared among all parties. So, in the case of Silje Redergard, the Norwegian government had nothing to gain by using the crime as a political issue; whereas in Britain, the political culture is majoritarian, therefore all parties are vying against each other for public votes. By politicising the Bulger case and responding to public angst over crime, it was in fact an ideal opportunity to exploit a crisis and use it as a bargaining tool to outdo the opposition.

Consequently, in Britain there was a strong sense of urgency by the New Labour Government to make its political agenda more appealing to voters. On the contrary, in Norway: 'because fewer players are excluded from policy making and all tend to contribute, there are fewer incentives for members of one political party to attack their opponents' (Green, 2008: 208).

Emma Kelly, Leeds Trinity University

FACT 12

Between 2004 and 2017, 33 people were fatally shot by the police in England and Wales

Laura Riley

When the life of a citizen is taken, whether by accident or design, by a representative of the state, without a trial and with no access to due process, it can send shockwaves through society. In some cases, extensive press coverage, furious protests and lengthy court cases can ensue. This anger and increased scrutiny can be cumulative, each case like a body blow to collective faith in the police and the criminal justice system as a whole, as we have seen recently in the Black Lives Matter movement in the United States and in the way that the police fatal shooting of Mark Duggan acted as the prelude to the English riots of 2011.

In the UK, the number of people whose lives are lost following police contact each year is a matter of public record (National Statistics, 2016). Shootings which result in a fatality (or fatalities) are carefully scrutinised, not only by academics and the public but also by the media and the Independent Police Complaints Commission (IPCC). The same cannot be said for the US.

In the UK, it is primarily the responsibility of the IPCC to investigate all police fatal shootings and their legitimacy and context (Davenport, 2017). The organisation has not been without controversy, and allegations of 'insensitivity' from relatives of some of those killed led it to 'review its own practice' in 2014 (Shaw, 2014). Nevertheless, the IPCC reinvestigates cases on the request of relatives, has been instrumental in seeking legal redress following fatalities, and has referred cases to the Crown Court (Wiredgov, 2013).

The Home Office collates information from the IPCC and makes reports available to the public through its own website (National Statistics, 2016). These are not the only reliable sources of data on those killed by firearms officers; for example, the charity Inquest also examines these cases (Police Shootings, 2017). This abundance of information is in stark contrast to analysis of such incidents in the US.

In the US, the notorious unreliability of statistics concerning police shootings has led Richardson et al (2016) to suggest that trauma unit staff might act as alternative sources of data on non-fatal police shootings. The structure of the US law enforcement agencies allows police departments to choose whether or not to report statistics on shootings to the FBI, meaning that no source can provide official statistics on relevant fatalities across the entire country, much to the chagrin of American journalists (Robinson, 2014). Attempts to redress this and provide more rigorous accountability, and perhaps intervention, have been strongly and successfully opposed at local, state and national level (McGregor, 2016). It is notable that the FBI's *Uniform Crime Report* records the data collated as 'justifiable homicides', described as: 'The killing of a felon by a law enforcement officer in the line of duty' (FBI, 2017).

This is, of course, not indicative of an unbiased source of raw data (FBI, 2013). This framing of fatalities in this way has not escaped the notice of researchers. Gilbert and Ray (2016), for example, address this conception of events and consider the overrepresentation of African American males in police shootings. Brown (2016) considers not only the events surrounding deaths via police shootings, but also the impact on communities. In an attempt to provide the necessary scrutiny, researchers have focused on specific police departments, and examined both the impact of citizen activism and the weaponry available to the officers in question (Hutto et al, 2016). Police departments might have good reason to limit knowledge of the scale of fatalities involving law enforcement. Research by Weitzer (2002) suggests that those incidents which do attract public attention tend to have a negative impact upon the public view of the police. This appears to be most dramatic among African Americans, but is also notable in White and Hispanic communities.

In addition to the inconsistency in availability of data, there is a marked difference in the historical tradition of police cultures in the UK and US, although British attitudes do appear to be shifting. The concept of 'Suicide by Cop' (where evidence suggests that an offender is attempting to behave in a manner that necessitates the police shooting him/her) is a well-established American phenomenon (Patton and Fremouw, 2016). However, there is evidence that this method of self-destruction has become more prevalent in the UK in recent decades, although still not as common as in the US (Best et al, 2004).

It must be noted that American officers police a population with the legal right to carry guns, a right which is severely restricted in the UK. Until 2017, any British firearms officer who discharged his/her weapon would be automatically suspended from duty while the circumstances of the shooting were investigated, yet in March 2017 the then Home Secretary, Amber Rudd, announced that this would no longer be the case (Powell, 2017). This represents a shift in the balance between scrutiny and security in the UK, following police-involved shootings ending recent lethal terrorist attacks.

British police differ from their American counterparts in their traditional lack of weaponry, so sacred is the great British tradition of the 'unarmed police officer' that the introduction to police operations of CS gas and Taser sparked controversy (Tyler and King, 2000). Yet concomitantly, a point of contention is the apparent lack of power that British police possess in comparison to their American fellow officers, owing to the comparative rarity of firearms officers, which has not escaped critical and negative attention (Bletchly, 2017). However, according to a survey by the Police Federation, while a slim majority of British police are prepared to be armed with guns, it is only a 55% majority and the routine carrying of firearms remains extremely contentious (Donald, 2017). Perhaps one reason for this absence of enthusiasm is the scrutiny to which British police are held if they discharge a firearm – an accountability which is more lacking in the US.

The most recognisable response to fatal police shootings and other killings of (predominantly young, black, male) civilians has been the movement 'Black Lives Matter', initially in the US. The movement's message has powerfully permeated a wider global public consciousness through protests and social media and has given voice to a demographic that has traditionally felt ignored and disenfranchised (Lowery, 2017). The movement has spread to the UK, however it has been met with controversy regarding its choice of targets, which have included commercial airlines (BBC, 2016). In any case, the reaction to fatal police shootings in the US and the UK has inspired a more global discussion, not only of controversial police tactics, but also of all forms of perceived racial injustice.

Greater transparency in the UK does not mean that when the police shoot someone dead, there is little impact on community relations. As mentioned previously, the shooting of Mark Duggan was a catalyst for the riots in England in 2011 (Bridges, 2012). Events may have preceded the birth of 'Black Lives Matter', but the shock and outrage were still palpable. Despite the comparative rarity of police shootings in the UK, researchers still scrutinise the use of deadly force, and there remains a tension between security and the principles of liberty and police accountability, when police use lethal force (Kennison and Loumansky, 2007).

Despite public outrage from sections of the wider community, there are no signs that all police departments in the US will begin to reveal statistics on their use of deadly force. With the election of President Trump, who suggested he regarded 'Black Lives Matter' as an organisation that utilises 'horrible' and 'divisive' rhetoric, it seems unlikely that the Federal government will change course. Until then, citizens in the US will be less aware of the full impact of the actions of their (armed) police than their British counterparts.

Laura Riley, Birmingham City University

Part Four
The police

FACT 13

There were 298,949 police stop-and-search incidents in England and Wales in 2016/17 – a rate of 5 per 1,000 people

Aidan O'Sullivan

The police have a range of statutory powers of stop and search available to them, which vary depending on the circumstances. In most cases, these powers necessitate an officer having reasonable grounds for suspicion that an unlawful item is being carried. The one thing the powers mutually share is that they permit officers to detain an individual who is not under arrest to search them or examine their vehicle for an unlawful item. Unlawful items include, for example, drugs, weapons and stolen property and, depending on what the police find on you during a search, you could be arrested.

It is important to note here that, along with stop and search, the police are also capable of conducting stop and question, in which they ask such questions as: what your name is; what you are doing in the area; and, where you are going. You do not actually have to stop or answer these – or any – questions. If you do not and there is no other reason for the police to suspect you, then this alone cannot be used as a justification to search or arrest you. Where this form of police power differs from stop and search is the element of 'reasonable grounds', and this can only be circumvented if permission is given by a senior police officer. For permission to be given, there needs to be one or more of the following factors:

- they suspect that a serious violent crime could take place;
- you are carrying a weapon or have used one;
- you are currently in a specific location or area.

There are, of course, several important issues surrounding the term 'reasonable grounds'. For instance, there has been a history of disproportionate stop and searches conducted on individuals from ethnic minorities with, as the Home Office (2018) report demonstrates, people from an ethnic minority background are three times more likely to be stopped and searched than White people.

It is important to note that the numbers of stop and searches have fallen for all ethnic groups over the period presented (2006/17); however, they have fallen at different rates for different groups. While White people saw the most significant decrease at 38%, for ethnic minorities, the decrease in stop and search was lower, with a decrease of 8% for Black people, 16% for Asian people, 19% for those of mixed ethnicity and 25% for other categories. So, compared to the five stop and searches for every 1,000 White people, there were 31 stop and searches for Black people in 2015/16. It has since been announced that new and standardised stop-and-search training will be implemented across England and Wales, to reduce such disparities between ethnic groups (Dodd and Gayle, 2016). Despite these recent changes, the question remains as to how such disproportions arose in the first place.

To gain an insight into the context behind these stop-and-search figures, it is important to consider the day-to-day duties and activities of lower-ranking police officers who carry out the majority of stop and searches. First, it is essential to acknowledge that most low-ranking officers enjoy the power of 'discretion' in how to apply the law and ultimately use their powers. There are various longstanding aspects of the police role in society that makes it possible and necessary for this to be the case. The legal codes and regulations they are tasked to enforce are finite in their formulation and cannot cover every conceivable scenario they might face. The day-to-day routine of the police is infinite in the number of possible scenarios they might have to respond to (Kinsey et al, 1986). In that regard the police officer must be able to have a degree of freedom in deciding what law, if any, to assign to each situation.

With this freedom, though, comes the risk of an individual's potential bias or prejudice to influence their decision making – with how they decide to implement stop and search. This was echoed by the then Home Secretary, Amber Rudd, who stated:

> 'While today's statistics show that our stop and search reforms are working, with a continuing fall in the overall number of stops and the highest ever recorded arrest rate, it is completely unacceptable that you are six times more likely to be stopped and searched if you are black than if you are white.' (Dodd and Gayle, 2016)

These figures create severe issues around police relations with the local community. From its foundation, the police are supposed to police by consent, meaning that their ability to enforce the law is through the consent of citizens who allow them this power (Home Affairs Committee, 2009). If stop and search is perceived as disproportionately targeting ethnic minority suspects, this can serve to reinforce the perception of racism and ethnic profiling. During the August riots of 2011, several cities in England experienced severe disorder and running battles with the police. Several participants in a major research project in the wake of the riots cited anger at stop and search as one of the reasons they felt disillusion with the police and spurring them on to take part in the riots. They felt that street encounters with the police were often ones of harassment and discrimination.

There is also the question to what degree stop-and-search powers are effective. Section 44 of the Terrorism Act 2000 allowed stop and search to be conducted without reasonable suspicion in authorised zones that were meant to cover areas that were more susceptible to terrorist attack. These zones grew in coverage, to the extent that they began to cover all of Greater London between 2009 and 2015. While over 200,000 searches were conducted, only 0.6% resulted in an arrest. This meant that a lot of ill-will was created between the police and the communities. This led the Home Office to suspend Section 44 and revert to previous legislation that relied on officers to demonstrate reasonable suspicion when conducting stop and searches (Rowlands, 2010a, 2010b). While this legislation is shaped in Parliament and the police are entrusted with enforcing it, how they do so can result in them being overzealous in how it is enforced, as the numbers around the use of stop and search show.

However, one factor that is changing the practice of discretion, and perhaps an important reason why the overall number of stop and searches across all ethnic groups has reduced, is the increasing visibility in which the police work. This is because mobile recording equipment that can visually or audibly document police practice is now available to everyone via a camera phone. This means that members of the public, or those with whom the police interact, can record the encounter. This can highlight abuses in how police officers enforce the law in a way that was not available before (Haggerty and Sandhu, 2014). Policing scholars have called this 'The New Visibility' (Goldsmith, 2010). Invisibility was a police resource that allowed patrol officers to enforce the law as they saw fit (Ericson, 2005), but now this is not as present as it was before. This has already led to several exposures of police abuse, such as racist verbal abuse endured by one man after an arrest (Lewis, 2012). As of October 2016, 22,000 Metropolitan Police officers were given body cameras in order to 'allow the Met to demonstrate the professionalism of officers, gather evidence and demonstrate their professionalism' (Metropolitan Police, n.d). Brown suggests that filming can create more accountability in the police than policing review boards, training or top-down bureaucratic initiatives could ever achieve (Brown, 2016a).

It is important to acknowledge that the role of stop and search is an integral part of policing and has undoubtedly been a vital tool in a police officer's ability to carry out their duties. Despite this, after more than a decade of statements of intent, policy documents and recommendations, the police power to stop and search continues to have a strikingly disproportionate impact on members of the ethnic minority communities.

Dr Aidan O'Sullivan, Birmingham City University

FACT 14

The police and security services are keeping 3,000 people in the UK under surveillance for suspected terrorist activities

Melindy Brown

In 2017 it was revealed that the police and security services were handling on average 500 active investigations of 3,000 people for suspected terrorist activities (Casciani, 2017). These figures have been made available to the public through a number of newspaper sources, as the official numbers are difficult to determine.

Terrorism has come to be an ever more central aspect of discussion in the criminal justice system of England and Wales, where it is largely understood as a premeditated act with the purpose of manipulating policy through fear or threats of violence, often for political, religious or ideological gain (McLaughlin, 2006). However, terrorism is not a new concept. Many groups, such as the Irish Republican Army and Euskadi Ta Askatasuna (more commonly known as ETA, an armed leftist Basque nationalist and separatist organisation in northern Spain and south-western France), have used terror and intimidation in an attempt to make political and religious change in the past (Carrabine et al, 2009).

Under the Terrorism Act 2000, the UK's Home Secretary may proscribe an organisation, if they believe it is involved in terrorism, making it a criminal offence for an individual to be a member. In 2016, the Home office stated that there were 74 international terrorist groups that are proscribed under the Terrorism Act 2000 and 14 groups in Northern Ireland that were proscribed under previous legislation, with the last addition being the neo-Nazi youth group 'National Action' in 2016 (Home Office, 2016). Jack Renshaw, a member of that group, pleaded guilty to preparing an act of terrorism, by buying a machete to kill MP Rosie Cooper (Khomami, 2018). While discussion of terrorism can tend to focus now on Islamic extremism, the UK faces terror threats from a wider array of groups than is sometimes suggested.

In recent years, and particularly with the growth of concern regarding Islamist extremism post 9/11, criminology has begun to incorporate into its lexicon theories and models that were traditionally more the preserve of political science and international relations. Part of this has been a growth in criminological concern that has sought to explain the reasoning behind radicalisation (for example, Laquer, 2003; Borum, 2003; Moghaddam, 2005). The basis of radicalisation is often an individual's frustration at the state, society or their personal lives, leading to them becoming involved – and often taking part – in – events with other like-minded people that can result in terrorism (Precht, 2007).

In the UK, it is an offence under the Terrorism Act 2006 (Section 5) for any person to engage in, prepare, attempt, or assist others in any acts of terrorism. To do so carries a maximum sentence of life imprisonment. One of the highest numbers of terrorism-related arrests, since records began, was noted at the end of the financial year March 2017. Of 304 people arrested, 108 were charged, of whom 84% were charged for terrorist activity, with international terrorism accounting for the majority (Home Office, 2017d).

The police and security services have a responsibility to monitor possible terrorist activity and respond to actual terrorist incidents. However, the anti-terror legislation has come to the fore in debates about balancing civil liberties with the need for security. Academics have long expressed concern about the unintended harms of creating 'suspect communities', for whom anti-terrorism measures and legislation can have far-reaching and serious impacts on civil liberties (Hillyard, 1993). It is therefore important to consider the role of the state in aiming to protect against the potential for alienating communities. Some academics have noted the potential for unnecessarily intrusive surveillance to increase hostility, ultimately contributing to conflict. Others have highlighted the more collaborative relationship between the police and security services, such as MI5. Collaborating alongside highly technical surveillance equipment and identification checks are essential in the fight for security (Zedner, 2000). Certainly, it is now not uncommon to see terrorism and organised crime being discussed as if these phenomena are invariably connected.

Yet, again, there are conflicting views relating to policing and security strategies, and the extent to which these should be conflated: should the response to terrorism follow traditional policing methods, or does the fight against terrorism require special tactics? In the wake of terror-related incidents, legislation has been passed that, in turn, appears to have given more power to the police (Walker, 2011; Newburn, 2013). One of the key pieces of legislation that helps police to monitor terrorism activity is the Investigatory Powers Act 2016. This legislation provides security services with the power to intercept, survey and record communications and internet use of the whole population in the United Kingdom.

It has been reported that 13 terror attacks were prevented between 2013 and March 2017, with a further five being prevented between March and May 2017 alone (Kentish, 2017). In the year ending December 2016, some 483 'stop and search' interventions were conducted by the Metropolitan Police Service under section 43 of the Terrorism Act 2000 (Home Office, 2017c). It is clear that a great deal of surveillance and monitoring is being conducted by the police and security services in the name of prevention. The crux of this issue is: who is being monitored, and what are the ramifications of such state actions? Such questions are important when we consider how the police spent £3 million on targeting Muslim communities in Birmingham over a two year period (Lewis, 2010).

Consequently, it would be reasonable to consider this level of surveillance as a developing strategy to deal with terrorist threats. It is therefore understandable to question the disparity between surveillance results in 2015 in comparison to 2016. One would expect these results to be higher due to the increase in terrorist activity; however, that is not the case. For example, from 2015 to 2016, there was a 30% decrease in the number of people questioned leaving or entering the country, an 8% decrease in the number of terror-related arrests, and a 30% decrease in the detaining and searching of those suspected of terrorist activity (Home Office, 2017c).

Yet a clear challenge facing the police and security services is the threat posed by lone attackers, who are the most difficult to monitor. Additionally, there is a lack of resources available to allow for 24-hour surveillance of each person suspected of being at risk of engaging in terrorist activity. The cost of 24-hour surveillance means that it is only used to monitor those who pose the highest risk to society (MacAskill, 2017).

While it might be understandable in the current climate that the police and security services have 3,000 people under investigation for suspected terrorist activity, this process is far from transparent. Moreover, the fact that the UK intelligence agencies and police now possess the most sweeping surveillance powers in the Western world ought to be at the forefront of debates about crime, power, liberty, citizen and state.

Melindy Brown, Birmingham City University

FACT 15

The Metropolitan Police Service examines approximately 40,000 digital forensics devices annually

Jonathan Jackson

The popularity of forensic crime television shows such as CSI: Crime Scene Investigation and Law & Order: Special Victims Unit have fuelled debate about the potential social impact of media representations of forensic science on public perceptions of crime investigation processes (Brewer and Ley, 2010). When the public are asked to give their impression of forensic science, they may immediately conjure up ideas of it as a vital crime-fighting tool and overestimate its use in real criminal justice.

While it is certainly true that forensic science has had a hugely positive impact on police work, much of forensic science has become heavily glamourised through fictional media, depicting a 'crime science' that can produce instant and infallible results. However, science is subjective, and these fictional portrayals often give an unrealistic vision of its capabilities and realities in order to satisfy the public demand for entertainment and escapism.

The truth is far more complex but by no means less interesting or exciting. Research into the contribution that forensic evidence makes to the investigation of crime in the United Kingdom (and in a broader global context) is very limited, but it is certain that scenes of crime officers in the UK do not throw themselves through windows or carry firearms. What they do is to provide vital information, which can assist the police in securing convictions and building a court-ready case.

Around 80% of the public's knowledge of policing comes from the media (Newburn et al, 2007). As a result, much of the public's understanding of the work of scenes of crime officers and forensic investigators is blurred, and the 'CSI effect' is typical of a distorted public view of the realities of forensic science (see Rowe, 2014). For many, while this may seem like an irrelevance, it is important to consider that the Criminal Justice System is staffed by members of the public who may hold distorted views on the actual nature of forensics. With such assumptions being made on the credibility of the science to ensure guilt, it could prove the difference between securing a conviction and a suspect walking free.

Forensic science remains a hugely broad and diverse subject, and encompasses a vast range of disciplines. Historically, the identification of fingerprints marked the summit of science and criminal investigation. With the advancement and accessibility of technology, the skills required of forensic officers has far surpassed fingerprinting and now encompasses investigations in both the physical and digital worlds. Forensic investigators have also had to adapt to far more science- and technology-savvy criminals, who have become adept at creating avenues of disinformation as well as protecting their identities. This often leads to the wasting of time and resources, both of which the forensic science service and the police have far less of. Both these points are ignored in fictional representations, with criminals often being portrayed as ignorant of such concepts, and resources being portrayed as vast and unending (Baskin and Sommers, 2012).

Yet contemporary forensics are likely to be transformed as the number of people using digital devices grows. In 2000, only 36% of UK adults owned a mobile phone compared to 93% in 2015. As the amount of digital data encountered in crime investigations grows, there has been an increase in demand for digital forensics. For example, the Metropolitan Police Service reports that it now examines approximately 40,000 digital forensics devices annually (Houses of Parliament, 2016), and the government suggests that demand for digital forensics might replace much of the traditional crime science of fingerprints and DNA in the near future.

The process of forensic investigation follows three key phases, which are enacted by both police and scenes of crime officers. The first is carried out by first responders, who must protect and secure the area and preserve what evidence is available. This is followed by an evidence-gathering stage, in which officers explore designated sections, to identify pieces of evidence relevant to the investigation of the incident. Finally, the evidence gathered, and the methods of collection, must be examined for mistakes or discrepancies, and must be prepared for the scrutiny of the courts (Baskin and Sommers, 2012).

The first distinctive myth generated by the 'CSI effect' is the timescale within which all three of these processes operate. It is often shown in dramas that all three stages are carried out within a 45-minute window. The reality is that the quicker this process, the greater the exposure to contamination and the incorrect analysis of evidence being presented. Large-scale forensic investigations can take (on average) weeks – but more often months – to ensure safe conclusions.

Throughout the different stages, the risk of contamination and loss of evidence is high. The stage in which this risk is at its greatest is the initial one, when crime scenes are often unprotected and unsealed. The realities of police work will often destroy vital evidence at a crime scene, much to the dismay of forensic officers (Genge, 2004). Lack of training, resources and time will often mean that areas remain exposed to public intrusion, creating doubt about the legitimacy of the evidence.

As with all other policing tools, forensic science is regulated through numerous pieces of legislation, most notably the Regulation of Investigative Powers Act (RIPA, 2000) and the Police and Criminal Evidence Act (PACE, 1984). Both pieces of legislation are designed to ensure that police work is monitored and able to stand up to scrutiny (Rowe, 2014). Legal representatives will conduct their own investigations into the evidential collection process, often with the intention of discrediting such information, to provide doubt of their client's guilt. The actions of many fictional detectives may provide the public with an entertaining evening, but would never be able to be justified under the rigours of such investigations or the restrictions placed on officers by legislation (Cook and Tattersall, 2008). Nor should police investigations be immune from boundaries, with the historical case of Stefan Kiszko highlighting the importance of regulating the actions of those placed in a position of authority (Manchester Evening News, 2010).

Police officers themselves are trained to focus on the lockdown (or sealing) of scenes, using cordons and barriers. In the case of murder, officers will follow the 'Murder Investigation Manual', which advises them on the core requirements of scene perseveration. Crime scenes can often be in multiple different locations, increasing the pressures on ensuring that evidence is not at risk of contamination (Becker and Dutelle, 2013). Many such areas are often difficult to control and are hampered by the elements themselves, which act as a barrier for forensic officers. A rain- and wind-swept hillside may seem an ideal setting for a dark crime drama, but such conditions often destroy the very things that are needed to carry out an effective forensic science investigation and can hamper the processing stage.

A question long debated by investigators, forensic scientists and criminologists alike has been the distinction between evidence and truth. In principle, this discussion has attempted to recognise the fallibility of forensic science and to dispel the untruths that are so dominant in fictional crime dramas (Baldwin, 1993). It does not aim to diminish the outstanding work of forensic science and its contribution to securing convictions and ensuring that dangerous and violent offenders are removed from society. However, the question remains as to whether evidence is truth.

Forensic science can often not explain the circumstances behind the events that led to the incident taking place. In drama, such outcomes are often shown as being derived from the scientific evidence gathered. The margin of error is, however, so great that simply placing suspects at a crime does not necessarily imply guilt. Roles are often not focused on prosecution, but rather on the establishing of facts in a case. This would suggest that forensic science is a tool to search for the truth, and should be used in conjunction with other methods of criminal investigation.

Throughout countless fictional dramas, there has always been a blurring of the line between reality and fiction, particularly when it comes to the portrayal of crime and its subsequent police investigations. It is impossible to regulate creative licence, and producers are eager to provide entertainment that will shock and intrigue audiences. It is also important that this is balanced with a dose of reality now and again, to ensure that the fictional representation of forensic science does not become the accepted public truth.

Jonathan Jackson, Birmingham City University

FACT 16

Police officers comprise only 60% of the police workforce in England and Wales

Kelly J. Stockdale

If you ask people what comes to mind when they think of 'the police', they are likely to picture a police officer in uniform – a symbolic and iconographic representative of 'police' and crime fighting in general. Similarly, if you were to pick up any criminological text or newspaper article discussion on 'the police', it would mostly relate to police officers. Yet police officers account for just over 60% of the police workforce. Police staff, police community support officers (PCSOs) and designated officers (police staff who have specific designated powers) make up approximately 40%, with staff occupying a diverse range of roles beyond 'back office' administration.

The modern police workforce has expanded rapidly over the last 15 years. Today, many staff work in a frontline capacity: indeed, police staff roles are present from the initial crime report to the final court session, and all aspects of the criminal investigation in between. For example, if you are a victim of crime, your first contact with the police is likely to be a police staff member, rather than a warranted officer (a Warrant Card is a proof of identification and authority carried by police officers or special constables to perform the functions of the office held); whether it be reported via telephone to police staff call handlers or to a front counter clerk or on the street to a PCSO. Crime scene investigation is predominantly a police staff role. A police staff investigator might be responsible for the case, from the initial report right through to court. Similarly, if an arrest is made, a suspect would be processed and cared for by designated officers in a custody setting. Furthermore, in some forces, hierarchical shifts have occurred, to enable police staff to occupy senior management roles equivalent to deputy chief constable.

This discussion explores the role of non-warranted officers in the police. It gives a brief history to the 'modern police family' and the development of police staff roles. Using Wiltshire Constabulary as a case study, it outlines some of the diverse roles that police staff occupy. It concludes by highlighting some of the barriers that police staff face, compared to police officers, in terms of their professional development and career growth within current police organisational frameworks. The aim is to encourage readers to think beyond traditional discussions that frame 'the police' as a homogenous entity and to recognise the need to be alert to the contemporary realities that make up and operate within the police as a broad organisation.

To understand the police in England and Wales, it is important to consider its historical backdrop: it is within this history that the mission, structures and image of the police are embedded. Reiner (2010) provides a detailed historical development of the police, setting out the raft of changes and adaptations that have occurred since the Metropolitan Police Act 1829, and locating these shifts in social, political and economic environments. While police staff have existed within traditional police force structures, it is since the post-millennium policing period and policy changes concerning workforce modernisation that a new, extended policing family has emerged.

Following criticisms, particularly in relation to the lack of diversity within the police force and 'institutional racism' as identified in the Macpherson Report (Macpherson, 1999), the New Labour government proposed a series of reforms to strengthen frontline policing, to provide a more 'visible' police force within communities, and to increase public confidence in policing. The White Paper *Policing a New Century: A Blueprint for Reform* (Home Office, 2001a) set out the government's intentions to increase the capacity of police officers, by enhancing the role of police staff and allowing them to carry out certain policing functions that were traditionally carried out by police officers. It also proposed the implementation of 'community support officers', employed as police staff but wearing a similar uniform to warranted officers who would be a visible presence in the community. With a remit based around community engagement, reassurance and visibility, they would also have basic (limited) powers in relation to dealing with minor offences and anti-social behaviour. These proposals, including the newly created post (renamed as police community support officers or PCSOs), were subsequently introduced as part of the Police Reform Act 2002, which relinquished the need for warranted officers to perform traditional policing roles and extended some powers of policing activity to this new, wider 'policing family'.

Over the following decade, the number of police staff increased exponentially: figures from the Office for National Statistics (ONS, 2013) and Unison (2014) detail 130,000 police officers across the 43 forces in England and Wales, with a further 65,000 police staff performing a wide variety of roles across all areas of policing. In addition to police officers and staff, a further 14,000 PCSOs are employed. There also exist 18,000 Special Officers (a voluntary role, whereby trained members of the public carry out the same services and functions of a warranted police officer); and 9,000 Police Support Volunteers (another voluntary and unpaid role, providing various support within a policing environment in a non-frontline capacity).

While there has been a decrease in numbers with government-driven austerity measures today, recent workforce numbers still show similar staff/officer proportions: 2017 data shows an overall workforce of 198,684, comprising 123,142 officers, 61,063 police staff, 10,213 PCSOs and 4,255 designated officers (Home Office, 2017).

Yet the introduction of police staff has not been without difficulty. While research distinguishes different police cultures that operate among officers (see, for example, classic works by Chan, 1996; Waddington, 1999b), little attention is paid to police culture in England and Wales and police staff's role within this. Police civilian staff, including PCSOs, may be part of an 'extended family' (Mawby and Wright, 2012), but that does not mean they have been fully accepted and integrated within existing police structures. There has been little research into civilian police cultures. However, research into PCSOs' acceptance shows a certain amount of hostility (Caless, 2007); and the conflict and 'culture clash' between police staff working as intelligence analysts and police officers has also been highlighted (Cope, 2004). In particular, Cope's research points to a lack of understanding between police officers and police staff, both in relation to one another's skills, their remit and their role in the organisation (2004: 192-3). This lack of understanding has an impact in relation to issues surrounding hierarchy and status, and thus potentially limits the ability for police staff to pursue leadership roles in the organisation.

The issue of hierarchy needs to be considered: police staff grades are difficult to compare to those of police officers, due to the difficulties of police hierarchical structures to fully reflect non-warranted police staff expertise and experience. For example, Cope's (2004) findings suggest that the role of intelligence analyst would be equivalent to a sergeant or detective inspector, yet this hierarchy is not recognised. These issues indicate a potential for conflict and tension between staff and officers. It is therefore crucial to recognise the specific roles and subcultures in the modern police family, when researching and discussing 'the police'.

Yet there are interesting developments: as the numbers of police staff have increased, forces are adapting and (partly due to austerity measures and spending cuts) workforces are undergoing significant modernisation, including substantial reviews of their force operational models. In some forces, there have been radical transformations, with a flattening of police officer hierarchy and greater opportunities and roles for police staff in terms of leadership roles and creation of new opportunities for professional development in the force. Wiltshire Constabulary is an example of this. Since 2015 the force has removed traditional police hierarchical structures, with many areas of the force now showing a 50% divide between staff and officers in leadership roles.

While there are many promising developments in police forces – and the role that police staff play in the organisation is being recognised, developed and incorporated into new force structures – the language and understandings of 'the police' have failed to adjust and keep pace. However, greater change may be on the horizon again, particularly with the Policing Education Qualifications Framework that is set to turn the police in England and Wales into a graduate profession (College of Policing, 2017). How this will impact upon traditional police–public relations may be significant, as the National Policing Curriculum and National College of Policing may hint at the significant changes in how we view and conceive of the police in time to come.

Dr Kelly J. Stockdale, York St John University

FACT 17

An individual police officer will attend to approximately 150 non-crime-related issues per year

Claire Davis

Police work is typically understood in terms of crime. When police officers are appointed, they swear an oath before a magistrate. The police constable's oath of attestation states:

> I do solemnly and sincerely declare and affirm that I will well and truly serve the Queen in the office of constable, with fairness, integrity, diligence and impartiality, upholding fundamental human rights and according equal respect to all people; and that I will, to the best of my power, cause the peace to be kept and preserved and prevent all offences against people and property; and that while I continue to hold the said office I will, to the best of my skill and knowledge, discharge all the duties thereof faithfully according to law.

This is a public declaration that crime is central to the police role. Research on police culture has also captured the attachment to crime-fighting as in most media portrayals as characteristic of 'real police work' (Cockcroft, 2013). Reiner (2010) has identified the action-centred orientation and sense of mission as core features of police occupational culture. Police work, in other words, is characterised by police officers in terms of the risk and danger of dealing with crime (Skolnick, 1975). As Waddington (1999a: 4) explains: 'The traditional image of policing, to which the police themselves tenaciously hold and fictional portrayal reaffirms, is that of the proverbial "thin blue line" protecting society from lawlessness'.

The emphasis on crime-fighting in police occupational culture is reinforced through promotion processes. Chief constables, for example, rarely use their operational powers of arrest. Therefore, as Wall (1998: 309) explains, 'there is no practical need for chief constables to possess operational experience'. Yet there is considerable prestige and credibility attached to the 'street policing' experience of police leaders (Rowe, 2006; Smith, 2008).

Yet, much of what the police do is unrelated to crime. The police have a central role in dealing with issues around vulnerability, public protection and safeguarding. According to the College of Policing (2015), in 2012/13 there were 19.6 million non-crime incidents recorded by the police, which equates to approximately 150 per police officer per year. We have seen a shift from the term 'police force' to 'police service', to capture the role of the police beyond crime (Reiner, 2010). The College of Policing (2015: 16) confirms that this non-crime demand 'now represents a greater share of what the police do'. In short, the police largely do not 'fight crime'.

Dealing with people with mental health problems is a large part of this non-crime work. The Independent Commission on Mental Health and Policing (BBC, 2013) estimated at least 20% of police time is spent dealing with people with mental health issues. The police are also required to attend suspected suicide incidents, and with contemporary suicide rates increasing, this represents a growing demand on the police service. We also expect police officers to deal with missing people, which is particularly important with the increased focus of the police service on protecting children and vulnerable adults from maltreatment (Shalev Greene and Pakes, 2013).

The recognition of the diverse nature of police work is in keeping with academic research, which has long recognised the role of the police beyond crime control. In the first empirical study of the police in Britain, Michael Banton (1964) described the role of the police as 'law officers' and 'peace officers' and argued that the police officer is primarily a 'peace officer'. Banton (1964: 127) explains: 'Relatively little of his time is spent enforcing the law in the sense of arresting offenders; far more is spent "keeping the peace" by supervising his beat and responding to requests for assistance'.

This 'peace officer' function of the police captures an array of activities performed by them, and includes, as Reiner (2010: 7) reminds us, 'a bewildering miscellany of tasks, from controlling traffic to controlling terrorism'. Maurice Punch (1979) provided an early insight into what he described as the 'secret social service' function of the police, and explains the role of the police as dealing with individuals in crisis. Like Banton, Punch argued that policing cannot be characterised exclusively in terms of law enforcement. He explains:

> Policemen frequently have to act as untrained and temporary social workers, vets (with injured animals), mental welfare officers, marriage guidance counsellors, welfare officers, accommodation officers, child-care officers, home-help to the infirm, and also as confidant and counsellor to people alone and in need of guidance. (Punch, 1979b: 107)

Similarly, Bittner (1990) also considers the activities of the police beyond crime. The police, Bittner (1990: 251) explains, deal with events where 'something-that-ought-not-to-be-happening-and-about-which-somebody-had-better-do-something-now'. The public's expectations of the police therefore are virtually limitless (Bittner, 1990).

In preserving the myth of the police as crimefighters, crime is positioned as exclusively a police responsibility, a police problem. The police are judged on their performance in reducing crime and their ability to reduce rising crime rates associated with police activity (Waddington, 1999a). Yet crime is inherently complex, a product of a variety of social, cultural, economic, political and psychological processes, and informal and formal social controls (Reiner, 2010). The police have an important role in responding to crime, but they are one part of the formal social controls. As Reiner (2010: 159) explains, 'it is chimerical to see them as the primary means of controlling crime levels'.

This attachment to crime-fighting also preserves what has been described as 'the cult of masculinity', where police officers are expected to be physically and emotionally strong, so they are able to effectively deal with crime (Waddington, 1999b). Fielding (1994) describes police culture in terms of 'hegemonic masculinity', which refers to the centrality of stereotypical masculine values such as aggressiveness, physical action and preoccupation with conflict. The peacekeeping function of the police, as Bittner (1990: 33) describes, is not seen as 'a skilled performance'. The positioning of crime control as real police work fails to recognise the legitimacy of the broader remit of the police (Punch, 1979b). This has many important implications for the police service in Britain, including acting as a barrier to the recruitment and retention of women (Heidensohn, 1992). Police work, with the emphasis on crimefighting, is understood as 'men's work'. Silvestri (2011: 31) explains: 'Police work becomes a means whereby men differentiate masculinity from femininity, a reason for constructing oneself as a real man. With the perception that police work involves strength, action, danger and male fellowship, the work of policing becomes securely defined as men's work'.

Despite the reality that much of police activity involves non-crime, the role of the police is still understood primarily in terms of crime. The perception of the police as exclusively crimefighters does not reflect the diversity of police work, the expectations from the public and, likewise, the complexity of crime control. To fully understand the role of the police, it is important to challenge misunderstandings and falsehoods about the nature of police work. Police work cannot, and should not, be understood solely in terms of crime.

Dr Claire Davies, University of Leicester

Part Five
Prison realities

FACT 18
Contrary to what people often think, a life sentence does last for life

James Treadwell

In debates about imprisonment, it is quite common to hear people say that 'a life sentence should mean life'. Indeed, that very sentiment was expressed by none other than Conservative Prime Minister David Cameron in 2014 (The Telegraph, 2014). However, while that view is a popular statement and a 'soundbite' that accompanies a lament on 'British justice', the reality is that few people recognise the complexities of a life sentence and what it means.

Of course, a first point worth making is that while there are often appeals to British justice, there is in reality no such thing. In the United Kingdom, there are three separate systems: in England and Wales; in Scotland; and in Northern Ireland. Each In the UK, specifically when it comes to those convicted of murder, life is the mandatory and only sentence that the courts can pass for the crime and it has been so since the Death Penalty was abolished in 1965.

In England and Wales, life imprisonment is a sentence that lasts until the death of the prisoner, hence the sentence lasts for life. 'Life' is a life sentence. Perhaps confusion is caused, because, as Appleton states, 'A Life Sentence does not mean, and never has meant, that the convicted offender must be imprisoned for the remainder of his or her natural life' (Appleton, 2010: 1). So, a life sentence lasts for life – it's just not necessarily always the case that the entirety of that sentence will be spent in prison.

Seemingly, what people mean when they express the view that 'life should mean life' is that the offender should spend their entire life in prison custody, and that is arguably a more complex matter. For murderers, this is the case and they actually will. It has been reported that there are around 100 cases since the first introduction of the whole-life order in 1983, according to which prisoners convicted of murder are likely to die in custody (although a significant percentage of these prisoners have since died whilst in prison or had their sentences reduced on appeal). Infamous murderers such as Joanne Dennehy (a female spree killer), Michael Adebolajo (one of the murderers of Fusilier Lee Rigby) and Thomas Mair (the murderer of MP Jo Cox) are subject to whole-life tariffs and are unlikely ever to be released from prison. The worst murderers, or those whose offences are deemed to merit the criteria, are now given these whole-life tariffs. This means that they will never be released, however safe it may be, except on compassionate grounds if they are thought to be dying (with the approval of the Home Secretary).

In England and Wales today, the Criminal Justice Act 2003 (and particularly section 269) requires judges, when setting the minimum term to be served by a convicted murderer, to have regard to the principles set out in Schedule 21 to the Act, which provides three starting points, including (for the first time in legislation) whole-life imprisonment as the maximum penalty. Judges are not obliged to follow the guidelines, but must give reasons if they depart from them. The guidelines recommended that multiple murderers (who murder two or more people), whose crimes involved sexual abuse, pre-planning, abduction or terrorism, should never be released from prison. Such a sentence is known as a 'whole-life order'. The murder of a single child following abduction, or sexual or sadistic conduct also qualifies, as does the murder of a police or prison officer during their duty (since 2015) and murder committed to advance a political, religious or ideological cause.

Previously, the Home Secretary reserved the right to set the 'tariff' or minimum length of term for prisoners sentenced to life imprisonment. In July 1990, the then Conservative Home Secretary David Waddington decided to impose a whole-life tariff on Myra Hindley, one of the 'Moors murderers'. His decision was then confirmed by successive Home Secretaries. In the case of Hindley, the House of Lords held that there was no reason in principle why a crime, if sufficiently heinous, should not be regarded as deserving of lifelong incarceration for the purposes of pure punishment. From this basis of 'principle', the High Court ruled that a whole-life tariff would not be illegal in principle (see Appleton and Grøver, 2007).

However, in November 2000, the Home Secretary lost the power in relation to defendants aged under 18, following an appeal to the European Court of Human Rights by the murderers of two-year-old James Bulger: Robert Thompson and Jon Venables. In 2002, a successful legal challenge by convicted double murderer Anthony Anderson removed from the Home Secretary the final say on how long a life sentence prisoner must serve, before the prisoner's eligibility for parole could be considered, including the right to decide that certain murderers should never be released.

Yet most 'lifers' do not spend the rest of their lives in jail. The trial judge sets a minimum term, known as a 'tariff' (the minimum length of time a prisoner must spend behind bars before becoming eligible for parole), and the length of that tariff will depend on the seriousness of the crime and some factors involving the offender. Life imprisonment is only applicable to defendants aged 21 or over. Those aged between 18 and 20 are sentenced to custody for life. Those aged under 18 are sentenced to detention (imprisonment refers to specific state of being incarcerated or confined in an institutional setting such as a prison, a custodial sentence is a sentence given by a court that involves a term of imprisonment, and a Detention Training Order combines detention with training and will be used for young people who commit a serious offence or commit a number of offences) during Her Majesty's pleasure for murder, or detention for life for other crimes where life imprisonment is the sentence for adults. However, people under 21 may not be sentenced to a whole-life order, and so must become eligible for parole. Once this minimum 'tariff' has been served, the prisoner is eligible for release on licence. The only issue is whether release would be safe. This is decided by the Parole Board on evidence that is as objective as possible. While there are no guarantees when predicting the future, 'lifers' released on licence are closely supervised by the probation service and are subject to restrictive conditions – for example, banning alcohol or contact with victims' families. A breach of licence or threatening behaviour can lead to recall to prison (Cullen and Newell, 1999). There is no court hearing, and the offender is just returned straight back to custody.

In England and Wales, tariff terms for lifers are getting longer and longer. Average tariffs for mandatory and non-mandatory life sentences have increased by 32% and 75% respectively in under a decade (Howard League, 2016a). Additionally, it has been claimed that more people are serving indeterminate prison sentences in England and Wales than in the other 46 countries in the Council of Europe combined (Howard League, 2016).

Although some released lifer sentence prisoners are returned to prison, few commit further offences, let alone kill again after they are released (or paroled) from their sentence. It is important to stress that those lifers who are released are never simply at complete liberty. They remain on that life licence for the rest of their lives, subject to recall to prison, should their behaviour cause alarm.

The whole-life order has proven a little more controversial. In 2012, three convicted murderers (whole-life prisoners), Jeremy Bamber, Peter Moore and Douglas Vinter, applied to the European Court of Human Rights in Strasbourg, for the court to declare that it is a contravention of the European Convention on Human Rights for someone to be sentenced to lifelong imprisonment. The court ruled that because the whole-life orders were imposed by a judge only after consideration of the facts of each case, and because the life prisoners could apply to the Home Secretary for compassionate release, their whole-life orders did not breach their human rights. A later appeal by the same men led to a ruling in July 2013 that there must be a prospect of review of whole-life tariffs, and that any impossibility of parole would violate their Article 3 rights under the Convention. In 2015, the European Court upheld the lawfulness of whole-life orders, on the ground that they can be reviewed in exceptional circumstances, though in reality such review is unlikely unless a subject is terminally ill and nearing death.

Whole-life sentences have also been criticised in some quarters for giving offenders no incentive to behave well and cooperate with prison staff, or make any serious attempt at rehabilitation or reform. In 2016, Victor Castigador, a whole-life prisoner, admitted murdering another prisoner at HMP Long Lartin. At least two other whole-life prisoners have seriously wounded other inmates in prison. Just after being jailed for life in 2005, spree killer Mark Hobson poured a bucket of boiling water over Ian Huntley (murderer of schoolgirls Holly Wells and Jessica Chapman, who is not subject to a whole-life order but a 40-year tariff). In 2012, convicted double murderer Gary Vinter admitted slashing Roy Whiting (the murderer of schoolgirl Sarah Payne) with a sharpened toilet brush handle. Four years later, Vinter also admitted the attempted murder of another inmate who sustained a brain injury and was blinded in one eye.

The whole-life order has been criticised, on the basis that it offers no hope, leading some penal reform charities to propose a 'faint hope clause' that would enable people sentenced to an indeterminate term, and who had made an

exceptional effort, to apply for earlier parole eligibility –
even those who have committed the most heinous crimes
(Howard League, 2016a).

Professor James Treadwell, Staffordshire University

FACT 19

The average yearly cost of keeping one person in prison in England and Wales is £35,182

David Sheldon

Since the early 1990s, the prison population of England and Wales has more than doubled and, as of June 2018, stands at approximately 82,989 (BBC News, 2018). This dramatic increase has resulted from a rise in the use of custodial sentences and an increase in the average sentence served by prisoners. This is the consequence of a growing political rhetoric concerned with 'being tough on crime', which began with former Conservative Home Secretary Michael Howard stating that 'Prison works' (Travis, 2010), and subsequently a political arms race in Britain between the Conservatives and New Labour, with each party seeking to outdo the other on the topic of crime.

The result of having a large prison population is the large financial cost it brings. In 2017 the average cost of imprisonment for a person for a year in England and Wales is approximately £35,182 (Ministry of Justice, 2017c). This equates to an overall financial cost to the taxpayer of roughly £3 billion a year. This is not just from having to clothe, feed and provide adequate living conditions for prisoners, but also the cost of prison security, prison staff and maintenance of the prison buildings.

A substantial number of the prisons in England and Wales were constructed in the Victorian era, and the cost of maintaining the buildings is becoming exponentially more expensive over time. This means that new prisons must be built as cheaper alternatives to the high maintenance costs of older prisons. HMP Oakwood and HMP Berwyn are examples of such estates. The price of such establishments is best displayed by HMP Berwyn, which opened in February 2017 at a total of £212 million (Ministry of Justice, 2018).

The people held in prison have committed a variety of offences – from failure to pay council tax all the way through to convictions for murder and terrorism. Those convicted of a crime will often have had a sentenced passed upon them determining the number of years they will be imprisoned for. However, not everyone in prison knows how long they are going to be held in custody. This is because they could have received a (now defunct) sentence known as Imprisonment for Public Protection (IPP), where they were given an initial minimum sentence but could be held longer (of which 4,500 still are), if they are deemed to still represent a risk to the public.

Alternatively, individuals awaiting trial, who have been refused bail, may also be remanded into custody. The refusal of bail can occur for several reasons, including the probability of the person absconding, the likelihood that they will commit further crime if placed on bail and the potential for them to intimidate witnesses to their alleged crimes. Those who are denied bail are remanded into custody. In 2012/13, some 48,584 people were remanded in custody to await trial, of whom 73% were remanded to await sentencing. Of the men and women who were remanded into custody, 13,900 did not receive a subsequent prison sentence (Prison Reform Trust, 2011). These remand prisoners contribute to the strain and growing number of the prison population in England and Wales, ultimately increasing the cost of imprisonment.

The average cost of imprisonment, however, is vastly misleading in deciphering the real costs of imprisonment. Prisons are not uniform and differ greatly, depending on who they are designed for. Prisoners in England and Wales are categorised across a spectrum ranging from Category A to Category D. These categories represent the risk and danger that the prisoners represent to the public if they were to escape. Category A prisoners include notable murderers, such as Joanne Dennehy (female spree killer), Thomas Mair (the murderer of MP Jo Cox) and Ian Huntley (murderer of the Soham schoolgirls Holly Wells and Jessica Chapman). Thus, these prisoners would represent a distinct risk to the public, if they were to escape from captivity.

Due to the risk represented by Category A prisoners, they are often held under much more stringent conditions than other prisoners. These prisoners will be imprisoned in one of the UK's dispersal prisons, such as HMP Belmarsh, HMP Manchester (often referred to as 'Strangeways') and HMP Frankland. These prisons have the highest levels of security, to make the prospect of escape near impossible. However, the increase in security precautions, such as higher levels of staff and increased perimeter precautions, impacts upon the cost of imprisonment. This means that a Category A prisoner will often cost in the region of £50,000 per year – far above the national average.

Category A prisoners only account for around 5–10% of the overall prison population. As prisoners pass through their sentence, it is considered that the risk they represent decreases. However, this is not always the case. For example, Charles Bronson, a notoriously violent inmate, has remained as a Category A prisoner despite his prolonged imprisonment. Nearly all other prisoners will progress through the prison estate from Category A status, until they are eventually moved to an open prison (Category D) or released from less secure custody.

Nearly 40% of prisoners will be Category C prisoners, meaning they are nearing the point where they can be held in open conditions. The practicality of this means that prisoners will often become cheaper throughout their sentence, as the need for enhanced security measures decreases. Category C prisoners only cost on average £20,000 per annum, markedly cheaper than a Category A prisoner. This is largely due to the lower security arrangements needed for their prolonged captivity. The risk that a prisoner represents, then, has a demonstrable effect on the cost of their imprisonment.

Moreover, the average cost of imprisonment fails to consider the cost of incarcerating specific types of offenders. Sex offenders currently account for 17% of the overall prison population (MOJ, 2016). This has resulted in eight of the nation's prisons being devoted solely to the imprisonment of sex offenders. These individuals are often very different to other types of prisoners. They are often older and come from middle-class backgrounds (Mann, 2012, 2014). Further, given their offence type, they are treated as being qualitatively different to other types of offenders. This means they are required to undertake special courses, such as the Sexual Offender Treatment Programme designed to quell their deviant sexual tendencies and rehabilitate them (Hudson, 2005). Providing these specialist courses and professionals requires great expense. However, these prisoners tend to be more conformist and create fewer behavioural problems for staff. So these types of offenders, although largely hated by society, are some of the cheapest to imprison. Indeed, sex offenders cost on average £19,000 to imprison per year, placing them well below the average cost of imprisonment.

In recent years, there have been concerted efforts to reduce the cost of imprisonment. This has resulted not only in governmental cuts in the wake of economic austerity, but also through the privatisation of prison establishments. Beginning most prominently in the United States and subsequently Australia (Ludlow, 2015), the process of privatisation in Britain began in the 1990s and has resulted in three private security firms (G4S, Sodexo and Serco) being responsible for the management of 14 prisons across England and Wales. This has led to a process known as 'benchmarking' being introduced by the former Secretary of State for Justice, Chris Grayling.

This 'benchmarking' process of creating cheaper and more cost-efficient prisons is a result of the public sector competing with the private sector. This has meant that public-sector prisons have had to match the cost-saving regimes of private prisons – meaning fewer staff, alterations to the core prison regime and fewer layers of management. The implementation of benchmarking was based on the premise that private prisons could imprison people for less, thus making them a model of success for the public sector to follow. This is despite evidence to the contrary that private prisons, although only accounting for 18% of the entire prison estate, account for 23% of the overall prison budget. Private-sector prisons, then, are in fact more costly than public-sector prisons, which raises questions as to the value of benchmarking and of following their commercial model. It has also arguably led to a decrease in prison standards, with less money available for a burgeoning prison population. Rather than reducing the cost of imprisonment, benchmarking has decreased the safety of those imprisoned.

The reality is that although cost per inmate is falling, imprisonment remains expensive, despite recent and ongoing attempts at its cost reduction. The cost varies massively across the prison estate, dependent on the type of prisoner and the establishment in which they are being confined. If real efforts are to be made to decrease the cost of imprisonment, a reduction in the number of people being imprisoned must occur, along with alternatives to imprisonment offered. Yet while many accept the view of Douglas Hurd, the former Foreign Secretary, that prison is 'an expensive way of making bad people worse' (Brown, 1997), the current projections continue to be for a rising prison population in England and Wales in years to come.

David Sheldon, University of Birmingham

FACT 20

In 2016, almost 289,605 extra days (or 793 years of imprisonment) were added to prisoners' sentences

Kate Gooch

When an individual is sentenced to imprisonment, we might assume that the length of their confinement will be determined in open court at the point of sentencing. However, the pronounced sentence rarely accounts for the various ambiguities and complex rules regarding release, nor the possibility that an individual's conduct *during* a custodial sentence may result in extra time being added during a hearing taking place *outside* the criminal/appellate courts and within the prison itself.

In the last 10 years, there has been a dramatic decline in safety and security across the prison estate (HM Chief Inspector of Prisons for England and Wales, 2015; 2016). The incidence of prison violence and self-harm continues to increase (Ministry of Justice, 2017a) and, in many prisons, conditions are declining, with more prisoners spending the vast majority of their day confined to their cell and in cramped, overcrowded and 'squalid' conditions (HMIP, 2017). A range of explanations have been offered for such trends, including staff shortages, staff inexperience, the use of psychoactive substances, and the increased use of drones and illegally held mobile telephones. In response, the government released a White Paper, *Prison Safety and Reform,* which among measures designed to reconfigure and modernise the prison estate, introduced a raft of measures emphasising punishment and enhanced security (Ministry of Justice, 2016b, 2017b).

Set against this background and symptomatic of the desire to regain order and control, prisoners are increasingly receiving 'added days' for breaching prison rules. The Prison Rules 1999 and Young Offender Institution (YOI) Rules 2000 specify those actions deemed unacceptable and inappropriate in a prison, ranging from relatively minor misbehaviour – such as intentionally refusing to work – to more serious and otherwise unlawful behaviour – such as physical or sexual assault, hostage taking, concerted indiscipline and escape attempts. This legislative framework is accompanied by policy guidance in the form of Prison Service Instruction entitled 'Prisoner Discipline Procedures' (24/2011). Taken together, a prison governor is empowered to hear charges against prisoners for breaches of Prison/YOI Rules during an 'adjudication' and to impose punishments if those charges are proved.

Adjudication hearings mirror court hearings in many ways but take place in the prison and are inaccessible to the public or the media. Prisoners must:

- be informed of the nature of the charges against them in writing and within a specified time limit;
- have an opportunity to hear the evidence against them;
- have an opportunity to offer a plea;
- have an opportunity to make a statement;
- have an opportunity to seek legal counsel.

Generally, the officer or staff member charging the prisoners is asked to attend the hearing and give their evidence in person. Other evidence can also be obtained, including witness statements, CCTV footage, the result of drug tests, body-worn camera footage, photographs or evidence seized. It is for the governor to decide if the charge has been proved beyond reasonable doubt (applying the criminal standard of proof) and to then award penalties according to a fixed tariff. Thus, unlike the criminal court process, there is no need for an independent prosecutor or sentencing judge. Rather, the finding of guilt and the levying of punishment is made by a prison governor from the same institution as both the prison staff bringing charges and the prisoners against whom charges are being made. Claims of neutrality may appear hollow if such hearings are not conducted with procedural fairness.

Sanctions typically include a loss of earnings for work or employment, loss of television, loss of association and cellular confinement in the segregation unit. If the governor thinks that 'added days' may be appropriate, they may refer the case to the Independent Adjudicator (IA), who has the power to add 42 days to a custodial sentence for each charge.

Awarding additional days to a prison sentence was, until 2002, within the range of powers given to a prison governor. However, following the case of *Ezeh and Connors v UK* (2002) 35 EHRR 28 and a successful challenge under Article 6 of the European Convention on Human Rights, this authority was placed in the hands of an IA, typically a district judge or deputy district judge, who presides over hearings in the prison. In part, this removal of powers from the prison governor introduces greater procedural fairness.

That said, there has been an increasing trend to refer matters to the IA. The reasons for this trend are unclear, but it is likely that a combination of increased contraband seizures, increased prison violence, a decline in conditions, and the desire to gain control and enforce boundaries are contributory factors. Although generally governors will refer the most serious cases to the IA – such as serious assaults, possession of contraband, and large amounts of property damage – it is notable that in 2016, one-third of charges resulting in 'added days' were for 'disobedience' and 'disrespect'. Such vague language does not indicate whether such disobedience constitutes behaviour that might include something more akin to a small or low-level 'riot', or whether it is effectively behaviour that could more appropriately be dealt with through less punitive means.

Moreover, the desire to regain order and control with 'added days' will not address the wider, systemic problems that are causing people to violate prison rules. For example, prisoners may misuse substances for a range of reasons, including boredom and long periods of inactivity. Punishment does not reduce demand for contraband and is unlikely to act as a deterrent. Moreover, punishing prisoners for acts of frustration born out of poor conditions is unlikely to improve the legitimacy of the prison.

The policy of awarding added days does not operate equitably. Not all prisoners are eligible. For example, added days cannot be awarded to prisoners who are on recall, serving indeterminate sentences or against young people serving detention and training orders (short sentences only available for those under 18). Those on remand may have added days awarded prospectively, only to be served if subsequently convicted of an offence and awarded a custodial service.

Moreover, and despite the extra time added to their sentences, prisoners who appear before the IA may not have legal representation. Unlike adjudication hearings, prisoners can still seek legal aid when faced with being brought before the IA. However, uptake is poor.

The decisions of both adjudicating governors and IAs can be appealed within specified timeframes. Other avenues of redress include the Prisons and Probation Ombudsman and judicial review applications to the High Court. It is possible for prisoners to apply for a remission of added days due to good behaviour. However, it is unclear how many do so or how many are successful.

Dr Kate Gooch, University of Leicester

FACT 21

3.5% of those serving a sentence in the criminal justice system in England and Wales are former military personnel

Emma Murray

Former military personnel (veterans) occupy a special and often privileged position in the public's imagination. Providing a continued reminder of the sacrifices made by the Armed Forces community, those who have served in the military represent and embody a central part of a nation's defence and security system. The impact and scars of battle are typically framed as a mark of their bravery and courage in popular discourse – a social and cultural expectation.

With an estimated ex-military population of 6.1 million in the United Kingdom (4 million in England and Wales) (Pozo and Walker, 2014), and an estimated 17,000 people leaving the UK Armed Forces each year (Supporting UK Service leavers and their families in the transition to civilian life, 2016), how individuals transition from the military into civilian society is a political concern. While it is important to note that the majority transition without interaction with health, welfare or correctional services, the issues facing a minority of veterans are of grave importance. Homelessness, unemployment, drug and alcohol dependency and post-traumatic stress disorder are all well documented. Each year, the problems experienced by a difficult transition are captured numerically. In 2015, this number is said to have reached 66,090 – costing the UK taxpayer £98 million (The Transition Mapping Study, 2013).

For almost a decade, veterans' involvement in crime has also received significant political attention. The National Association of Probation Officers report, which claimed that veterans were disproportionally represented at each stage of the criminal justice system in England and Wales, played an important role in raising awareness of the potential numbers of veterans who are convicted on an offence (Ford et al, 2016). Although inconclusive, figures released by the Ministry of Justice (2017b), note that 3% of those who responded to the question 'have you served in the armed forces' when entering prison disclosed a military past. The figures of those on licence are forthcoming, but the Ministry of Defence in 2016 suggested that former military personnel accounted for 3.5% of those serving a sentence in custody and a similar number was reflected in those on community sentences (Ministry of Defence, 2016). In anticipation of the figures gleaned by the systematic identification instructed by the Phillips Review (2014), military culture and veterans' reluctance to disclose their military pasts is important to bear in mind (Ford et al, 2016).

Of course, to acknowledge that those who have served their country may also serve a sentence in the criminal justice system is not new. Indeed, as Emsley (2013) notes, increasing crime rates, attributable to veterans in immediate post-war periods, can be traced after both World Wars. Scholarship concerning a possible relationship between war and crime, and the criminogenic properties of the military institution, can also be traced back this far (see, for example, McGarry and Walklate, 2016).

What is new, is the identification of veterans in the criminal justice system as a unique criminal population, requiring a tailored response in policy and practice. The very idea of a 'veteran-offender' is complex and problematic. However, few writers in criminology have offered a critical qualitative commentary about the inherent conflict in an identity that represents dogmatic understandings of who are the 'good' and who are the 'bad' in society – or how we might understand it. That said, calls have been made for criminology to ask questions that implicate the state and the military institution in future debates, particularly within the growing scholarship of war (see Murray 2014, 2016; Treadwell, 2016). Important insights about the demographics of veterans who offend, the nature of their offences, and how the criminal justice system might respond, have been offered.

Research has focused on men, and while questions have been raised about the glaring omission to investigate female veterans in the criminal justice system in England and Wales, Defence Analytical Services and Advice (2010) found that 99% of those convicted with military records were men, with 81% having served in the Army with the remainder comprising those that have served in either the Royal Air Force or Royal Navy. A number of studies have found that the crimes committed were violent in nature. In 2011, James Treadwell led the Howard League for Penal Reform National Inquiry into Former Armed Service Personnel. This highly influential report found no evidence that military experience makes an individual more likely to end up in custody than their civilian counterparts. Yet, those with military experience were twice as likely to be convicted of a sex offence and more likely to engage in violent offending more generally (Howard League, 2011).

Similarly, a study in the *Lancet* later noted that young men who have served in the Armed Forces in Britain are three times more likely to be convicted of a violent offence than their non-combatant peer group. The report concluded that, of their sample of 2,700 young men under 30 with military experience, 20.6% had a violent conviction and that the figure was 6.7% for their civilian counterparts (MacManus et al, 2013). One question that needs to be asked next, however, is: how do female veterans experience crime and criminal justice?

As information about this new offending population has emerged, there have been rapid advances in criminal justice practices in response. Underpinned by the Armed Forces Covenant, which states that those who have served should not be disadvantaged by services, and sometimes should be given special consideration, the Phillips Review (2014) noted limited national provision for veterans in the criminal justice system. There is evidence of excellent practice in some areas; while in others, both information and resources are lacking. In the absence of a national policy, debates about what amounts to best practice endure.

To be a veteran is not a crime, nor a formal category of diversity or metric of risk, which can cause anxiety and confusion for practitioners working with this unique offending population (Murray, 2014). Yet, as research and decentralised initiatives continue to emerge, Ford et al (2016) warn against commissioning projects that do not combine research and policy development and that do have the expansion of knowledge at their core.

Dr Emma Murray, Liverpool John Moores University

FACT 22

Prisons are now the largest provider of residential care for older men in England and Wales

Sophie Rowe

People over 60 are the fastest-growing age group in prison, with numbers tripling between 2003 and 2018: 3,175 are in their 60s, with a further 1,561 prisoners aged 70 or older (Prison Reform Trust, 2017).

Of course, with the general population ageing, you may expect to see a similar reflection in prisons. However, there is a combination of factors affecting the increase in older prisoners:

- the introduction of harsher sentencing policies;
- the number of people serving indeterminate sentences;
- convictions for historical sexual offences.

This demographic shift presents a significant number of specific challenges for the Prison Service.

Changes in legislation have seen an increase in the average custodial sentence length in England and Wales, such as the introduction of mandatory life sentences for those convicted of a second serious sexual assault. Not only this, but people serving a mandatory life sentence are staying in prison for longer – on average spending 16 years in custody, up from 13 years in 2001 (Prison Reform Trust, 2017).

It is also worth noting that England and Wales have the highest use of indeterminate sentences in Europe – more than France, Germany and Italy combined (Aebi et al, 2015). Over 10,000 people are currently in prison serving an indeterminate sentence. This accounts for 14% of the sentenced prison population, up 5% since 1993 (Prison Reform Trust, 2017).

Another factor affecting old age in prison is the use of Imprisonment for Public Protection (IPP) sentences. Until the Parole Board is satisfied that the offender no longer posses a risk to the public, then IPP prisoners are liable to be detained without limitation of time. Despite the abolition of these controversial sentences in 2012, there are still 3,162 people serving an IPP sentence, many for minor crimes, with 86% serving beyond their original tariff and with no idea of when they might be released (Ministry of Justice, 2017b).

In addition to the issues raised above, a series of high-profile cases have contributed to the ageing prison population. Following the exposure of abuse committed by Jimmy Savile and other celebrity figures in 2012, increasing numbers of victims are coming forward to report sex offences, many for historical sex abuse. Subsequently, the Crown Prosecution Service's prosecution and conviction rate for rape, domestic abuse, sexual offences and child abuse cases has been increasing year on year. In cases where there has been a long period between the offence taking place and a conviction, the offender is often an older person. The oldest prisoner currently serving time is 101-year-old great-grandfather Ralph Clarke, convicted of a number of historical sex offences against young children. While prisons were not designed with the needs of older prisoners in mind, judges are not obliged to take age into account when sentencing. Consequently, an increase in historical convictions has meant that on average prisoners are much older than previously upon their first entry to prison.

To put this into perspective, prisons are now the largest provider of residential care for older men in England and Wales. However, there is overwhelming evidence to suggest that the Prison Service is ill equipped to meet the needs of older prisoners. Most notably, the prison estate has not been designed or properly resourced to accommodate disability and palliative care needs. The majority of prison buildings are Victorian, previously designed to hold young, healthy men, with lots of stairs, narrow doorways and bunk beds. As a result, old age comes with many unique difficulties in a prison environment. Typically, among the older prisoners there are those who require a wheelchair-friendly setting, including: ramps; wide doors; handles to lift themselves; grab handles in showers and toilets; and minimum use of stairs. This is rarely the reality in prison. Those struggling with mobility often end up spending long periods in their cell, excluded from meaningful activity, because it is not feasible for them to access certain parts of the prison.

Incarceration of older people is especially punitive when considering the increasing number of inmates diagnosed with, or showing signs of dementia, who struggle to understand where they are. Adopting a cost-saving approach, it has become increasingly common for older prisoners to be allocated another prisoner as care provider, to help assist with the daily routines of prison life.

Provision for end-of-life care is another complex challenge that comes with an ageing population. As the number of older people in prison increases, inevitably more people will die of old age or from chronic disease. In fact, the number of deaths from natural causes in prison has doubled in only eight years, with 164 people aged 50 or over dying of natural causes in prison in 2016 (Prison Reform Trust, 2017). This presents significant practical and emotional challenges for staff and other prisoners working closely with these individuals. While a small number of prisons have developed palliative care suites – such as HMP Whatton and HMP Norwich – it is not easy to implement these specialised facilities across the prison estate, given the design of Victorian prisons. There is also the added difficulty of maintaining prison security protocols, while safeguarding human dignity. The former

Prisons and Probation Ombudsman for England and Wales, Nigel Newcomen, had repeatedly raised concerns about the treatment of terminally ill prisoners, highlighting the inappropriate use of restraints on prisoners who are at the end of their life (PPO, 2017).

In a review of end-of-life care, the level of restraint was found to be inappropriate in at least 32 cases while in hospital or a hospice and in at least 21 cases when a prisoner was restrained during treatment (Prisons and Probation Ombudsman, 2013). Disturbingly, one prisoner was restrained while in a coma, while another died handcuffed to a prison officer. However, despite identifying some clear failings in care for older prisoners, it is important to note that palliative care suites have been found to deliver an exemplary level of care.

The increase in elderly prisoners is no demographic glitch. So it may be likely that we can expect to see purpose-built prisons for older prisoners in the not-too-distant future.

Sophie Rowe, Birmingham City University

FACT 23

The female prison population accounts for just under 5% of the total prison population

Nicola Harding

When a woman is sentenced to a period of imprisonment, the implications extend far beyond those experienced by individual women 'doing time' in prison. Criminalised women are often the main carer for children or other dependants such as grandchildren. The Howard League for Penal Reform estimates that 'more than 17,000 children under 18 years in England and Wales were forcibly separated from their mother in 2010' (Howard League, 2016b: 1). Incarceration has negative implications for both imprisoned women and their children.

This discussion examines the instrumental role of short sentences in maternal separation, and the prevalence of self-harm among female prisoners, by considering some of the insights of a study by Lucy Baldwin and Rona Epstein (2017), 10 years on from the recommendations made by Baroness Corston in her report (Corston, 2007). With the number of women committed to the prison estate higher than ever, and levels of self-harm within prisons growing, it is time to consider whether imprisonment is an appropriate method of punishing criminalised women.

In 2006, the deaths of six women at Styal prison prompted the creation of the 'Corston report; a review of women with particular vulnerabilities in the criminal justice system' (Corston, 2007). This set out to address some of the gender-specific failings of the criminal justice system, proposing a 'distinct, radically different, visibly led, strategic, proportionate, holistic, women centered, integrated approach' (Corston, 2007: 79). This included 43 recommendations, one of which was that 'defendants who are primary carers of young children should be remanded in custody only after consideration of a probation report on the probable impact on the children' (Corston, 2007).

Many of the formal considerations embedded into sentencing structure because of the Corston report's (2007) recommendations have not been fulfilled, and women with dependent children are still sentenced to prison. This can occur because of a lack of detail about children or dependants in pre-sentence reports, with key information about the impact upon any children routinely excluded. Therefore, sentencers are not always aware of dependent children. Alternatively, and even more worryingly, the Prison Reform Trust (Minson et al, 2015) identified that judges and magistrates believe that considering the impact upon dependants is discretionary, rather than subject to case law.

Ten years after the publication of the Corston report (2007), Baldwin and Epstein's (2017) study indicates that little progress has been made to divert mothers from custody, with the 17 imprisoned women in their study cumulatively leaving behind a total of 50 children. The impact on such children's futures currently fails to be fully understood, as there is no systematic or formal recording of what happens to the children of imprisoned mothers (Baldwin and Epstein, 2017). However, reports state that a child whose parent has been in prison will have a higher risk of going to prison themselves and is at increased risk of experiencing behavioural problems (Murray and Farrington, 2008; Epstein, 2014), which will ultimately negatively affect their future life chances.

Despite the recommendations made by Corston in 2007, more women than ever are incarcerated, with increasing numbers of mothers going to prison. The female prison population has consistently risen, with women now accounting for just under 5% of the total prison population (Baldwin and Epstein, 2017). Yet this increase is not as a result of an overall increase in women committing crimes, but an increase in the severity of sentencing. Short prison sentences are common for women, with one in every three women sentenced to imprisonment in England and Wales spending less than six months in prison (Baldwin and Epstein, 2017). The women involved in Baldwin and Epstein's (2017) study served between two weeks and 23 weeks, for non-violent, sometimes first-time offences. The Corston report (2007) also identified that 'women tend to be located further from their homes than male prisoners, to the detriment of maintaining family ties, receiving visits and resettlement back into the community' (Corston, 2007: 3). A short stay in prison, for a relatively non-serious offence, renders women at risk of losing their children, their support networks and their home.

While we may not be able to fully understand the long-term effects on the children of women in prison (Murray and Farrington, 2008), we are able to observe the immediate harm that imprisonment causes the women themselves. A report by Corston in 2011 that reflected on progress since the 2007 Corston report identified that, while the suicide rate is higher for men than for women in the wider community, gender roles are reversed when in prison. Women show far higher levels of suicide and self-harm while detained in prison: 'women still make up 52% of the self-harm incidents in prison despite constituting only 5% of the total prison population' (Corston, 2011: 9). Such high levels of self-harm and suicide, coupled with the practical implications of completing prison sentences, such as losing accommodation, mean that a seemingly 'short' sentence can have far-reaching and sometimes permanent implications for both woman and child. By imprisoning a mother, her punishment is extended to her children and other dependants, with consequences that can be felt long after the sentence has been fulfilled.

With a criminal justice system that is increasingly imprisoning women for less serious, non-violent offences and the rising use of short prison sentences for both men and women, growing numbers of parents are being separated from their children due to parental incarceration. This has implications for the future life chances of their children, yet the effects of maternal imprisonment are immediate and can leave children homeless, cared for by extended family, or in the care of the state.

Women who leave their children to go to prison are faced with conditions that lead to unprecedented levels of self-harm. Sentenced often to short sentences for non-violent crimes, or subject to recall to prison for non-payment of fines for offences that would not have warranted a custodial sentence, women are separated from their children indiscriminately, harming both mother and child. Sentenced often to short sentences for non-violent crimes, or subject to recall to prison for non-payment of fines for offences that would not have warranted a custodial sentence, women are separated from their children indiscriminately, harming both mother and child. Evidently, This has a significant and immediate impact on the day-to-day lives of all those involved.

The publication of the Corston report (2007) aimed to improve conditions experienced by women in the criminal justice system, with specific recommendations made for mothers facing potential custodial sentences. However, as Baldwin and Epstein's (2017) study shows, little progress has been made in this area. The proliferation of self-harm and death by suicide and the implications of short sentences and maternal separation affect some of the most marginalised women and children in England and Wales. Put simply, this is 'a disgrace for our society' (Baldwin and Epstein, 2017: 6).

Nicola Harding, Leeds Trinity University

Part Six
Criminal justice

FACT 24

Around 84% of all offenders who appear before the courts are convicted

Susie Atherton

A very good way to learn about court processes and to see justice being done is to visit any magistrates' court in England and Wales, where you will observe the culmination of a series of events which begin with the act of crime, and proceed to detection, arrest, conviction via referral of the case to court by the Crown Prosecution Service. This can be an opportunity to reflect on the workings of criminal justice.

Perhaps some of the best-known sentiments on the machinations of justice are:

- the famous Lord Sankey speech (in the case of Woolmington in the House of Lords), which noted that: 'Throughout the web of the English Criminal Law one golden thread is always to be seen that it is the duty of the prosecution to prove the prisoner's guilt' (Woolmington v DPP, 1935);
- Blackstone's formulation that: 'It is better that ten guilty persons escape than that one innocent suffer' ('Commentaries on the laws of England', 1893).

Yet if the function of the court is to deliver justice, we might ask why is it that they so often do this by finding those appearing before them guilty? Indeed, the number of offenders convicted at all courts remains broadly stable – at around 84% of all those who appear before them. While the courts might not get the attention of many of the more headline aspects of the criminal justice system, it is worth understanding some of the roles, functions and operations of the courts.

A myriad of criminology or criminal justice texts will tell you about the adversarial system of justice in England and Wales, where defence and prosecution are pitched against each other to win the case and see justice done (for example, Carrabine et al, 2014; Newburn, 2017; Liebling et al, 2017). The extent of the sparring between the two depends on the case. In a magistrates' court, you are more likely to encounter a very routine presentation of facts and discussions about the outcome, focused on the sentencing decision. This is because 95% of cases dealt with in the magistrates' court involve defendants who have pleaded guilty (Davies et al, 2015), and therefore their defence may be to offer mitigating circumstances, presenting a case to persuade the magistrate to show leniency.

To understand the rationale behind sentencing, Canton (2017) has presented an introduction to the philosophy of punishment, which assesses the evolution of the response to crime and suggests debates and points of discussion that are useful to develop critical analysis of the system of justice that we currently have. In addition, the previous sentiments mentioned earlier will all provide a useful overview of the purpose of punishment and rationale behind magistrates' and Crown Court judges' decision making.

There are traditions in courtrooms that have held sway for decades, bound up in legal requirements and regulations, which ensure due process and fairness in the delivery of justice. The aims of the criminal justice system in England and Wales are to protect the public, to administer justice, and to manage penalties and the reintegration of offenders (James and Raine, 1998). To what extent these aims are achieved in a system that seems to be based largely in praxis on securing conviction is debatable. It suggests that in reality the function of the justice system favours crime control (Garland, 2001), which emphasises the promotion of imprisonment (Simm, 2009), and a concern with risk assessment and management (Kemshall, 2008).

When examining the work of the courts, it is also important to understand the principle of 'due process' – a requirement to guarantee individuals' legal rights when they are involved in the justice system (Davies et al, 2015). The criminal justice system in England and Wales is presented as operating under an evidence-based and objective ethos, independent of government, and aiming to offer all citizens access to justice, and to maintain confidence in and respect for the system.

Yet we also ought to examine who is most adversely affected by the criminal justice system, specifically the bias and prejudice demonstrated in statistics on race and gender and the 'imprisonment of the poor', to understand how the odds are stacked against those on lower incomes achieving fair justice (Wacquant, 2009). Then, we can more critically examine the aims of the criminal justice system and, specifically, of the court service, and ask: is it fair? Is there access to justice for all citizens? Another very good way to examine this is to explore cases that led to a review and change in practice, whether as represented by racial bias in the criminal justice system (see Foster et al, 2005 on the Stephen Lawrence case) or miscarriages of justice due to reliance on expert witness testimony, such as that of solicitor Sally Clark (Batt, 2005).

In the magistrates' court, magistrates (also known as Justices of the Peace) have a legal advisor, to ensure that due process considerations are met and to advise the bench of three magistrates, as this includes 'lay magistrates', who are volunteers from the local community (Davies et al, 2015). Each bench in the courtroom also has a district judge, a legally qualified magistrate, to ensure that cases are heard within the remit of the law.

In a magistrates' court, sentences can range from discharge (where no punishment is imposed) to 12 months in prison. The seriousness of the charge (an indictable or either way offence) may warrant referral to Crown Court, where judges can impose a longer custodial sentence. In addition, in cases where a defendant pleads not guilty, as they have a right to, they will be heard in a Crown Court and the outcome will therefore be determined by a jury of their peers. Non-guilty plea cases can still be heard by magistrates, depending on the seriousness of the offence.

However, more recently, a different form of doing justice has been introduced in England and Wales, imported from the US, in the form of community, or problem-solving courts. The latter label more accurately describes the approach used in the UK, in existing magistrates' courts, where staff can seek to help defendants address the causes of their offending and make use of partnerships and access to other services to do this. Problem-solving courts are based on community justice centres, which are described as having a dual role: 'to change lives of offenders and also to improve the quality of life in communities' (Berman and Feinblatt, 2005). This is done through the prevention of reoffending, but also reaching out to those at risk of offending and offering a focal point for residents to access services such as advice on housing, education and mental health treatment.

This model was implemented in the UK in 2006 in North Liverpool (see Llewellyn-Thomas and Prior, 2007; Mair and Millings, 2011) and based on the US model, for example the Red Hook Community Justice Centre in Brooklyn (see Berman and Feinblatt, 2005). Mair and Millings described it as 'a unique court process with wider community resource provision' (2011: 3), which offers a problem-solving approach and co-location with other agencies. These courts were developed to fulfil a need identified by many, including Bowen and Whitehead (2013), who suggested that a more innovative, fairer, faster and 'people focused' court was needed, to cut crime and reduce costs in the UK. The innovations are underpinned by fairness, focus on victims and offenders as people needing help, authority in sentencing decisions and acting swiftly in response to breaches of court orders.

Ward (2014) describes this as 'therapeutic jurisprudence' (2014: 2), represented by court processes which enable offenders and others to develop different self-identities, where they engage in lawful and purposeful activity, or 'a criminal justice model that has wellbeing at its core, and puts a human face to the delivery of justice' (Ward, 2014: 2). For Donoghue, problem-solving courts present a way to do justice that is more 'socially meaningful' (Donoghue, 2014: 141).

The Crown Court is the setting where the more serious criminal cases are heard. It is also a place where the adversarial system happens in practice – the contest to be won by the state (prosecution) or by the defence. The most well-known Crown Court in England is the Central Criminal Court, colloquially known as 'the Old Bailey' in London, where high-profile cases are played out and reports of case outcomes are presented in front of the iconic image of the court.

Juries are part of the system of justice and usually constitute a group of 12 members of the public, drawn from the electoral register, aged between 18 and 70 years old. There are exemptions, based on mental ability, occupation and capacity to be part of a jury. Juries are a vital component in upholding the principle of due process (Newburn, 2017). The use of juries is often debated, with the central concerns being: how well equipped the public is to deal with complex case such as fraud and organised crime; whether their prejudices and uninformed views can sway their judgement; whether they are vulnerable to lawyers' manipulation (remember, the lawyers are trying to 'win'); and how influenced they are by external factors (Davies et al, 2015).

Courts are just one part of the criminal justice system, but they represent a pivotal part of implementing the aims of the criminal justice system, and a point where justice can be observed. The types of court represent different arenas, where the whole range of criminal and civil cases are subject to legal and objective assessment of the facts, which will determine the outcome. However, in most cases, we know that the outcome in the courts will likely be a finding of guilt. It is therefore not hard to suggest that, overall, the role of the courts is also in reality that of ensuring conviction.

Susie Atherton, University of Northampton

FACT 25

Judges in courts in England and Wales do not use gavels

Shona Robinson-Edwards

Many readers will be familiar with the gavel, the official name given to the small ceremonial mallet often seen in dramas, being wielded by judges in courts of law. Indeed, the gavel is often a staple of court crime drama, whether it is set in the United Kingdom or elsewhere. As a dramatic device, the gavel can be banged ferociously on the desk before the presiding judge, to call the court to 'order'. The only problem with this is that fictional drama uses fictional devices, and although many people do not realise it, judges in England and Wales do not use gavels.

Tracing the origin of the gavel raises a number of complexities, as opinions differ as to where and when it was invented. Some trace it back to medieval England; others suggest that the gavel existed in many parts of the world long before its use became mainstream in the medieval era. The gavel is defined as a tool used by a judge to command attention or to confirm legal action (Grana et al, 2002), further symbolising the notion of power and authority that the judge possesses (Stanko et al, 2004). The judge's strike of the wooden gavel in the courtroom is a feature recognised as commonplace in courtrooms around the world; however, although it is claimed that the gavel originated in England, the gavel is predominantly used in courts of law in the United States. The gavel, which is sounded in a decisive and striking manner, brings an element of animation to the courtroom.

However, gavels are not exclusive to the courtroom; they are also frequently used worldwide in auctions. The auctioneer presents an item and begins the bidding, with the familiar phrase, 'going once, going twice', followed by the strike of the gavel.

Television shows, such as *Judge Judy*, which features the judge dealing with criminal court cases in front of the camera, became very popular in the US and in the UK. This form of Americanism has become so entertaining that now we have our own version of televised court cases in the form of *Judge Rinder*, which makes for entertaining daytime television (for some). In addition, films and comedies frequently show the judge shouting 'order' or 'order in the court', while striking the gavel. So of course we cannot be blamed for associating judges and gavels in courts in an English and Welsh context, can we? It is also an excellent illustrative example of how inaccurate and fictionalised representations can frame people's perceptions – and misperceptions – of crime, punishment and the legal process.

The inaccurate perception of gavels being used in courts in England and Wales is well documented (Rentoul, 2016). The English criminal justice system needs to be presented in an accurate manner, but the fact is that the judge's use of the wooden gavel in England and Wales is largely a myth (Rentoul, 2016). Nor are gavels used in Scottish courts (Rentoul, 2016). Dean (2015) argues that such myths are perpetuated in television dramas that have portrayed the English courtroom incorrectly in the past. Many people learn about crime and criminal justice from what we see in the media (Surette, 2015). Essentially, we live in the media (Dueze, 2012); when we look at mediation, it is important to acknowledge that our perceptions are shaped by factors such as journalists, newspaper editors and media platforms. Therefore, our perceptions of criminal justice will be shaped by the wider media's representation of both historic and current criminal justice processes. :So why are gavels presented in almost every courtroom irrespective of the locality around the world? Why have courtrooms in

England and Wales been misrepresented? And why does such misrepresentation connect so well with public views?

It may be because criminal courts in England and Wales are quite mysterious: most people have never been to a court, or seen a judge, jury or defendant. Therefore, the portrayal of the courtroom by popular media outlets is not only a form of entertainment but also educational – albeit in some instances with incorrect information. More critically, seeing the judge using the gavel to obtain order, alongside hearing the strike and the bang, does give more of a dramatic effect. However, the line between fact and fiction needs to be clear, even if this mean the English and Welsh courtrooms are a bit more dull and sombre. After all, it is a courtroom – not a place for entertainment.

The inappropriate use of the gavel in British TV drama has not gone unnoticed. Legal writer Marcel Berlins wrote a piece for the *Guardian* (Berlins, 2009), highlighting the inaccuracies of TV shows. However, this went beyond a simple newspaper article and consequently there was the creation of the 'Inappropriate Gavels' blog and Twitter page – which brings to light the misrepresentation of gavels on TV, in newspapers and elsewhere (Dean, 2015).

Such mistakes do accentuate stereotypes (Hyde, 2015) and, in some instances, the courtroom is depicted as a dramatised theatre piece, emphasising visual clichés. However, although gavels are not used by judges in England and Wales, in future they may have an increasing presence in some courts. For example, clerks in the Inner London Crown Court use gavels to alert parties in court to the entrance of the judge into the courtroom. However, against the often-misinformed media representation, the fact remains that judges in courtrooms in England and Wales do not use gavels.

Shona Robinson-Edwards, Birmingham City University

FACT 26
The Home Office claims that around 100,000 people are responsible for half of all recorded crime

Katie Brooker

It has been suggested that there are two main types of offender in society: the adolescence-limited offenders, essentially those who exhibit anti-social behaviour only during adolescence and youth and who then desist from crime; and a second group, called 'life-course persistent offenders' by Moffitt (1993), who begin to behave anti-socially early in childhood and continue this behaviour into adulthood.

While Moffitt coined the term 'antisocial behaviour' instead of crime (due to the differing definitions of 'crime' among cultures), essentially her work has been hugely influential in criminology in understanding who commits crime. Indeed, life-course persistent offenders have been studied for a number of years, and many of these studies suggest that they commit a significant proportion of overall crime. Yet in England and Wales (under the New Labour government), by the mid-2000s it had become a largely unchallenged wisdom in some quarters that a significant proportion of all crime was committed by a relatively small group of persistent or prolific offenders. It was argued that targeting these individuals would be one of the most effective ways of delivering further falls in crime.

Recidivism, more commonly known as reoffending, is when a perpetrator commits a further crime (or crimes) after their release from prison. Recidivism is likely to occur with persistent offenders, as a strong predictor of future offences is a history of past convictions (Walters et al, 2008). Unfortunately, this is a current issue within the criminal justice system in the United Kingdom. Although figures suggest that recidivism might be slowly declining, it has remained relatively stable over the last decade (HM Government, 2017). UK prison statistics for 2014/15 show that 44.7% of adult reoffenders had 11 or more convictions, compared to 7.5% of those with no previous offences (HM Government, 2017). This supports the argument that those with previous convictions are likely to reoffend.

Another variable that indicates a higher reoffending rate is age. Juvenile offenders show a higher reoffending rate than their adult counterparts; with 74.5% of those juveniles with 11 or more convictions reoffending within a year, compared to 24.6% of those juveniles with no previous convictions (HM Government, 2017). However, it should be remembered that reoffending rates do not necessarily include punitive sentences, but do include those who receive cautions (HM Government, 2017). This could account for the higher number of recidivism by young offenders.

Research also suggests that there is an overlap with juvenile victimisation and offending, meaning that these offenders have more than likely been a victim of crime at least once (Finkelhor et al, 2007; Posick, 2013; Cops and Pleysier, 2014). Reoffending rates were also a stronger predictor among males (McKillop et al, 2017). The correlation between victimisation and reoffending has likewise been shown among adult offenders, with other indicators of reoffending, such as substance abuse or mental health. This indicates a vicious cycle for persistent offenders.

Figures from crime statistics in 2015, for example, show that 36% of adults convicted of an indictable offence (crimes serious enough to be eligible for trial by jury in a Crown Court) in 2015 had a long criminal record (15 or more previous convictions or cautions) compared to 24% in 2005, suggesting that any attempt to reduce serious recidivism had been ineffective. Moreover, it was also suggested that half of persistent offenders (those with eight or more convictions or cautions) were given their first official sanction for a theft offence.

As Roberts has pointed out, despite very diverse approaches to punishing crime, all Western jurisdictions tend to punish repeat or recidivist offenders more harshly. This is a practice known as the 'recidivist sentencing premium' as opposed to flat rate sentencing, where previous offences have no impact on the sentencing for the crime under consideration. For many repeat offenders, their previous convictions have more impact on the penalty they receive than the seriousness of their current crime (Roberts, 2008). Additionally, Roberts asks the essential moral and ethical question: does punishing repeat offenders more severely amount to double punishment and undermine the legitimacy of the criminal justice system?

There has been some research that supports the assertion that a small cohort of offenders are disproportionately responsible for a very high volume of all crime. For example, in work based on Swedish crime statistics, Örjan Falk et al (2014) have suggested that just 1% of the population is accountable for 63% of all violent crime convictions, and that the majority of violent crimes are perpetrated by a small number of persistent violent offenders. They suggest that the perpetrators are typically males, characterised by early onset of violent criminality, substance abuse, personality disorders and non-violent criminality. However, discussions of the impact of 'persistent offenders' are problematic. The recent emphasis in criminological theory and research on what are termed habitual, chronic and persistent offenders assumes that involvement in crime is concentrated among a small group of offenders (rather than being widespread in the population). Yet the evidence is far from conclusive.

That said, for over a decade it has been suggested that persistent offenders constitute a significant crime problem in their own right. In 2004, the UK government talked of 100,000 so-called 'persistent offenders' apparently being responsible for half of all crime, and stated that within that is a smaller group of prolific offenders. Thus, the Home Office Strategic Plan in 2004 stated:

> A large proportion of crime is committed by a small number of people. In any one year, approximately 100,000 people commit half of all crimes and just 5,000 people commit about 9 percent of all crimes – around one million crimes in total. (Home Office, 2004c: 32-33)

The problem is, we simply do not really know that this is the case, and the issue is complicated by the fact that what constitutes a persistent offender is not legally defined in statute, but can vary a great deal. Sometimes it is based on a volume number of previous convictions. The government's theory of persistent offenders was based on an interpretation of the Offenders Index, a database containing the details of all individuals convicted of standard list offences in England and Wales since 1963. A 2001 Home Office study used this data to examine various groups of offenders born between 1953 and 1978 (Home Office, 2001b). Looking at those offenders born in 1953, the study found that one-third of males and 9% of females had been convicted of at least one standard list offence before the age of 46. The study also looked at the number of times individuals born in 1953 had been convicted of an offence. In the case of male offenders, half of these had only been convicted once before the age of 46; 17% had been convicted on two occasions; and 8% had been convicted three times. A relatively small group of male offenders, approximately 25% – accounted for two-thirds of all convictions.

But while this data tells us that a relatively small number of men are convicted of a disproportionate number of offences, there is little to substantiate claims that some 100,000 criminals are responsible for half of all recorded crime.

Katie Brooker, Birmingham City University

FACT 27

In 2017 there were 260,000 offenders in the community under statutory supervision by the criminal justice system in England and Wales

Cristiana Cardoso

The National Probation Service for England and Wales is a statutory criminal justice service, largely responsible for the supervision of high-risk offenders in the community and the provision of reports to the criminal courts, to assist them in their sentencing duties. It was established in its current form by the Criminal Justice and Court Services Act in April 2000, but it has existed since the passing of the Probation of Offenders Act 1907. Its role, remit and function have been reformed considerably over time. Today, the service is part of the Her Majesty's Prison and Probation Service, which is part of the Ministry of Justice.

The National Probation Service (NPS) comprises 42 probation areas, which are coterminous with police force area boundaries. In recent years, it has been subject to the most significant shake-up in its history under former Secretary of State for Justice, Chris Grayling, as part of his controversial Transforming Rehabilitation Strategy in 2015. That programme has involved the outsourcing of a large portion of the traditional statutory probation function to charities and non-statutory agencies, leaving the NPS solely responsible for those deemed high risk in the community.

Arguably, the core function of the NPS is to assess and manage offenders' risk. In criminal justice, the term 'risk' relates to both the risk of future reoffending within a timescale (usually two years, and this may include cautions) and the risk of harm – will the offender commit a harmful offence; and, an offence that will cause 'serious harm' to the public? However, while the term 'risk' in criminal justice is somewhat imprecise, it does now delineate which agency will manage offenders in the community. Today the NPS manages those classed or categorised as high-risk and very high-risk offenders (those who are likely to offend in a serious harmful manner); and 21 community rehabilitation companies (CRCs) are responsible for the management of low- to medium-risk offenders in 21 areas across England and Wales. The CRCs also now have responsibility for supervising short-sentence prisoners (those sentenced to less than 12 months in prison) after release.

Today, the NPS advises courts on sentencing all offenders, and manages those offenders who present a high or very high risk of serious harm, or who are managed under licence by the NPS. Yet while collectively over 260,000 are now under direct supervision of the NPS and CRCs each year, the NPS only manages a proportion regarded as presenting the highest degree of risk of serious harm to the public.

This is a notable shift from the origins of probation in England and Wales, which began largely in an ad hoc manner, in which prior to the passing of the Probation of Offenders Act in 1907 staff were merely volunteers and referred to as 'Court Missionaries'. With the passing of the 1907 Act, such volunteers were given official status and thus became the first probation officers. On 8 May 1907, the Liberal Home Office Minister Herbert Samuel, moving the short second reading debate in the House of Commons, told MPs that the measure was needed so that offenders whom the courts did not think fit to imprison because of their age, character or antecedents might be placed on probation under the supervision of these officers, whose duty would be to 'advise', 'assist' and 'befriend' them. This last phrase about 'advise', 'assist' and 'befriend' continued to ring down the decades, until it was dispensed with in favour of 'public protection', 'enforcement' and 'rehabilitation' in the late

1990s. Indeed, 'risk' was to become a major element in the practice of probation from the 1990s onwards. Its rise to prominence in relation to the management of persons deemed 'at risk of causing serious harm' came about from the 1990s onwards with a more unified political consensus on the need for criminal justice to be tough and interventionist, particularly regarding the risk assessment of sexual and violent offenders, who were regarded as presenting a significant risk to the public (Kempsall, 2001).

The Criminal Justice Act 2003 under New Labour provided for the establishment of Multi-Agency Public Protection Arrangements (MAPPA) in each of the 42 criminal justice areas in England and Wales. MAPPA is not a statutory criminal justice agency, but is a mechanism through which agencies (police, prison, probation, and other public and involved services) can better discharge their statutory responsibilities and protect the public in a coordinated manner. MAPPA allows agencies to assess and manage offenders on a multi-agency basis, by working together, sharing information and meeting to ensure that effective plans are put in place. Each agency retains its full statutory responsibilities and obligations at all times, while probation staff retain case management responsibilities, including management planning for the offender.

Since 2014, the number of individuals charged with a serious further offence committed while under probation supervision has risen by some 20%, from 429 to 517 (HM Inspectorate of Probation for England and Wales, 2017). A significant proportion of this number are convicted of murder, manslaughter or a serious sexual offence. However, in comparing numbers before – and after – the government's 'Transforming Rehabilitation' reforms in 2015, it ought to be remembered that it is no longer comparing like with like, as 40,000 extra individuals (those on short sentences) are now under probation supervision post-release.

The proportion of individuals charged with a serious further offence has remained relatively stable at just 0.2%. On 31 March 2017, there were 76,794 MAPPA-supervised offenders: 72% were Category 1 offenders (Registered Sexual Offenders); 27.6% were Category 2 offenders (Violent Offenders); and less than 0.5% were Category 3 offenders (Other Dangerous Offenders) (Ministry of Justice, 2017d).

This speaks volumes about how effectively most of those considered dangerous in the criminal justice system on release are being supervised. However, what the figures aptly illustrate is that a great deal of work with offenders, including those deemed high risk and potentially dangerous, goes on unseen every day as part of the criminal justice system – and much of it is very successful.

Cristiana Cardoso, Birmingham City University

FACT 28

It's (nearly) impossible to go to jail for not paying your debts, but mass indebtedness nonetheless remains an entry point to many crime problems

Mark Horsley

In the not-too-distant past, failing to pay outstanding debts was a criminal offence, carrying the possibility of an indefinite custodial sentence. Debtors were imprisoned at the pleasure of their creditors, confined to a system of privately owned, profit-oriented debtors' prisons that expected inmates to pay for their accommodation and their upkeep, as well as making meaningful payments towards their debts. To that end, debtors' prisons were usually open during the day, allowing inmates and the public to come and go in order to support families, make a living or sell their wares. Inmates were often encouraged to continue a trade or to find work, but the equipment required to do so, including any furniture, would also come with a fee payable to the institution.

Nevertheless, debtors' prisons were a fixture of English life for at least five centuries – Southwark's Marshalsea, one of the most infamous examples, was probably built during the 14th century and finally closed its doors in 1842. Many of them acquired a rather fearsome reputation for dark and squalid conditions, corruption, profiteering and debauchery, profiting by incarceration while implicitly encouraging creative ways of making the next payment.

This approach to indebtedness neatly reflects the early history and development of the English criminal justice system in its distinctly co-evolutionary, mutually developmental relationship with the earliest strains of modern capitalism. Just like the 'Bloody Code' – the wide-ranging system of capital statutes available in English law, mostly for the protection of property – imprisonment for unpaid debts was only enacted in a minority of cases, supplemented by loose private arrangements, merciful write-offs or abscondments. According to White (2016: 269), for example, 'of 12,000 bailable writs against debtors issued [in 1791] only some 1200 led to imprisonment, the rest paying up in some form, absconding or proving such hopeless cases that creditors ... let the matter drop'.

In the cases that ended in prison, however, debtors were consigned to relatively lawless spaces that inspired a degree of monetary creativity, allowing further profits to be drawn from the inmates as well as encouraging them to a dynamic, competitive disposition in service of their creditors' interests and their own release. In other words, debtors' prisons simultaneously worked to punish and repress non-payment, while stimulating the productive forces of interpersonal and economic competition (see Horsley et al, 2015), encouraging indigent debtors to adopt the creative habits of entrepreneurialism. In the Marshalsea, for instance, more established prisoners extracted 'garnish' from new arrivals, using their position to run a protection racket that helped them pay off their own debts.

At the beginning of the 19th century, as much as half of the English prison population had been confined indefinitely for unpaid debts. Many did not stay long – most only served fairly short sentences, before scraping together enough cash to satisfy their creditors. But with fairly high turnover, more than 10,000 people were committed year on year (Ware, 2014), while a number of campaign groups, influenced by the likes of Charles Dickens (whose father was imprisoned as a debtor), sought to end the practice. After much debate, the Debtors' Act 1869 pretty much eliminated the spectre of indefinite imprisonment, ensuring that most debtors kept their liberty, while anyone who ignored court orders or flatly refused to pay could still find themselves subject to a maximum term of six weeks.

If we take the letter of the law at face value, the England and Wales legal system still works roughly along these lines. It's still theoretically possible to acquire a jail term through non-payment but, in practice, it's also distinctly unlikely for anything other than cases of extreme intransigence. As long as the debts in question were obtained honestly, non-payment remains a civil matter and cannot lead to any kind of criminal penalty, unless the debtor refuses to comply with repayment planning processes, financial mediation services and with court-ordered recovery devices such as 'Attachment of Earnings' orders (a legal innovation that allows creditors to recover funds from a debtor's wages). In such circumstances, there is an ultimate threat of 14 days' imprisonment but more as a consequence of 'contempt of court' than direct refusal to pay debts. Beyond that, the only realistic prospect of substantial jail time comes with evidence of a criminal offence linked to 'credit fraud' or 'identity theft', where funds are acquired on false pretences.

Nevertheless, the criminological significance of outstanding personal debt connects into a number of different but interrelated fields of study, based on the wider function of debt within our social and economic form and the growing prevalence of debt-financed payment means as our collective exposure has risen over the last few decades (see Horsley, 2015). In the United Kingdom, only about 3.5% of the money supply currently exists in the form of notes and coins, the rest is created as bank deposits – electronic payment means – by the process of credit creation. When a bank is presented with a potentially profitable lending opportunity – anything from reasonable spending on a credit card, an application for mortgage finance on an appropriately valued property or an evidenced business plan – there are no reserves of precious metals to transfer from one vault to another; the required amount is simply created out of thin air as a claim on the future (Werner, 2014). It doesn't come from anywhere, it just appears as integers on a balance sheet.

Once approved, however, it is spent just like any other form of money. It can be withdrawn from a cash machine, waved away on a contactless credit card or transferred from one account to another, as if the value it represents is more than a prospective claim on future income. The availability of debt sustains payment means over and above the availability of concrete resources, providing the vital lifeblood of a consumer economy, by allowing us to buy and spend now on a promise of future payment, ensuring that the production and disposal of physical value does not constrain economic expansion, at least in the short term. It's difficult to overstate how integral this process of credit creation is to our social and economic structures. Without payment means created as debt, our economy could not function in its current form. There would be no 'liquidity', nothing to spend, no capacity to buy. But just as the process of borrowing and lending sustains legitimate economic activity, it also represents an entry point into a multifaceted sphere of crime and harm that also has implications for the criminal justice system.

In the last few years, the UK economy has experienced another rapid growth in consumer lending and household debt. Unsecured lending on credit cards and the like grew by around £14 billion or 8% in the year to July 2017 alongside stagnating wages, price inflation and an ageing governmental austerity programme that seems to be strangling incomes. As a result, more of these debts are finding their way into courtrooms. According to the Registry Trust, the number of County Court Judgments against consumers in England and Wales has risen 35% in the year to April 2017 and is now higher than it was at the time of the financial crisis (Jones, 2017). Meanwhile, the average value of debts requiring courtroom arbitration has fallen 17% to a historic low of

£1,495 – for further comparison, the average was £3,500 in 2008 – suggesting that a larger portion of the population is struggling to pay smaller debts, taxing already strained aspects of the criminal justice system.

In the field of corporate and white collar offending alone, the last couple of decades have seen successive cases of lenders and their employees misrepresenting loan terms, overselling certain products and colluding with each other to the detriment of their customers' interests. The 'Libor scandal' that broke in June 2012, for instance, implicated a number of banks, including high street names, in artificially inflating or deflating interest rates, generating increased profits or improving market share. If banks kept the Libor rate artificially high, it's pretty much inevitable that the payments attached to outstanding loans and mortgages followed suit, potentially extracting millions of pounds in additional revenue from bank customers. Conversely, managing the rate downwards would have the same effect for savers. Those with substantial deposits would receive artificially low interest payments, again working in the banks' favour.

We tend to adopt a very euphemistic turn of phrase when dealing with such offences, often implying accident rather than criminality, by speaking of 'mis-selling' and 'misrepresentation' rather than 'crime' and 'fraud', but Libor fixing is not an isolated case. Without even mentioning the practices that went into the financial crisis, many UK banks have been implicated in a series of illegal practices and suspect products over the last few decades, following the freer and more open regulatory approach adopted towards the end of the last century. Endowment mortgages – an interest-only mortgage that came with a secondary investment product, which was supposed to mature at the end of the term, paying off the capital portion of the loan – continue to leave borrowers with shortfalls that run into the thousands despite a compensation effort, because lenders failed to adequately explain the risks of relying on long-term market performance. In a very similar vein, the same institutions have also been implicated in aggressively upselling expensive Payment Protection Insurance since the early 1990s, sometimes adding as much 50% to the cost of mortgages, personal loans and credit cards, without ever explaining that it was an optional extra. The resultant compensation programme is set to continue until June 2019, despite repayments already totalling more than £24 billion to 12 million customers.

Elsewhere, research from the United States (see Kubrin et al, 2011) suggests that there might be at least a correlation between the prevalence of 'fringe finance' lenders – payday loan operators, cheque cashers, pawnshops, rent-to-buy shops and the like – and higher localised crime rates. There is evidence that illegal markets might find a use value for otherwise legitimate forms of credit, with ongoing research in and around North East UK heroin markets pointing to a blurring of lines between legal and illegal payment means (Horsley, 2017).

It is also possible that outstanding debt might be partially implicated in levels of criminal recidivism – a longstanding problem for criminal justice systems around the world – because offenders released from prison into insurmountable debts and the clamorous demands of multiple creditors are probably even less likely to steer clear of established habits. Finally, the growth of illegal online markets, identity theft and credit fraud would probably be all but impossible without the proliferation of electronic payment means and multifarious techniques of credit creation.

What should we take from this? If nothing else, it certainly suggests that crime and deviance might be inseparable from broader socio-economic trends, that criminality often is not a separate and distinct phenomenon that can easily be studied in isolation. Instead, it tends to hang off, and intermingle with, other aspects of our social order – and the development of a highly debt-financed economic form over the last few decades is no exception.

Dr Mark Horsley, University of Chester

Part Seven
Black market Britain

FACT 29

The number of suspected victims of trafficking and slavery in the UK increased by 35% in 2017; of the 5,145 suspected victims from 116 countries, 2,118 were minors

Sarah Page

It is estimated that there are 27 million victims of human trafficking globally. While the true extent of these crimes is invariably difficult to document, in 2017 the UK's National Crime Agency (National Crime Agency, 2017a) suggested that the number of suspected victims of trafficking and slavery in the UK increased by 35% in 2017. Of the 5,145 suspected victims from 116 countries, 2,118 were minors. Most cases involved forced labour or sexual exploitation.

Human trafficking is a crime that involves organised groups of criminals recruiting and transporting people to a different geographical location, to exploit them for financial gain. Traffickers often deceive, drug, coerce, threaten and/or force the person to travel with them (Cree, 2008), meaning that some victims do not realise that they are about to be exploited and agree to travel under the illusion of migrating to work legitimately. Other victims are sold to traffickers by family members in desperation, or are kidnapped. Individuals and groups of people might be trafficked at any one time. In the UK, under the Modern-Day Slavery Act 2015, trafficking includes being forced into slavery within your own country borders, as well as when someone has crossed country borders and is enslaved. This means that if someone who is living in the UK is abducted or deceived and then enslaved within UK borders, this is also human trafficking. Another term for this is 'domestic trafficking' (UNODC, 2009).

Human trafficking is often referred to as 'modern slavery', a reminder that slavery and the transportation of slaves is still an issue in today's society, long since slavery was abolished in Britain in 1865. While slavery remains illegal today, the enforced servitude of human beings still occurs in the UK, spurring a new generation of abolition activists to advocate that the British government needs to do more to protect people and prosecute the traffickers and slave-controllers. Friesendorf (2007) points out that today there is still keen activism within anti-trafficking campaigns, who present a Christian moralistic argument for governments to do more to tackle this social problem. In England and Wales, the Salvation Army is contracted by government to manage adult victims of human trafficking.

Modern-day slaves are forced to be involved in a range of occupations – from forced prostitution to car cleaning and building construction. Those who are sexually exploited may experience daily rape and sexual violence, potentially via forced marriage, or through work in the sex industry. Furthermore, victims may end up with sexually transmitted diseases, which may not be treatable and can destroy future fertility, as well as being life threatening. Victims who contract AIDS or other significant health issues may be deemed unfit to work by the traffickers and abandoned or killed (Lusk and Lucas, 2009). Certainly, in the UK, trafficking people (whether a baby, child or adult) is increasingly regarded as an organised crime that generates significant income for the criminals involved (Di Nicola, 2005).

The begging industry is also lucrative, and children can be forced to beg and give the money they receive to those controlling them (Lusk and Lucas, 2009). Illegal drug production and transportation are also jobs that trafficked individuals find themselves involved with, while yet further victims may be forced into committing crimes. If caught by the authorities, victims may well face yet further prosecution and punishment for crimes they have been compelled to commit. Lobasz (2009) highlights the injustice when a victim of trafficking is treated as a criminal for crimes that they have committed under duress and the harassment of a trafficker, including the initial crime of illegal immigration.

Other examples of forced labour may involve having a job but not being paid, or not being paid much for very long hours and poor work conditions. Victims may find themselves in debt bondage, where they are told that they owe the traffickers for accommodation and protection. A trafficked victim may find themselves working in the building trade or being a domestic servant in a home. While some jobs may not sound as if they could be harmful, consider how you would feel having no freedom and no (or little) money. Many victims are controlled with violence, fear and coercion, with restrictions on their daily movements. Imagine living in a country where you do not know the language or do not know who, out of the limited number of people you meet, are safe and can be trusted. Even the police, in some nations, have been guilty of colluding with traffickers, utilising sexual services and behaving in a way that alienates victims from seeking help (Lusk and Lucas, 2009).

In some countries, people are trafficked for their organs. For example, kidneys are removed from their bodies and sold to others. This is known as 'organ harvesting'. Other forms of harvesting are connected to human slavery. You may be eating chocolate made from cocoa beans harvested by trafficked adults and children, who are being brutally treated and work long hours; you may be wearing a diamond ring that was mined by a child abducted from the family home and forced to work in dangerous conditions,; or you may be wearing clothes made by forced child labour. While those trafficked on cocoa bean farms or cotton farms, or in diamond mines and textile factories may not be living in the UK, the consumer marketplace of the UK – and the affluence of the West – certainly impacts upon their lives.

We simply do not know how many people are being recruited, controlled and enslaved by human traffickers. As with all official statistics, there is a hidden number of people who are victims but have not been found or officially regarded as victims of the crime of human trafficking. In the UK, the National Referral Mechanism (NRM) is the official route for victims to be formally identified as victims of human trafficking and to get support while their case is being investigated. It is reported that around 3,805 people were referred to the NRM as potential trafficked victims in 2016 (NCA, 2017), yet many charities working with victims throughout the world suggest that there are significantly more than this.

The UK system has been criticised for how victims of human trafficking are treated. When trafficking is detected, one of the following will occur:

- If the victim is a UK national and found in the UK, then they are supported and placed under some form of protection while investigations occur (for example, safe house accommodation). They are then free to return home, or are supported to set up home somewhere else in the UK.
- If the victim is not a UK national, they are supported and receive emotional support and medical attention while their case is reviewed. If it is unsafe to return to a home country, the victim can apply for asylum here in the UK.
- If the victim is not a UK national, they are deported back to their home country with minimal medical and emotional intervention.
- Regardless of their nationality, the victim is imprisoned for a crime that they were forced to commit by a trafficker.

Hence victims of human trafficking found in the UK may not be getting adequate support to fully address the trauma of what they have endured. Victims of human trafficking on their journey of recovery are often referred to as 'survivors'. However, many victims are vulnerable to re-victimisation when support levels are compromised. There have been cases where a person has escaped the hands of one trafficker, received limited intervention and support', and then become vulnerable to being trafficked by another trafficker, especially if they are deported back to their home nation (Lusk and Lucas, 2009; Lobasz, 2009). It is therefore imperative that governments make more effort to assist victims through to sustainable survival. There is growing recognition of this in the UK.

Governments need to join forces to share intelligence and interrupt human trafficking networks and routes of travel. However, stricter border control policies can result in more of a punitive approach towards victims who are illegal immigrants (Yen, 2008; Lobasz, 2009). Countries with good policies promoting anti-exploitative practice in the workplace make it harder for corruption through trafficked and enslaved labour to occur. Countries are often discouraging with regard to the demand for exploitative labour, especially in the sex industry (Yen, 2008).

Punishment for those involved in recruitment, transportation and exploitation of people is also important.

In Britain, many frontline service providers, such as those working in the NHS, are now being trained on how to spot potential victims of human trafficking and how to share information with the relevant authorities and refer the case to the NRM. Organisations such as STOPTHETRAFFIK, Hope for Justice and the Salvation Army distribute information on their websites on indicators of someone being a victim. Some common points include:

- being dressed inappropriately for the weather;
- having poor English;

- looking particularly anxious, sleep deprived and malnourished;
- deferring to another to answer for them;
- not knowing where they live;
- not having any ID;
- having bruises on their bodies and poor dental care.

The United Nations Office on Drugs and Crime also has a helpful guide to spotting trafficked persons.

There is a lot of work still left to be done to raise awareness with professionals and the public about human trafficking and how to respond to potential cases of trafficking. Yet the battle to reduce the pains caused by trafficking may require better public knowledge. Everyone can play a part in helping to reduce human trafficking,, by shopping ethically to ensure that workers get paid fairly, and increasing knowledge about the signs for spotting someone who could be trafficked, hence raising public awareness.

What is certain is that while we do not fully appreciate the numbers, we do know that offences of slavery, servitude and forced or compulsory labour and human trafficking are very real crime problems in the globalised and consumerist Western world today – and they do not only occur overseas and out of view.

Sarah Page, Staffordshire University

FACT 30

The fake medicine trade has now overtaken marijuana as the world's largest market for criminal traffickers

Charlotte Stevens

Fake medicines are attempts to pass off counterfeit products as legitimate pharmaceutical products. These items can range from legitimate products, to copies that contain incorrect doses, wrong ingredients or no active ingredients at all.

With regard to the type of fake medicines that consumers in Britain appear to have a demand for, 6.2 million doses or medical devices were seized in 2015. Of these seizures, there were: 2 million doses of erectile dysfunction drugs, narcolepsy pills, abortion pills, diabetes medication, hair-loss drugs, cancer medicines (particularly for breast and prostate); slimming drugs (some of which can increase the risk of heart attacks and strokes); and medical devices, including fake condoms (Gallagher, 2015).

What is striking to note is that these drugs are not always being used for their medical purposes. For example, breast cancer drugs have been reportedly used by some bodybuilders, in order to reduce their breast tissue (Fiore, 2014). It has also been reported that many packs of narcolepsy pills were seized en route to universities, where students take them for 'cognitive enhancement' – staying awake around exam time (Pells, 2016).

It is considered that individuals buying such drugs are made up of those who think they are buying genuine medicines, those who believe that their doctor would not prescribe what they are seeking, and those who believe the legal alternative simply costs too much money (Gallagher, 2015).

There are, of course, a number of health risks that the fake medicine trade presents. For example, counterfeit medicines (Hall and Antonopoulos, 2016) pose an increasing danger to public health, including death and insufficient healthcare as a consequence of self-medication (Jackson et al, 2011). According to Jackson et al (2011), another particularly worrying concern is that counterfeit medicine includes cancer and heart drugs, which are aimed at individuals with serious health issues.

With regard to the actual ingredients found in such medicines, 'variable concentrations of active ingredients or even dangerous toxins, such as arsenic, boric acid, leaded road paint, floor and shoe polish, talcum powder, chalk and brick dust and nickel' have been found (Jackson et al, 2012). While it is difficult to determine the number of fatalities due to fake medicines in the UK, the World Health Organization has put the annual death toll from counterfeit drugs at approximately 1 million. Within this estimate, the largest single group of those affected is concentrated in Africa, where around 200,000 deaths each year are attributed to fake anti-malarial drugs (Clark, 2015). This is even more striking when we consider that there are no recorded instances of anyone dying from a fatal dose of marijuana alone (Wing, 2017). Despite this, the question remains as to how this illicit market has come to overtake other illegal markets.

The illicit drugs market, which involves the distribution of cannabis, cocaine and heroin (to name but a few), is undoubtedly one of the largest criminal trades in the world. This can be largely attributed to the global 'War on drugs' policy of the United States. This initiative comprised a set of drug policies that were intended to discourage the production, distribution and consumption of psychoactive drugs that the participating governments and the UN had made illegal (Eldredge, 1998). The term was propagated by the media shortly after a press conference given in 1971 by President Richard Nixon, when he declared drug abuse 'public enemy number one' (Bertram et al, 1996). The UK adopted a similarly strategy, launching the Misuse of Drugs Act in 1971, which witnessed the further criminalisation of the possession and supplying of particular prohibited substances.

In 2018, approximately 46.3% of inmates incarcerated in the US were convicted of drug-related offences against around 15% in the UK. Despite an increasing number of organisations such as the Drug Policy Alliance in the US voicing their concerns and criticisms towards such policies, there still appears to be strong political will and support to continue the prohibition policy.

The majority of governments around the world currently choose to focus extensively on the 'illicit' drugs trade. As stated, the US prison population is disproportionately filled with offenders who have engaged in such trades. Meanwhile, the endemic problem currently sweeping the US in relation to legal prescribing of OxyContin and various other substances has been allowed to proliferate. This response has largely been echoed internationally, with the disproportionate focus on the 'illicit' drugs trade, allowing other dangerous and economically damaging markets to emerge – including the fake medicine trade.

With the UK following the US example, it has become increasingly difficult for drug traffickers to import their product across the border into the UK. Those who traffic drugs, such as marijuana, also risk facing harsh penalties and lengthy prison sentences (McSweeney et al, 2008). This has resulted in large criminal organisations losing a large amount of trade. It is also important to consider that the demand for imported marijuana has also decreased, due to more and more individuals and criminal groups domestically cultivating marijuana (Potter, 2008). While this illicit trade poses a number of challenges for traffickers, the fake medicine trade seems to be going from strength to strength, with an estimated annual global turnover of US$200 billion (Finlay, 2011). This is in stark contrast to the annual global turnover of marijuana, which was projected at US$46.4 billion in 2016 (Yakowicz, 2017).

One of the primary reasons why this trade has flourished is due to the recent advancements in information and communication technologies (Keeling, 2014). Specifically, the internet provides counterfeiters with opportunities to supply their products with a reduced 'paper trail' (Hall and Antonopoulos, 2016), which reduces accountability and results in weak enforcement. The internet also gives consumers convenient opportunities to buy medicines in relative anonymity. Hall and Antonopoulos (2016: 9) also suggest that the internet 'presents opportunities for the global trade in illicit medicines without the face-to-face interaction experienced by the patient and professional in traditional healthcare'.

It is important to note here that this theme of anonymity is something of a misnomer, and that a customer's information is not quite as hidden as they believe, with their online details and home address (needed to deliver products) often being traceable.

The internet also provides the means for suppliers to advertise their products to potential buyers. Specifically, while it is currently illegal for any pharmaceutical supplier in the UK to advertise their products via direct-to-consumer advertising, the internet has witnessed a significant increase in user-generated content. This provides ample advertising opportunities for illicit suppliers. For example, while nearly 1,400 websites were closed as part of an operation conducted in 2015 (Gallagher, 2015), Hall and Antonopoulos (2016) conducted a Google search using the key words 'online pharmacy UK' and 'buy medicine no prescription' and found 42,000,000 and 59,200,000 results respectively.

In summary, it is evident that the fake medicine trade is quickly becoming the 'go to' market for criminal organisations and entrepreneurs. Alastair Jeffrey, the head of enforcement of the UK's Medicines and Healthcare products Regulatory Agency, shared this view, noting that it is not a 'police priority, you can use the internet as a facilitator, the risk is low, and the profits are very high' (Gallagher, 2015).

One thing is certain, as the fake medicine trade continues to grow exponentially, the probability is that the number of deaths will increase – both in the UK and globally. With that in mind, more needs to be done to tackle and police this growing market, and individuals need to be suspicious of websites that offer prescription-only medication without a prescription or at considerable discounts.

Charlotte Stevens, Birmingham City University

FACT 31

Tackling drug trafficking costs the UK government £10.7 billion annually

Kevin Hoffin

The National Crime Agency has reported that the cost of combating drug trafficking, borne by the taxpayer, is £10.7 billion – a figure that includes policing, healthcare and court costs (National Crime Agency, 2017b). Of this full cost, an estimated £6 billion is spent on combating drug-fuelled thefts and burglary (Home Office, 2017c). The drugs market remains a lucrative industry for organised criminals – both domestic and international. Innovation in the narcotics industry has resulted in stronger strains/higher purity on the streets (Global Drug Survey, 2017; Winstock, 2017), increasingly complex methods of distribution (Buxton, 2013) and, until August 2018, the supply of so-called 'legal highs'.

Currently, global attitudes to drugs and drug use could not be more disparate. Numerous states in the US have moved towards the legalisation of marijuana. Meanwhile, the UK has tended to maintain its stance of 'war on drugs' regardless of the advice to the contrary given by various organisations. A report by right-wing think tank the Adam Smith Institute (Lavin-Morris, 2016) announced: 'The government must acknowledge that cannabis legalisation is the only workable solution to the problems of crime and addiction in the UK and modernise and legalise'. This explicitly states the common link between drugs and crime. While there are those who decry cannabis as a 'gateway drug' and therefore say that legalisation should not even be considered, the report claims that a 'legal cannabis market' would draw revenue close to £6.8 billion annually. This would include £1 billion for the Treasury. Costs on the criminal justice system would also decrease, as the 1,363 inmates incarcerated for marijuana-related crimes in 2016 would save the taxpayer £50 million (Lavin-Morris, 2016). In August 2018, some changes have come to fruition, namely the Home Office allowing a select few individuals (children) access to medical cannabis.

According to government statistics in 2017, just over 15% of prisoners in England and Wales were incarcerated due to drug offences (House of Commons, 2017: 10). This category of offence includes, but is not limited to, possession and possession with intent to supply by sharing or dealing. In the year ending March 2017, a total of 41,098 individuals were convicted for drug offences; of those, 8,638 were handed a custodial sentence (a custody rate of 21.4%). This varies from the previous 12 months, when 45,714 convictions resulted in 8,846 custodial sentences (a custody rate of 19.7%). In effect, there were fewer drug-related convictions overall in 2016/17, but more were sentenced to imprisonment (Ministry of Justice, 2017a: Q1.3). This trend has been in slow but stable decline since 2012, when the peak number of convicted individuals sentenced to imprisonment stood at 9,809 after a steady rise in the preceding years (Ministry of Justice (2017a: Q5.2).

One suitable conclusion may be the suggestion that the attitudes of judges and magistrates towards drug offences are changing, and offenders are being dealt with using alternative methods such as:

- fines
- community orders (perhaps with a focus on addressing drug use)
- suspended sentences
- discharges

Alternatively, the alteration of sentences results in less of a burden on the taxpayer. In 2017 the average cost of imprisonment for a person for a year in England and Wales is approximately £35,182 (Ministry of Justice, 2017c). Considering this, an estimate of the total cost that imprisonment due to drug-related offences between March 2016 and March 2017 was £561.47 million (assuming that all sentences handed out equate to a year; £65,000 x 8,638). A caveat is that any individual cases must be judged on their own merit, as not all offences are deemed equal. Add to this the costs of rehabilitation and reintegration into society, and we can start to build up a picture of the vast expenses involved.

The new drugs strategy unveiled in 2017 has four intentions: reducing demand, restricting supply, supporting recovery, and driving global actions (Home Office, 2017c). The associated research states that for 'every £1 spent on treatment, an estimated £2.50 is saved' (see Fact 33; Home Office, 2017c). By focusing on multiple areas, such a strategy not only casts a watchful gaze over the most vulnerable members of society (the most prone to becoming victims of drug abuse), but also systematically contributes to global policies and intelligence, to damage the proliferation of illegal substances at a more cost-effective rate.

A recent occurrence in the narcotics industry has been the increased purity of some Class A products, particularly cocaine (Global Drug Survey, 2017). This is partially due to the low satisfaction that users experienced from the drug (the initial purity of the dose could have been anywhere between 20% and 5% – deemed 'council cocaine' for its *relative* cheapness) (Winstock, 2017). The market forces controlling cocaine ushered in a response; producers augmented the purity of each dose, in order to stave off competition from other psychoactive substances. Now, the average cocaine 'hit' in the UK can be over 40% pure (Public Health England, 2016b), having doubled between 2013 and 2018.

The parallels between the drug market and more legitimate markets can be surprising but perfectly logical. Narcotics and psychoactive substances are commodities and are affected by supply and demand in much the same way as minerals, oil and grain. Cocaine of a higher purity places a higher burden of cost on the consumer and reflects society perfectly. As Winstock (2017) comments: 'It was a brilliant bit of remarketing that sat well with a society that says money gets you better quality things'. Of course, this increase in purity has had a negative effect on public health (Global Drug Survey, 2017), specifically citing the associated dangers of both cocaine and MDMA.

Distribution and sales networks are becoming increasingly complex, simultaneously aping the commodities market and confounding police forces (Buxton, 2013) – '[an industry] which is increasingly dynamic, innovative and quick to react to challenges and one which requires an equally dynamic, innovative and agile response across Europe' (EMCDDA and Europol, 2013). After all, drugs are a consumer product. The only real difference is their legal status. The National Crime Agency adds that: 'The traditional distinction between international importers and the UK-based wholesalers is becoming more blurred, with some regional wholesalers travelling to the continent to arrange their own imports' (National Crime Agency, 2017b). Organised crime operates at all levels of the drug trade, from importing to wholesale and street-level sales; with some foreign nationals who maintain ties to their (drug-producing) home countries taking responsibility for safe passage of products into the UK (National Crime Agency, 2017b).

The rise of 'legal highs' or synthetic substances with psychoactive effects occupies a curious position in the illicit market. Made in volume in equally illicit laboratories, products such as methamphetamine and MDMA are trafficked to the UK in higher demand than the rest of Europe. The name 'legal highs' is quite often inaccurate, as many contain controlled substances and would be distributed with their supposed 'legality' in mind. Easily available in locations as diverse as music festivals, clubs and a large representation online, their distribution was for a while only countered when certain strains were discovered, and the chemical composition (or stated intended use) altered to return the product to the legal 'grey area'. This created problems for police response and control.

The Psychoactive Substances Act 2016, enacted in May of that year, made significant progress, in that it is now illegal to produce a substance which works: 'by stimulating or depressing the person's central nervous system, it affects the person's mental functioning or emotional state' (Psychoactive Substances Act 2016, s.2 (2)). This excludes alcohol, nicotine, caffeine or tobacco products, food items and those already covered by the Misuse of Drugs Act 1971 (see Psychoactive Substances Act 2016, s.2 (3)). Although the legislation has received much in the way of criticism – from groups who protest over its apparent consequence of 'ban[ning] pleasure' (Scott, 2015) – the Act does not affect those who possess it with the intention of using it recreationally themselves unless in a custodial environment, or for scientific research (Psychoactive Substances Act 2016, s.11).

The National Crime Agency estimates that 18-23 tonnes of heroin and 25-30 tonnes of cocaine are imported to the UK each year (National Crime Agency, 2017a). The arrest of easily replaceable, low-level dealers barely makes an impact on an area's drug problem. To counteract these extremes, a 2017 focus on large-scale strike operations at both local and regional levels has resulted in a certain level of success. Numerous arrests and prosecutions (as necessary) and seizure of illicit products have been reported (Kreft, 2017a, 2017b; Waldron, 2017). The focus on these operations is aimed at ensuring that the authorities can both arrest influential distributors and seize the contraband before it hits the wider markets, thus minimising the sheer number of smaller operations necessary. These operations are currently the UK government's best hope in taking drugs off the streets, while HM Revenue & Customs works diligently with the tools at its disposal to aid the prevention of drugs entering the country.

Kevin Hoffin, Birmingham City University

FACT 32

Alcohol-related crime in the UK is estimated to cost the economy between £8 billion and £13 billion per year

Craig Kelly

In 2016, the UK alcohol industry was worth £39.9 billion in sales. While this points towards the sheer profitability in the industry's sale of alcohol, the frequent connection between alcohol and criminal behaviour raises important questions around why a fundamentally harmful substance has proliferated under extraordinarily loose regulations in modern free market economies.

According to research into the household expenditure on alcohol in the UK in 2015, a total of £17.2 billion was spent (Office for National Statistics, 2018). From this, HM Revenue & Customs collected around £10 billion from alcohol duties in the fiscal year 2012/13. This amounts to 2% of overall tax receipts, increasing further to just below £11 billion in 2016 (HMRC, 2016). However, once the actual cost of alcohol is appraised from a criminological perspective, the actual cost to society is much greater. While the income generated by the alcohol industry produces an indelible contribution to the UK via its taxation, to what extent do the repercussions of alcohol and the night-time economy cost the nation? How exact is this figure?

Led by the examples set by Scotland and Wales, the Home Office (2012) sought to assess the viability of the introduction of a minimum price threshold per unit of alcohol, and in doing so, estimated that alcohol-related crime cost British taxpayers £11 billion per year; yet this figure was based on data available for the period 2010/11. Pertinently, this statistic should be treated with caution for the very fact it was detailed in a report commissioned by a government lobbying for an increase of taxes within a lucrative tertiary economy. Therefore, it is likely that the true figure is closer to the conservative estimate of £8 billion per annum. These reasons include, but are not limited to, the exclusion of victim populations from these surveys (Spalek, 2017) and the ubiquitous complex realities of measuring crime. However, the actual estimate is that alcohol-related crime costs British taxpayers £13 billion per annum.

The link between increased violence and alcohol has long been established. Data from the period 2013/14 from the Office for National Statistics (2015) highlights that victims of violent crime perceived the offender to be under the influence of alcohol in 53% of violent incidents. This equates to alcohol being a factor in over 700,000 self-reported violent incidents within a 12-month period in England and Wales alone. Within this subsection of victims assaulted by those under the influence of alcohol, the data also displayed a notable trend for an increased severity of injury as a result of the incidents.

Alcohol-related sexual offences have also been widely researched (Lacasse and Mendelson, 2007; Hovarth and Brown, 2007; Beynon et al, 2008). Research conducted over the last four decades (Binder, 1981; Finkelson and Oswalt, 1995; Allen, 2007; and Wolitzky-Taylor et al, 2015) indicates that sexual offences are often alcohol-related. Ullman (2003) presented research indicating that when alcohol is involved in a rape or sexual assault, the victim and offender are predominantly unknown to each other beforehand, meeting in a nightclub or house party, but alcohol is a factor in a much broader array of sexual violence.

However, the costs of alcohol more broadly often do not feature in contemporary discussions of crime, because of its inherent pettiness. Examples of this might be the university student who, during a drink-induced haze in freshers' week, acquires a traffic cone to adorn their new flat; or those stopped by the police for being under the influence of alcohol while riding a bicycle (Guillory, 2014). Such offences will not be included in the typical analysis of alcohol-related crime, yet the cost of a police officer's time in stopping the person on the bike or the thousands of traffic cones having to be replaced each year between September and October are a small part of the social costs.

Despite the fact that the exact scale of alcohol-related crime remains shrouded in mystery, the financial implications are dramatic. But in monetary terms, how does the billions per annum cost of alcohol-related crimes compare with the costs of other forms of criminality? In the 2016/17 fiscal year, the annual counter-terrorism policing budget totalled £670 million (Parliament, 2017). For the fiscal year 2014/15, the British Retail Consortium (2016) estimated the cost of retail crime to total £613 million. Utilising data from 2010/11, Mills et al (2013) attempted to estimate for the Home Office the economic and social costs of organised crime in the UK. They discerned that the social and economic costs of the illicit firearms trade in the UK totals approximately £160 million, while the cost of organised crime groups committing fraud totals £8.9 billion. Using the figures presented to demonstrate the economic implications of alcohol-related crime, therefore, the combined costs of these crimes equate to significantly less than the full cost of alcohol-related crime per annum.

This discussion has focused so far on the economic cost of alcohol-related crimes and the inherent difficulty in precisely evaluating the subject. However, it has been estimated that in a community of 100,000 people each year, 1,000 people will be a victim of alcohol-related violent crime. In 2010, the Coalition government listed a reduction in alcohol-fuelled violent crime among its core priorities in its Alcohol Strategy; and today's Conservative government highlights drugs and alcohol as one of the six key drivers of crime in its Modern Crime Prevention Strategy. However, people often do not think of alcohol as a drug in the way that they do with illicit narcotics. Yet where crime is concerned, it is very often the first and most prevalent drug – and this can only partially be explained by its availability.

Yet while its harms in monetary costs are contested, the unarguable facts are that 64% of stranger violence, and 70% of violent incidents at the weekends, in the evenings and at night are alcohol-related (Alcohol Policy UK, 2015). In 2015, there were over 8,000 drink-driving accidents in the UK, including 220 fatalities and 1,160 serious injuries.

This shows that discussion of the economic cost of alcohol-related crimes alone is limited. While the economic costs can seem staggering, the human costs may be far starker.

Craig Kelly, Birmingham City University

FACT 33

For every £1 spent on drug-related treatment, there is a £2.50 benefit to society

Loukas Ntanos

Drugs and crime are, as concepts, frequently perceived as being intimately linked. In this discussion, drugs are viewed as substances that are otherwise alien to the body, which influence the central nervous system once ingested, inhaled or otherwise introduced. Of course, substances such as caffeine (and alcohol) fall within this remit, but for this discussion, the proposed definition focuses primarily on those substances that are criminalised in UK law.

Levine (1978) details that addiction to drugs has been in the public consciousness for around 200 years. The relationship between drugs and crime, however, is a vague one, still the subject of examination and interpretation in academic discourse., Numerous academics have proposed a variety of perspectives on the matter, including the view that drugs and crime simply co-exist (Mott, 1975), and that sociological and environmental factors potentially lead to criminal behaviour or drug use. A perspective commonly found in the mainstream media, however, is that drug use leads to crime.

Drugs are perceived to have a facilitative effect on crime, in the sense that they affect the mood, capacity for judgement and self-control of the offender (Walters, 2014). Economically oriented crime, for instance, is frequently committed so that drug offenders can support their drug use (Walters, 2014). A considerable number of crimes committed in the UK are indeed related to drugs, the cost of which has been estimated at £13.5 million for England and Wales (UK Drug Policy Commission, 2008). It is important to note here that this number is far lower than the estimated cost of alcohol related crime, which is estimated at £11 billion (Home Office, 2012). Stemming from the existing debate in regard to the causality between crime and drugs, there is no consensus as to whether drug offenders (that is, drug addicts found guilty of a crime) should be punished or sent for treatment instead.

To contextualise the existing debate, we need to examine the way in which society has chosen to deal with drug offenders. In particular, much of this has involved a narrow policy of prohibition. The first modern law in Europe for regulating drugs was the Pharmacy Act 1868 in the United Kingdom. There had been previous moves to establish the medical and pharmaceutical professions as separate, self-regulating bodies, but the General Medical Council, established in 1863, unsuccessfully attempted to assert control over drug distribution. The Act set controls on the distribution of poisons and drugs. Poisons could only be sold if the purchaser was known to the seller, and drugs, including opium and all preparations of opium or of poppies, had to be sold in containers with the seller's name and address. Despite the reservation of opium to professional control, general sales did continue to a limited extent, with mixtures with less than 1% opium being unregulated.

More recent prohibition occurred as part of a response to rising drug use among young people and the counterculture movement. Government efforts to enforce prohibition were strengthened in many countries, but particularly in the US from the 1960s onwards. Support at an international level for the prohibition of psychoactive drug use became a consistent feature of US policy during both Republican and Democratic administrations, but grew exceptionally in the 1970s with the declaration of a 'War on drugs' by President Nixon. This became so entrenched that, subsequently, US support for foreign governments has often been contingent on their adherence to US drug policy. Unarguably, it is prohibition-driven drug policy that has accompanied the increased use of incarceration in the US and the UK.

Prisons in the UK offer limited opportunities for drug offenders to embark on treatment, but overall criminal justice-based drug interventions are not particularly effective. The problems have been raised by offenders, who entered the prison with an alcohol problem and thereafter expressed dissatisfaction regarding alcohol treatment services in custody (Alcohol and Crime Commission, 2014). The effectiveness of drug treatment in prison is additionally hindered by the fact that prisoners continue to take drugs while in custody. In fact, more than 37% of male and 31% of female prisoners have reported that it was easy for them to find drugs in prison (Prison Reform Trust, 2016). Indeed, there are multiple ways in which prisoners can access drugs:

- they can bring drugs themselves into prison;
- visitors can sneak drugs to them;
- corrupt prison staff can provide inmates with drugs;
- drugs can be thrown over prison walls.

There have also been instances in which prisoners became addicted to painkillers prescribed by prison doctors (Bean, 2014). The inconsistency of drug treatment in prison falls in line with the considerably low record of the prison system for reducing reoffending. Reports indicate that 46% of prisoners are reconvicted within just one year of release (Prison Reform Trust, 2016). The high reoffending rates are usually of drug offenders.

Drawing on her own experience in prison and her professional background as an economist, Vicky Pryce (2013) has promoted the provision of drug treatment instead of custody for drug offenders, summarising that society could save up to £200,000 per offender in costs over the offender's lifetime. Indeed, a closer examination of drug treatment indicates that it is less expensive than the incarceration of drug offenders. A full year of methadone maintenance treatment, for instance, was estimated to cost between £3,000 and £5,000 per patient (Laurance, 2009), whereas a full year of custody cost far more.

Furthermore, drug treatment appears to be more effective than any alternative. From 1 April 2015 to 31 March 2016, some 64,166 drug addicts who started treatment managed to overcome their addiction and were subsequently discharged as treatment completed (Public Health England, 2016a). Swanswell, a drug recovery charity, offered treatment to 7,767 drug addicts in 2014; 83% of people who started a programme with the charity completed it successfully. Notably, 90% of those who completed their programme managed to maintain the changes they had achieved six months later (Swanswell Charitable Trust, 2015).

In 2017, the National Treatment Agency for Substance Misuse suggested that for every £1 spent on drug-related treatment, there is a £2.50 benefit to society (Public Health England, 2018). In particular, the combined benefits of drug and alcohol treatment amount to £2.4 billion every year, resulting in savings in areas such as crime and improvements to health and social care. In demonstrating this line of thought, there were approximately 203,808 people engaged in drug-related treatment between 2015 and 2016, and if they had not been in such treatment, they could have cost the NHS over £1 billion (NHS Digital, 2017a). To provide a more specific example, needle and syringe programmes cost approximately £200 a year per injector and can provide up to £41,000 in savings for every prevented case of hepatitis C treatment and up to £42,000 a year for every prevented case of HIV treatment (Public Health England, 2018). It is also estimated that such treatment prevented close to 5 million crimes in 2010/11 and resulted in 4.4 million fewer crimes in 2016/17, with a 44% reduction in dependent individuals reoffending and a 33% decrease in the number of offences committed (Public Health England, 2017, 2018). When we consider the risk factors involved in drug misuse – which include socio-economic deprivation, homelessness, unemployment, poor job security and poor mental health – it is evident that a more treatment-based approach is beneficial, not only to the individual, but also to society in general.

It is also worth noting that many treatment schemes essentially function as community builders, assisting drug offenders in becoming productive parts of their families and of the wider communities to which they belong, thus helping them to abstain from criminal activity. The largest financial benefit of drug treatment is seen in avoiding incarceration and victimisation costs. This unavoidably raises the question as to why our society insists on prohibition and punishing drug offenders. Why do we invest money on a prison system that has failed to cater adequately for these individuals who suffer drug addiction – especially when harm reduction approaches have proven to be a much more effective and less expensive way of controlling drug problems?

Loukas Ntanos, Birmingham City University

FACT 34

If you get caught selling counterfeits, you can face a maximum of 10 years' imprisonment and an unlimited fine

Joanna Large

In England and Wales, it is an offence to manufacture, sell or be in possession of counterfeit goods with a view to sell, under the Trade Marks Act 1994 (Section 92). On indictment, the maximum sentence available for a person convicted of these offences is 10 years' imprisonment and/ or an unlimited fine. In addition, once someone has been convicted of an offence, they could be subject further to a confiscation order under the Proceeds of Crime Act 2002. This targets the 'criminal lifestyle' and has the power to recover assets (such as property) that are deemed to have been funded through committing counterfeit crimes.

Under the Trade Marks Act, the primary concern relates to the 'loss' to the trade mark owner associated with the copying of a trade-marked good. This forms one of the main arguments against counterfeiting – its detrimental effect on the legitimate manufacturer and wider associated industry and economy. However, counterfeiting is also stated to have broader social and economic impacts, and of particular concern is the relationship it is claimed to have with 'serious' and 'organised' crime (OECD, 2008).

Counterfeiting is recognised as a highly profitable business, which has natural allure to criminal groups and networks. Organisations such as the United Nations Office on Drugs and Crime (UNODC) highlight the evidence for 'organised crime groups' being involved in counterfeiting through national and international authorities' attention on counterfeit markets and supply chains. UNODC also identifies the 'strategic and operational links between counterfeiting and drug trafficking', for example (UNODC, n.d.). The Intellectual Property Crime Group (IPCG), based in the United Kingdom, further documents examples of the relationship between counterfeiting and criminal activities, citing 'many' cases where links have been found. These 'criminal activities' include 'money laundering, people trafficking, loan sharking and the exploitation of children' (IPCG, 2010: 15 (cited in IPCG, 2014)). The 'pitifully low sanctions' (or lack of enforcement) which many countries have for counterfeiting, alongside the profits which counterfeiters stand to make, are the reasons why money laundering and organised crime are becoming increasingly involved – 'from Paramilitary groups to international fraud organisations' (AIM, 2005: 1).

Despite (limited) recent attention of counterfeiting as a criminological issue, and the contemporary concerns about counterfeit goods, counterfeiting itself is not a new phenomenon. However, recent years have witnessed a movement away from the 'cottage industry' of counterfeiting (Vagg and Harris, 1998: 189) to a rapidly developing complex global market, which produces, distributes and retails counterfeit goods. The Organisation for Economic Co-operation and Development (OECD) argued in April 2016 that the global import trade in counterfeit goods amounts to nearly half a trillion US dollars, with 'much of these proceeds going to organised crime' (OECD and EUIPO, 2016).

Continued rapid advances in technology, most notably the growth of the internet, have transformed the nature of the market(s) for counterfeit goods. It is easier than ever to distribute, produce and manufacture goods (Heinonen et al, 2012; Treadwell, 2012; Wilson and Fenoff, 2014; Hall and Antonopoulos, 2016). In addition, the internet enables a heightened drive and desire for counterfeit (and legitimate) goods more generally (Heinonen et al, 2012; Treadwell, 2012; Lavorgna, 2014; Wilson and Fenoff, 2014; Hall and

Antonopoulos, 2016; Rojek, 2016). Alongside technological advancements, the nature of contemporary late capitalism and its resultant impact on consumer culture have all contributed to the rapidly changing nature of illegal markets.

In addition, as well as larger-scale criminality, counterfeiting is likely to be a key activity for smaller informal economies and illicit markets. A survey conducted by the IPCG asked authorities to comment on whether counterfeiting was linked to 'wider criminality'. The IPCG's report found that there was a range of links with 'lower level' types of criminal and anti-social behaviour, with benefit fraud being the most common (48%) (IPCG, 2010: 16 (cited in IPCG, 2014)). Current ongoing research on small-scale counterfeit markets and the transnational financial flows of counterfeit goods examines the differing scopes of production, distribution and end market supply of counterfeit goods, and the relationships between licit and illicit economies. Counterfeits are also noted for the potential to be commodities in which criminals can trade (UNODC, n.d.).

Therefore, there are growing political, industry and policing concerns about counterfeit goods at international, national and local levels. Law enforcement agencies (despite local and national variations), for the large part, have become more attuned to counterfeiting as a crime issue. In the United Kingdom, the launch of the Police Intellectual Property Crime Unit in December 2013 reflected some of these concerns. In addition, the National Trading Standards eCrime Team investigates online sales of counterfeit goods as part of its national online crime remit, which further supports the work of locally based Trading Standards authorities. 'Operation Jasper' is a recent example of a large-scale partnership enforcement approach that tackled the online sale of counterfeits through social media (Facebook and Instagram) in addition to offline wholesale retail points (Forster, 2017).

Despite these kinds of increased enforcement activities to tackle counterfeiting and remove counterfeit products from the market, policing and law enforcement agencies face several challenges in doing so. Therefore, alongside traditional enforcement activities, a consumer-responsibility initiative has developed (Large, 2015). This approach attempts to 'educate' consumers about the 'dangers of buying fakes' (AIM, 2005: 4). It is loosely based on the premise that if consumers are educated about the 'harms' of counterfeiting, then they will cease to purchase (at least in terms of knowingly purchasing) counterfeit products – and thus a reduction in demand will mean a reduction in supply.

The importance of this strategy is reinforced by the *Intellectual Property Crime Report* (IPCG, 2007 (cited in IPCG, 2014)), which after claiming that the National Intellectual Property Crime Strategy is starting to provide improved outcomes in dealing with counterfeiting, states that 'the biggest hurdle to overcome is to educate the general public' (IPCG, 2007: 5 (cited in IPCG, 2014)). This consumer-responsibility approach to enforcement raises various concerns. First is with the notion of 'educating' consumers with the aim of changing behaviour. Another concern lies with the implications of having a criminal justice enforcement policy that emphasises the role of the *non-criminal* participant.

Returning to the original point about the severe penalties associated with supplying and manufacturing counterfeits, it is interesting to note that to purchase a counterfeit in England and Wales is not in itself necessarily a criminal activity.

Joanna Large, University of Bristol

Part Eight
Violent Britain

FACT 35

There is no comprehensive national figure for the number of gangs or the number of young people involved or associated with gangs

Charlene Crossley

Media and political responses to youth gangs in the United Kingdom have heightened in the last 15 years. This has mainly been the result of a spate of tragic and high-profile criminal activity attributed to gang activity. As a result, it is often suggested that the UK has a gang problem – yet the ability to accurately quantify gang membership is ambiguous and is argued to stem from the inconsistent application of gang definitions.

Critical interest in gangs emerged in 2008 from the work of Hallsworth and Young, who, in their discussion of 'gang talk', challenged media and policy representations of gangs, arguing that it only serves to perpetuate the problem, thus glamourising the discourse. Therefore, rather than accepting the reality of gangs, do we instead need to consider if there is a problem?

In 2012, a report by the Metropolitan Police service (House of Commons, 2015) suggested that there were at that time 259 violent gangs made up of 4,800 individuals. Manchester has identified 66 urban street gangs totalling 886 individual gang members (Home Office, 2015). Despite these figures, the total number of individuals involved in gangs remains unclear, with no recent statistics other than a series of sensationalist headlines. As a result, the Home Office (2015) has concluded that there is no comprehensive national figure for the number of gangs or the number of young people involved or associated with gangs.

The term 'gang' in itself is problematic, with the media, the police, communities, young people, the general public and academics all having clear – yet often contrasting – views on the term. The lack of clarity as to the extent of the gang problem in England and Wales is problematic and is argued to be the result of varying definitions. Definitions have been suggested as far back as 2002. In 2009, a report commissioned by the Centre for Social Justice attempted to bring clarity and uniformity to the discussion of gangs, offering a definition that, it suggested, distinguishes it from the 'everyday activity of young people on the streets' (Centre for Social Justice, 2009: 11). This definition consists of the following: a relatively durable, predominantly street-based group of young people who (1) see themselves (and are seen by others) as a discernible group, (2) engage in a range of criminal activity and violence, (3) identify with or lay claim over territory, (4) have some form of identifying structural feature, and (5) are in conflict with other, similar, gangs (Centre for Social Justice, 2009: 21).

Despite this, uniformity in the application of gang labels remains problematic. Empirical research from Smithson et al (2012: 117) found that the label 'gang' was adopted by police despite the lack of an agreeable working definition. Added to this, Williams et al (2013) found that definitions were often misunderstood among practitioners and applied inconsistently. Therefore, although there has been a definition operating in the UK by virtue of the Centre for Social Justice since 2009, the lack of understanding and the inconsistent application has since led to further revisions.

The aim of the new definition serves to offer flexibility and a less prescriptive approach to defining gangs (Home Office, 2015). Therefore, the (in)ability to define and quantify gang membership goes some way towards providing evidence of whether a UK gang problem exists, or whether the continued focus is a result of inconsistent recording practices (Williams and Clarke, 2016) and the inability to identify a problem.

Contemporary evidence on gangs and gang definitions remains unclear. Despite the lack of evidence on UK gangs, the Ending Gangs and Youth Violence (see Ending Gangs and Youth Violence, 2011) strategy was developed in response to the serious disorders perpetrated in England in 2011. Ministers concluded that the riots were initiated and controlled by organised gangs, and the government emphasised a holistic approach, involving statutory and voluntary agencies, to support and protect communities and individuals. In pursuing this aim, the government prioritised £10 million in early intervention work for 2012/13, to support up to 30 areas that are most affected by gangs and youth violence (Ending Gangs and Youth Violence, 2011).

The post-riots era has, as demonstrated, caused a reconsideration of gangs in the UK. While the Ending Gangs and Youth Violence initiative could be regarded as a knee-jerk reaction to the riots, the continued focus on gangs shows no sign of abating and thus continues to inform both policing practice and legislation (Home Office, 2015). However, without a universal definition, the full scale of the gang problem cannot be accurately assessed (Bullock and Tilley, 2002), and this has obvious implications for research and policy creation.

Despite this, the government responded to the ensuing media narrative on gangs, by introducing into the Policing and Crime Act 2009 a new civil injunction specifically targeting gangs. Initially implemented in specific UK cities following the 2011 riots, David Cameron in his commitment to ensuring 'stamping out gangs' would become a national priority, which consisted of rolling out gang injunctions across the UK. The introduction of the gang injunction in early 2011 (often referred to as a 'Gangbo' in news media) enables the police and local authorities to apply to the courts to impose a wide range of indefinite restrictions or requirements on individuals identified as being involved in gang-related activity. As a civil order, rather than a criminal one, it carries a much lower burden-of-proof requirement, which is potentially problematic when identification remains unclear. Therefore, while the perceptions around gangs are heightened in the media, this is not evidenced through policy or the underreported use of gang injunctions. This is supported by Home Office statistics (2015: 5), which demonstrate that 'London, while experiencing the most gang-related violence of any area in the country, has obtained only fourteen gang injunctions'.

Treadwell and Gooch (2015) question the value of gang injunctions for addressing and reducing the serious gang violence for which the injunction was intended. The question, therefore, remains as to whether a gang problem exists in the UK, particularly to the extent that the media and policy suggest, or whether police and local authorities are recognising the gang injunction's usefulness in reducing gang activity. While on the surface it appears that the gang injunction signals to policy makers and communities that the issue of gang violence is being addressed, and that the welfare of those either targeted as being in a gang or on the cusp of involvement is paramount, arguably such initiatives lead to further stigmatisation.

Despite its exploratory nature, this chapter offers some insight into gangs and gang injunctions, and considers the links between gang identification and the underreported use of gang injunctions. Although it is not disputed that youth gangs exist, the lack of reliable, empirical evidence combined with media coverage has resulted in government responses that are targeted towards – and therefore stigmatising to – specific individuals. This raises various questions for consideration. What is the use of the gang label for making sense of the problem of youth crime more generally? Is serious youth violence, for example, best explained by a gang problem? Or should we begin to look at this in a different way?

Charlene Crossley, Manchester Metropolitan University

FACT 36

Britain's most prolific serial killer was Dr Harold Shipman, yet we are still uncertain how many people he actually killed

David Wilson

The term 'serial murder' is a social construction (Wilson et al, 2015). However, it is only the labelling of offences that is a social construction; the actual act of murder that these offenders engage in is very much a physical reality (Ferguson et al, 2003). Due to the classification of murder into numerous types – including single, double, triple, mass and spree murder – the term 'serial murder' was initially created to separate this distinctive form of murder from, most notably, mass murder (Hickey, 2006).

Many different, and often competing (Lundrigan and Canter, 2008), definitions have been produced to be the first to create a universal classification. These differences often centre on either the number of victims that are required, the amount of time that must have passed before an individual can be labelled a serial murderer, or both. While there are disagreements, the range of the number of required victims is typically two or three (Hickey, 1997). However, the issue of an approximate amount of time needed to be classified as a serial murderer has proven to be much harder to agree on.

This facet of serial murder has ranged between simply being an unspecified 'cooling off period' (Newton, 2006), most commonly associated with the Federal Bureau of Investigation in the US, to a much more specific 'period which is greater than thirty days' (Newton, 2006) between the first offence and the subsequent offences. While it is acknowledged that the term 'serial murder' is a loose and slippery concept, it is often agreed in the UK that a serial murderer is:

> An individual who has been found guilty in a court of law of the murder of at least three victims (or posthumously determined to be guilty), irrespective of motive, in a period of greater than thirty days, typically killing at least one person per killing episode, with a 'cooling off' period in between. (Lynes, 2017: 26)

While it is often enticing to get 'into the mind' of a serial killer – an approach often credited to the rise of offender profiling – this approach is rather limited in understanding the structural or societal context within which these killers exist. For example, my own research into the phenomenon of serial murder determined that British serial murderers tend overwhelmingly to target particular groups in society, including: sex workers; gay men; children; young women; and the elderly. While these groups may appear to be disparate, with little in common, they are each, in various ways, vulnerable and often marginalised members of society, which makes them easier targets for predators. While the scope of this book prevents an in-depth analysis of why each of these groups are at risk, a case study of Dr Harold Shipman – probably Britain's most 'notorious' serial murderer – provides a means by which to demonstrate how such vulnerabilities come into existence, and how individuals such as Shipman capitalise and exploit them.

Harold Frederick Shipman was born on 14 January 1946 in Nottingham, England, the second of four children of Vera and Harold Shipman, who was a lorry driver by trade. Growing up, Shipman was particularly close to his mother, who died of cancer when he was 17. If we attempt to explain the template for his future murder, his mother's death came in a manner similar to what later became his own modus operandi: in the later stages of her disease, she had morphine administered at home by a doctor. Shipman witnessed his mother's pain subside in light of her terminal condition, up until her death on 21 June 1963. His mother's death would have a significant impact on the young Shipman, and would be the precursor to his later murders.

Shipman received a scholarship to medical school, and graduated from Leeds School of Medicine in 1970. In 1974, he took up his first position as a general practitioner (GP) at the Abraham Ormerod Medical Centre in Todmorden, West Yorkshire. In 1975, he was caught forging prescriptions of pethidine for his own use. He was fined £600, and briefly attended a drug rehabilitation clinic in York. After a brief period as medical officer for Hatfield College, Durham, and temporary work for the National Coal Board, he became a GP at the Donneybrook Medical Centre in Hyde, Greater Manchester, in 1977. Shipman continued working as a GP in Hyde throughout the 1980s and opened his own surgery on Market Street in 1993, becoming a respected member of the community.

It would be this element of respectability – afforded to him by his occupation – that would ultimately assist in Shipman committing hundreds of murders over an estimated 23 years. Compared to most other serial killers who would have to break down a door or smash a window to gain access to their victims, Shipman was instead invited in and often offered a cup of tea and a biscuit by his patients (Wilson, 2009). Shipman was, for all intents and purposes, perfectly hidden in plain sight thanks to excellent 'occupational camouflage' (Lynes, 2017).

Another important factor in his ability to remain undetected was his previously touched on modus operandi. Shipman would follow a pattern of his administering lethal doses of diamorphine, signing patients' death certificates, and then falsifying medical records to indicate that they had been in poor health.

Another important factor to his 'success' as a serial murderer was the type of victim he targeted. The elderly – one of the vulnerable groups highlighted previously – are often considered a burden to a neoliberal capitalist society, in which those individuals who cannot compete and contribute to the economy are pushed to the background, subsequently marginalised and often ignored.

To fully understand society's role in creating vulnerable groups, it is important to consider the work of Young (1999), and the theoretical discussion on the transformation of Britain from an 'inclusive' to an 'exclusive' society. Young's (1999) *The Exclusive Society* argued that Britain was, at one stage, a society that placed great emphasis on community, locality and employment. This, according to Young, changed during the 1980s, when Thatcherism's anti-social welfare policies de-emphasised these very principles, which was concerned with materialistic consumption, individualism, anonymity, and less about 'traditional ties of community and family' (Young, 1999:6). As a result, certain groups became increasingly marginalised in society, with government policies that have, over a period, weakened the economic and social protection of the elderly, gay men, runaways, children, and women involved in prostitution (Wilson, 2007).

With the elderly already marginalised and made vulnerable, due to being unable to compete within an 'exclusive' society, Shipman's occupation as a well-respected GP, who offered the only home visit practice in the area (Wilson, 2009), provided the ideal means for him to kill at least 215 of his patients over 23 years. The true number may never be known.

When we look at the phenomenon of serial murder, it is easy to get lost in the 'mind of the serial murderer' and repeatedly ask ourselves what was different about them, and what led them to want to commit murder. With our unwavering gaze directed towards the killer, it is easy to forget the people who lost their lives to them. At its heart, an examination of serial murder lays bare society's nature, and reveals that some of its practices create vulnerabilities that serial killers exploit.

Emeritus Professor David Wilson, Birmingham City University

FACT 37

The average cost of a contract murder in the UK is just £15,180

Mohammed Rahman

> Crucially, a hitman's job is to 'shoot to kill'. The drift into this lethal practice not only involves hitmen separating their morally-responsible selves so as to be able to kill, but also depersonalising their intended victim. (Wilson and Rahman, 2015: 263)

Wilson and Rahman's observation, quoted here, explains the functionality of a hitman – one that accepts an order to kill a human being from someone who is not officially acknowledged as a legal authority regarding a 'just killing'. While the phenomenon of contract killing is actively woven into the fabric of British popular culture, there has been little academic discussion about hitmen and their 'hits'. However, in recent years, several scholarly sources have explored British hitmen, their motivations and the significance of space when executing a contract. MacIntyre et al's (2014) pioneering study on British hitmen concluded that the average cost of a hit was £15,180, with figures ranging from as low as £200 up to £100,000.

The point of interest here is the lowest sum, given that most people would consider £200 to be an inadequate payment for the taking of a life. This was the sum received by 15-year-old Santre Sanchez Gayle, who on 26 March 2010 murdered 26-year-old Turkish national Gulistan Subasi on her doorstep, in east London. Within the context of contract murder, Subasi's assassination was perfectly executed. While nearby CCTV captured Gayle executing the hit, the grainy footage was unable to identify him, and the hitman left no forensic evidence at the crime scene. Gayle was apprehended after bragging about the hit to his schoolmates. Subsequently, he was arrested, charged and convicted of murder at the Old Bailey in 2011 (Wilson and Rahman, 2015: 5). Gayle, who was also a low-level drug dealer, is serving life imprisonment, where he is, somewhat ironically, currently at risk of becoming a victim of a 'hit', having had a £50,000 bounty placed on him by the Turkish mafia. It is reported that he is now serving his sentence in protective custody.

In their four-division typology of British hitmen, MacIntyre et al (2014) categorised Gayle as a 'novice'. This description implies those who are young, new to contract killing, predominantly unemployed, involved in petty crime, and often apprehended through local intelligence. The authors argue that this is not to say that novices are 'unable to plan the hit, or carry it out successfully' (2014: 334). Subasi's murder was considered a 'professional' hit, which therefore would have categorised Gayle as a 'master' hitman in MacIntyre et al's typology, had he not bragged locally. It was Gayle's criminal immaturity and hedonism that led to his downfall – two characteristics that are often controlled or repressed by hitmen operating at higher levels.

Before exploring a contracted hit nearer to the average cost, it is worth briefly discussing the remaining three descriptions of MacIntyre et al's hitman typology.

- 'Dilettantes' are a step above 'novices'. These are contract killers, who kill based on personal or business motives. For instance, dilettantes may accept a contract to solve a financial crisis. Thus, dilettante hits are often disorganised, and their method of killing varies. They are often apprehended through confessions, forensic evidence and local intelligence.
- 'Journeymen' hitmen are more advanced than 'dilettantes', as they comprise killers who have backgrounds in violence

and are capable assassins. These encompass individuals who have experience in the use of firearms and other lethal weaponry. They leave the crime scene with little or no forensic evidence, and their contract motives are typically related to business or organised crime. 'Journeymen' are usually apprehended through local intelligence.

- 'Master' hitmen are the exceptional performers, who are highly skilled, organised, and leave no tangible or forensic evidence at the crime scene. A contract killer of this grade evades justice by existing in the periphery. MacIntyre et al (2014) note that the main reason why master hitmen evade justice is because they 'travel into the community where the hit is to take place and then leave that community shortly afterwards'. (2014: 338)

MacIntyre et al's (2014) typology has been crucial in unpacking the dynamic nature of British hitmen and their hits. The study also charts the reality of the contract killing world – one that is far from the popular cultural portrayals of hits being conducted by organised crime henchmen in five-star hotels, smoky bars and busy casinos.

However, the study surprisingly missed out a notable hit that received national press coverage. On 30 March 2000, 48-year-old Italian-born Mario Commatteo was gunned down at point-blank range at his home in Surrey, England. Commatteo was the wealthy boss of a catering company and was married to a 50-year-old Greek Cypriot, Angela Bristow. They met in 1991, and soon after married. However, in the latter years of their marriage, Bristow became bitter towards her husband and feared he would leave her in financial ruin if they divorced. For Bristow, bitterness turned into hatred, and she resorted to thoughts of killing her husband as she stood to gain more than £160,000 from Commatteo's insurance policies. Her initial plan to overdose Commatteo with ecstasy failed, which led her to seek external help.

Of note is the fact that Bristow requested the assistance of 35-year-old Paul Hayter, a car wash owner, who worked as security for Chelsea FC. Bristow, a regular customer of Hayter's car wash, offered him £10,000 to kill her husband. Hayter refused to execute the hit and instead negotiated a 'middleman' role, by approaching 35-year-old Raymond Ryan – who was short of money and accepted the contract. Ryan, a career criminal, earned money by selling used and stolen cars. Leading up to the hit, Ryan stole a red Ford Sierra and used it to shadow Commatteo for weeks. Witnesses described seeing the car near the vicinity of Commatteo's house in the days leading up to the murder. At around 5.45am on the morning of 30 March 2000, Commatteo was set to leave home, when Ryan forced him back inside his home. He then blasted Commatteo in the back of his head with a sawn-off shotgun (R v Bristow, Hayter, Ryan, 2006).

Immediately after the killing, police put Bristow under covert surveillance, which caught her making a joke about the murder to a delivery man only 15 days after the hit. Subsequently, Bristow was arrested and denied any relationship with Hayter. However, phone records proved she was lying and, soon after, Ryan confessed to his girlfriend of the killing, who then told the police. In court, Mark Dennis, prosecuting, stated that Hayter sent his girlfriend's teenage son to collect cakes from a shop in Whyteleafe, Surrey, but instead he was given a substantial amount of money inside a brown bag. The court also heard that Bristow approached customers and acquaintances and offered cash payments ranging from £2,000 to £50,000 for Commatteo's assassination. On 3 July 2001, all three defendants were found guilty. Before sentencing, The Recorder of London, Judge Michael Hyam, described the crime as a 'pitiless killing' (R v Bristow, Hayter, Ryan, 2006). Bristow was the first to be unanimously found guilty of murder. Hayter and Ryan were each convicted by a Jury Majority of 10-2.

Returning to the quote at the beginning of this discussion, the sole aim in this line of work is 'shoot to kill'. The murders of Gulistan Subasi and Mario Commatteo illustrate the stark realities of contract killings; a phenomenon that is low paid, and one that is *not* exclusive to secret services, organised crime firms and other media-portrayed examples. Thus, criminologically, contract hits are like various forms of interpersonal homicide, as there is often a small degree of separation between offender and victim. Indeed, it is the offender–victim nexus that often contributes to the high clear-up rate of homicide in England and Wales.

Some criminologists suggest that hitmen operate as arbiters of an alternative form of criminal justice – murder (Rahman and Lynes, 2017). The best hitmen are able to rationalise their victims as 'objects' for profitable gain. These are the movers and shakers, who are able to successfully repress their actions, and in doing so become 'criminal undertakers' (Hall, 2012) – individuals who value business more than human life.

Mohammed Rahman, Nottingham Trent University

FACT 38

Sex workers in the UK are 12 times more likely to be murdered than the general population

Kate Williams

Sex work, or prostitution – the selling of sexual services in exchange for money or goods (Overs, 2002: 2) – is one of the most dangerous occupations in the world. Sex workers in London are 12 times more likely to be murdered than someone from the general population. In the UK, it is estimated that at least 152 sex workers have been murdered since 1990 (English Collective of Prostitutes, 2016: 6). This is likely to be a conservative estimate; there are significant numbers of sex workers simply reported as 'missing', many of whom may also have been murdered (Kinnell, 2008: 164). Of course, this statistic also does not consider the untimely deaths of other sex workers (for example, from drug overdoses), which overall points towards a much higher mortality rate than that of a non-sex worker. Furthermore, sex workers face a higher risk of violence towards them, including beatings, rape, sexual assault and robbery; indeed, one survey found that 49% were worried about their safety (House of Commons, 2016).

There have been infamous cases of serial killers who have murdered sex workers – from Jack the Ripper, to the Yorkshire Ripper and, more recently, the Suffolk Strangler. The news media have played a significant role in making the killers much more famous than their victims, whose names are often quickly forgotten. These examples of infamous perpetrators encapsulate the reasons why sex workers are so often the favourite target group of the serial killer, but it is also because:

- the victim quickly and willingly gets into the car;
- her lifestyle means that she might not be missed for a long time, if ever;
- her disappearance, if noticed, may not be taken so seriously by the police or indeed the wider population – arguably because her prostitute identity contains not only an inevitability of risk and violence, but also has less importance than that of a 'normal' woman.

How prostitution is regulated has a profound effect on the practicalities – and therefore the safety – of sex workers' lives. Yet, it is an incredibly controversial and emotive issue, deeply bound up with within our morals, cultures and religions. For some, sex work is indeed 'work' – a profession like any other – and for others, from a radical feminist perspective, selling sex is fundamentally a violent act (Kinnell, 2008). In turn, these viewpoints impact directly upon the regulation of prostitution.

Campaigners have long been calling for a change in the law, in order to attempt to reduce the amount of violence against sex workers. While prostitution in the UK – contrary to popular belief – is actually legal, sex workers remain vulnerable due to the criminalisation of soliciting, kerb crawling and brothel keeping. Campaigners argue that the arrest and prosecution of sex workers and their clients, together with the illegality of working in pairs or groups, which could create a safer working environment, means that violent attacks can not only happen more easily but are also significantly less likely to be reported to be the police. While the House of Commons Home Affairs Committee (2016) has recommended that soliciting as an offence be removed, and sex workers be permitted to share premises, the current government response (2016) is that a better understanding of the nature of prostitution in England and Wales through further in-depth research is needed first.

In recent years, considerable favour has been shown towards the sex buyer law, which criminalises the client, as opposed to the sex worker. Often referred to as the 'Nordic Model', it was introduced in Sweden in 1999 and has now also been adopted in several other countries, including France, Northern Ireland, Iceland and Norway. This method could be deemed laudable in its view of prostitution as violence against women and contrary to gender equality (indeed, in 2014 the European Parliament in support of this model recognised sex work as contrary to human dignity). It controversially claims significant success in reducing the number of sex workers in Sweden (English Collective of Prostitutes, 2016). However, it has also been criticised for not actually protecting the workers, and in fact increasing their risks of violence, due to having less time to assess clients due to their fear of arrest, or working in more isolated conditions, for example (House of Commons, 2016).

In contrast, the decriminalisation of prostitution spearheaded by New Zealand's Prostitution Reform Act of 2003 provides a realistic alternative, and has received the support of the World Health Organization and Amnesty International. Crucially, decriminalisation should not be confused with the legalisation of sex work that can be seen in Germany or the Netherlands, for example. While legalisation creates laws to regulate how sex work operates, decriminalisation removes those laws, and instead seeks to prioritise the human rights and safety of prostitutes (New Zealand Government, 2008). Much research into legalisation has found evidence of an increase in trafficking and in the numbers of sex workers, whereas this has not been the case after decriminalisation in New Zealand. Furthermore, the English Collective of Prostitutes (2016: 5) found that, 'over 90% of sex workers said decriminalisation gave them additional employment, legal, health and safety rights … 0% reported that since decriminalisation they were more likely to report incidents of violence to the police'. As Amnesty International (Murphy, 2015) argues, 'what we want is a refocussing of laws to tackle acts of exploitation, abuse and trafficking – rather than catch-all offences that only criminalise and endanger sex workers'.

Yet until the laws on prostitution in the UK are changed, the National Ugly Mugs scheme (an initiative that alerts women to potentially violent clients) provides a helpful service to sex workers, by alerting outreach teams and the police of reports of violent clients to be avoided. However, as the English Collective of Prostitutes (2016) reminds us, the underlying reason for much prostitution is poverty: of the approximately 72,800 prostitutes in the UK, around 90% are female, and of those, a 'clear majority' are (often single) mothers. The other side of the coin, of course, is the need to change the often-unconscious acceptance of violence against women, especially those women who are viewed as somehow deserving of that treatment.

Dr Kate Williams, University of Wolverhampton

FACT 39
Not all violence is criminal
Victoria Silverwood

The concept of violence is intrinsically tied up with notions of criminality being one of the most serious of interpersonal crimes – and it is taken with the utmost seriousness by the criminal justice system. However, not all violent acts are crimes; a great deal of crime undertaken by individuals is legitimate, due to those who inflict the violent behaviour.

It is important to view violence outside the criminocentric gaze, away from the limitations of the label of crime (Jackman, 2002; Ferrell, 2004), to understand violence as human conduct. Violence does not have one clear definition. It can be used to explain a multitude of offences, from threatening language, to homicide and, to some, the social harms inherent in the capitalist economic system (Hall and Winlow, 2015). While one's first thought about violence might be the image of an assault during a street fight, it is a culturally mediated term, and one which needs careful engagement.

Historically, one of the key points of the civilisation of society and the emergence of our current legal and criminal justice system is that the state maintains the monopoly on the use of violence (Elias, 1978). That is to say, the state authorises certain key individuals and groups with the power to use legitimate forms of violence, for example the military and the police. These special liberties shape our understanding of the difference between civilians and those with power.

However, legitimate violence is not limited to that used by the police, private security firms (Winlow et al, 2001) and the military. Physical sport has long held a special dispensation for allowing violent acts, which remain acceptable despite being illegal in other forms (Collins, 2009; Ray, 2011). Acts of extreme interpersonal violence such as that seen in boxing and wrestling matches remain legal, despite the harm caused to those engaged in the sport. This constitutes a 'moral holiday' (Collins, 2009), allowing for behaviour that would not normally be acceptable to be tolerated, enjoyed and even celebrated.

The apparent exemption of certain sports from criminal laws stems from the idea that a person can consent to violence. The legal principle for this comes from the latin term 'Volenti non fit injura', which translates to 'to a willing person, injury is not done'. This allows for an interruption to the usual laws governing behaviour in certain circumstances that those involved in the sport can expect. This term is not without its problems, however, as it relies on the notion of implied consent., There remains a constant disagreement in the law about what one consents to and what is normal, both within the rules, and within the culture but outside of the rules.

The sport of ice hockey allows this to be seen most clearly. In ice hockey, it is not legal to engage in a bare-knuckle fist fight; indeed, that action is criminalised in all areas and in all other sports. However, many ice hockey leagues in many countries see culturally endorsed bare-knuckle fights in many games each week. This is due to the fact that violence in this context is tacitly permitted (Colburn, 1986) by the relatively low penalty of five minutes served in the penalty box for each player. This is a concurrent penalty that does not leave the team short-handed and simultaneously allows the fighters time to recover from the exertion of the fight., As such, some argue that it does not constitute a punishment at all.

In England and Wales, the legal precedent was set in R v Brown (1993), which allowed for acts that occur in the commission of the sport, but outside of the commonly agreed rules of the game, to be challenged in court (Pendlebury, 2006). However, in 2004, the case of R v Barnes allowed, for the first time, for sports participants to consent to physical violence that occurs outside of the agreed rules of the sport. This has led to a somewhat blurred, but deliberately broader, understanding of what is considered cultural consent (Groombridge, 2016). This point is often at the crux of legal cases regarding violent assault in sports. See, for example, the case concerning recreational ice hockey player Macauley Stones, where the judge ruling in the case slammed the 'legal vacuum' that exists (Black, 2017). In that case, Bradford Bulls player Stones pleaded guilty to grievous bodily harm after the attack on rival player Reece Glossop, of the Nottingham Lions, during a match on 19 September 2015. During a mass brawl on the ice, Stones repeatedly punched Glossop in the face while he was on his knees, causing serious facial injuries. However, a judge said it was not fair to 'put all of the sins of ice hockey' onto Stones, and suspended his nine-month sentence for two years. His conviction is in itself rare, as there are numerous instances where hockey players inflict injuries on one another that, if they were to occur and be charged in any other context might result in custodial sentences. The custodial sentence for grevious bodily harm as an offence against the person ranges between five years and life, depending on the category charged and the perpetrator's degree of intent and malice and the injuries caused.

While there are certainly those who do not agree that this type of behaviour is acceptable, it remains that violent and conflict sports are experiencing halcyon days in recent times. The popularity of wrestling, mixed martial art and combative sports demonstrates the desire of some to partake in, and to spectate on, this most violent behaviour in a legitimate, legalised context. It has been argued by Hall (2007) that increasingly within the civilised society, individuals have sought opportunities to engage in violent acts otherwise unavailable due to legislation. This is referred to as a pseudo pacification process. This can be particularly the case for men, who can see this form of sportised violence as a 'masculinity-validating experience' (Dunning, 1999: 229). Cultural criminologists (see, for example, Ferrell, 1999, who builds on the work of Katz, 1988) have built on this idea that engaging in violent behaviour can be exciting, and acknowledge the concepts of illicit thrills and the seduction of physical behaviour, which is often ignored in traditional criminological theory.

We can see, then, that violence is not limited to a criminocentric definition of physical contact, and it includes acts which are legal, or at least legitimised, in several contexts. The discussion of violence expands from criminal acts of violence, such as homicide and assault, through to violence that is legitimised due to its notion of being conducted by the state (for example, policing and military violence), as well as legitimised violence in sport. Violence can include a vast raft of human behaviour – from physical contact, to coercion or simply through words and language. Yet the important lesson for criminologists is that not all violence is criminal.

Victoria Silverwood, Cardiff University

FACT 40
You cannot consent to be harmed in sex, but you can in the boxing ring

John Bahadur Lamb

The *Fifty Shades of Grey* characters Christian Grey and Anastasia Steele brought to prominence in the public consciousness a form of sexuality that is often maligned and misunderstood: bondage and discipline, domination and submission, sadism and masochism (BDSM). BDSM covers a range of differing sexual practices, which all share the common element of consensual pain being inflicted, in order to create mutual sexual and psychological gratification. This leads these acts to fall into a legal grey area, as the participants in such 'kinky' sex are consenting to bodily harm. Consent is the cornerstone of these activities, with many BDSM practitioners using coded safe words to stop activities if true distress is caused – and even drawing up contracts, which specify what acts are consented to and what acts are not. In the views of one scholar on the subject, BDSM is 'Safe, Sane and Consensual' (Barker, 2013).

However, in the United Kingdom, an individual can only consent to bodily harm in very specific circumstances, where the harm has been legally judged to be in the public interest. As such, surgery, piercings, tattoos and sport are legally permissible, because they are deemed as being in the public interest. Despite these exceptions and the Sexual Offences Act 2003 defining a person as consenting if they 'agree by choice and have the freedom and the capacity to make that choice', BDSM activities are all considered chargeable criminal offences under the Offences Against the Person Act 1861 and the Sexual Offences Act 2003. Given that we, in the UK, can legally and publicly beat a consenting opponent senseless inside a boxing ring, it seems odd that the use of handcuffs and a spanking paddle in the bedroom could result in criminal charges.

So why does the government via the law and judiciary feel it has the right to legislate against the sexual practices of consenting adults? The answers are bound up with a now infamous case known as the 'Spanner Trial'. A police raid in 1987 found a videotape, which showed a group of men engaged in heavy sadomasochist activities, including genital abrading, bodily beatings and lacerations. Indeed, so serious did the physical harm appear that Greater Manchester Police actively pursued the case under the belief that at least one of the participants who took part in its making must have died from the injuries sustained. On investigation, the police discovered that not a single one of the 16 men involved in the video had any long-term injuries from their participation and no one had died. Despite this revelation and the genuine belief of all involved that they were consenting adults engaged in legal behaviour, at trial the court handed down sentences ranging from fines to four-and-a-half years in prison. These draconian sentences were given on the basis that consent offers no defence, as BDSM activities can never be in the public interest, as they pose both a public health and a 'moral threat to society' (R vs Wilson, 1996).

As such, it would appear that if you engage in BDSM activities, which result in marks or injuries that are more than transitory or trifling, in the UK you are committing both a sexual crime and a crime against the person and should face criminal sanction. It is this line of thought which sees this case continue to set the benchmark for what is considered legally acceptable sexual behaviour between adults, due to the failure of appeals against it at the House of Lords (1992) and the European Court of Human Rights (1997). Yet, the idea that BDSM is a public health and a moral threat to society does not stand up to scrutiny, and there also seems to be an element of discrimination against LGBT BDSM practitioners. For example, in another case, R v Wilson (1996), the courts decided that the branding of a partner using a heated knife was not grounds for criminal prosecution. The only difference between this case and the Spanner Trial case is that the defendants in Wilson were a married husband and wife instead of a group of single, gay men.

It would appear, then, that the law around BDSM is being applied inconsistently. This is backed up by conviction rates, with gay BDSM practitioners more likely to be arrested, tried and convicted of both crimes against the person and sexual crimes than their heterosexual counterparts. This leads us back to the core of the matter: that BDSM is evaluated by the courts largely on 'moral' grounds. It is only through a moral lens that we can understand how a heterosexual married couple engaged in fairly heavy BDSM involving branding can avoid prosecution. This is arguably because marriage between a man and woman is still considered the 'correct' form of a relationship, and thus the marital bed is deemed a private sphere and the consensual activities which take place between husband and wife are no concern of the state. Whereas, the engagement in BDSM by single, homosexual individuals represents a moral threat to this accepted and idealised form of relationship.

This muddled and confused legal and moral framework has become even more difficult to navigate, thanks to the introduction of yet another piece of legislation, which criminalises those individuals who enjoy watching BDSM pornography but have never engaged in such acts. The Criminal Justice and Immigration Act 2008 outlawed the possession, distribution or consumption of pornography that depicts any acts which threaten a person's life, will result in serious injury to breasts, anus or genitals and other acts. While this sounds perfectly reasonable, convictions have been handed down by the courts for pornography containing the wearing of gas masks; vaginal fisting and the use of unusual objects for penetration. A further piece of legislation, the Criminal Justice and Courts Act 2015, outlaws pornography that depicts simulated rape, rough sex or sex with individuals who are bound. Effectively, these laws ban all BDSM pornography, as it is up to the court to interpret what acts would cause harm or threaten life.

Thus, we can conclude by paraphrasing Lord Templeman during the 'Spanner Trial' appeal, that the legality of BDSM has little to do with harm and more to do with the belief that pleasure derived from pain is an evil thing, so long as sexual gratification and not body modification or sport is the driver behind it (Groombridge, 2016).

John Bahadur Lamb, Birmingham City University

Part Nine
Victims

FACT 41

64% of homicide victims are male

Anthony Ellis

The overwhelming involvement of men as perpetrators in incidents of violence, particularly violence that is lethal or causes serious physical harm, is a pattern that is so consistent across time and place that it prompted criminologist Steve Hall (2002) to remark that this statement is the closest that criminology has come to establishing a 'fact' about crime. He is not alone in making this assertion. Tim Edwards reached similar conclusions, when he claimed that from 'pub brawls to building bombs, and from forced prison buggery to battered wives, the problem seems to be men' (Edwards, 2006: 44). Reflecting on the number of men prosecuted in Britain during 2015/16 for offences against women, Owen Jones (2016), writing in the *Guardian* newspaper, described male violence as a 'pandemic'.

These assertions are supported by a considerable amount of evidence. The Crime Survey for England and Wales found that during 2014/15, in over three-quarters of incidents of violent crimes reported during that period, the victim identified the perpetrator as a male. In cases of homicide brought to the attention of the police during the year ending March 2015, 90% involved male perpetrators (ONS, 2016). Importantly though, men in contemporary England and Wales are often the victims of serious violence too: 2014/15a total of 64% of homicide victims in 2014/15 were male (ONS, 2016).

When examining the issue of violence from a global perspective, these aforementioned national trends are amplified. The United Nations Office on Drugs and Crime (UNODC) reports that 'some 95 per cent of homicide perpetrators at the global level are male; males also account for almost 8 out of every 10 homicide victims' (UNODC, 2013: 11).

When it comes to explaining this 'fact', it would appear logical, given the pervasive nature of male involvement in violent crimes, that there is a biological basis to this behaviour – that there must be something in the biological make-up of males that makes them more aggressive. Understandably, then, some criminologists have subjected the male body to deep scrutiny, convinced that the answer to this relationship lies in hormones, genetics or evolutionary psychology. Criminologist Adrian Raine (2013), a leading exponent of biological explanations for violent crimes, suggests that human evolution may provide a foundation to these patterns. This line of argument suggests that, ultimately, humans are driven by the selfish need to ensure that their genes are reproduced in the next generation. For males, this rests on their ability to acquire status and resources and to provide protection, which are attractive qualities to a potential female partner. Violence can provide these things, while eliminating other males, who may offer competition.

It is plausible that genetic evolution may play some role in the quite stark patterns of violent behaviour involving men that we see replicated in societies across the globe. Yet, while physically violent behaviour is in the vast majority of cases perpetrated by male bodies, there is further variability and complexity to this pattern. First, we must acknowledge the obverse to this 'fact', which is simply this: not all men commit physical violence against others. Immediately, this renders problematic the claim that male biology is responsible, while adding a layer of considerable complexity that continues to bedevil our attempts to fully explain what remains a very evident association. In addition, violence perpetrated by males is variable by space and place, as is the amount of violence committed by males at points in history, which suggests that other, non-biological factors play a significant role in this relationship. So, if the fact that some men commit nearly all violent crimes cannot be accounted for by biology alone, where else might we look for underlying explanations for this 'fact'?

For American psychiatrist James Gilligan (2000), a useful place to start is by to considering psychological and social factors. For Gilligan, male violence 'has far more to do with the cultural construction of manhood than it does with ... biology' (Gilligan, 2000: 223). Gilligan is concerned here with the various expectations and pressures that societies and their members can place upon males and how this affects them psychologically. The complexity of contemporary human societies, of social life and of patterns of violent crime indicates that our attention must be directed towards social, political and economic issues as well, and how these might affect human behaviour.

Feminist and pro-feminist scholars were among the first to give the consequences of the contemporary cultural construction of manhood and masculinity, that Gilligan alerts us to, the attention that it quite obviously requires. While feminist scholarship is diverse, what generally unites feminist arguments that address male violence is that this behaviour is at root a manifestation of the evident inequalities that exist between men and between men and women. Given that contemporarily and throughout history men have tended to occupy more privileged and advantageous positions within society than women, these patterns can be interpreted as symptomatic of these relations of power and dominance and the use of violence to maintain these, particularly if they are perceived to be coming under threat (Connell, 2005). Some dominant cultural constructions of manhood and masculinity are often regarded, then, as unhealthy and damaging for both women and men, because of their unrealistic expectations and the pressures they exert upon individual men to be strong, unemotional, competitive, domineering and successful.

Economic inequality is also an important factor in better understanding this relationship, with strong evidence that violent crime rates are higher in more unequal societies and largely concentrated among specific groups of socially and economically disadvantaged males (Hall, 2002; Wilkinson and Pickett, 2010; Ellis, 2016). To some extent this complicates the suggestion that physical violence serves as a strategy to consolidate male power in our society, as those men who hold positions of genuine power and influence, and who are wealthy, rarely achieve this through using physical violence themselves. Wealthy and powerful British men, such as business leaders and political figures, will no doubt have had to behave 'aggressively' and in a competitive fashion at times to reach the positions they occupy, but they largely do not amass their wealth and influence through using physical violence themselves.

It is, rather, some of those men with the least power in society who so often use violence most persistently and perceive a reputation for using violence to be a valuable personal asset. Men who use serious physical violence themselves are, rather, subjected to strong state repression and control, and often find themselves moving between prison sentences and living a precarious and insecure existence in impoverished communities. In-depth research conducted by criminologists that has enabled them to get up close and personal with such men reveals how strongly various social and economic disadvantages loom large within their lives – as do issues of substance misuse, family breakdown, physical and emotional abuse, and victimisation. Many of these men have complicated relationships with violence that are partially rooted in traumatic and humiliating personal experiences, social and economic disadvantage, as well as particular beliefs and assumptions about what it means to be masculine (Ellis, 2016; Ellis et al, 2017).

In summary, then, while the evident and strong relationship that exists between the use of violence and the male population constitutes as close to a 'fact' about crime as criminologists have arguably come, a more careful examination of patterns of male violence indicates that there is still much about this (albeit very strong) pattern that remains unclear and requires further exploration and explanation.

Dr Anthony Ellis, University of Salford

FACT 42

It is claimed that around one in 20 children in Britain are sexually abused

Saabirah Osman

It is claimed that one in 20 children in the UK have been sexually abused at some point in their childhood (Radford et al, 2011; The Lantern Project, 2012; NSPCC, 2017). However, when considering the nature of sexual abuse and the methods used for collecting crime data, this claim may be an underestimation of the prevalence rates of sexual abuse against children in the UK.

Defining sexual abuse is complex due to the historic, cultural, political and social perceptions. Thus, definitions vary and adapt as our understanding develops. For now, a useful definition is provided by the NSPCC (2013). It states that child sexual abuse is: 'Forcing or enticing a child or young person to take part in sexual activities, not necessarily involving a high level of violence, whether or not the child is aware of what is happening' (NSPCC, 2013: 2).

One development to the definition of sexual exploitation and abuse is the notion of grooming (Jay, 2014). By adding this concept to the definition, we understand that in the lead-up to, and the commissioning of, a sexual assault, a perpetrator may not need to engage in levels of force or physical violence; indeed, at times the child may be unaware of the grooming process (HM Government, 2015). There is also a misconception of who a 'typical' perpetrator might be: in their guide to inter-agency working, the government highlights that women and children are also perpetrators of sexual abuse, as well as adult males (HM Government, 2015).

Sexual abuse is often classified into two types of abuse: contact abuse and non-contact abuse. Contact abuse involves physical touching, whereas non-contact abuse involves exploitation, grooming, performing sexual acts on the internet, and so on (NSPCC, 2017).

Statistics show that in 2010/11, England and Wales recorded a total of 17,727 sexual crimes against children under 16 years (Lantern Project, 2012). By 2015/16, the figure had risen to 54,898, the largest increase in five years (Bentley et al, 2017). Further findings suggest that one in three children who have experienced sexual abuse by an adult, do not tell anyone (Radford et al, 2011). While the data presented demonstrates that child sex abuse is a significant issue, these figures must be understood with some caution. The nature of child sexual abuse means that:

- Such data, in the main, represents one assault per victim at a given moment in time, whereas sexual abuse is often experienced repeatedly over time;
- some children are so young that they are unable to report such abuse;
- many victims do not report abuse for fear of not being taken seriously or being ignored (Allnock and Miller, 2013; Lampard and Marsden, 2015) or not being believed, being afraid of the stigma and shaming their families (Coffey, 2006).

An example of this comes from the Independent Inquiry into Child Sexual Exploitation in Rotherham (Jay, 2014). Jay reports that, the scale of child exploitation in Rotherham remains unclear, as during her investigation in 2014, many victims were reluctant to come forward due to feelings of shame or fear. Indeed, according to Finkelhor (1984), this is not uncommon, as a child usually keeps the abuse a secret and if there is some disclosure, they only disclose part of the abuse. This is due in part to the sophistication of the grooming process, in which the perpetrator convinces the victim, over time, that the abuse must not be shared with anyone.

This process, proposed by Summit (1983), proffers children may keep their abuse a secret – through 'Accommodation Syndrome'. The 'Accommodation Syndrome' model explains that children may suppress details of the abuse, because of at least one of five key components:

- secrecy
- helplessness
- entrapment
- conflict as to whether to disclose
- retraction

Such techniques appear to be most effective with children who are already vulnerable. For example, with the component of secrecy, the adult (the abuser) misuses their authority to establish the act as a secret by using bribery, threat or intimidation (for example by saying, 'this is our little secret' or 'I will tell them what you did'); the abuser is able to increase the victim's compliance (Summit, 1983).

While the proposition presented here is that official data on child sexual abuse is an underestimation of the actual prevalence rates, this is not to say that child sexual abuse is increasing. There has been a recent surge in allegations and convictions of historical cases of child sexual abuse and institutional failures to respond to allegations, such as Jimmy Savile (McLaughlin, 2015), Rochdale grooming (Salter and Dagistanli, 2015), Rotherham child abuse (Jay, 2014), Newcastle sex grooming, and so on. However, it is important to recognise that this current phenomenon is more likely to be an indication of the challenges that children and victims face when attempting to report abuse.

One of the encouraging outcomes of this recent surge is that such exposure to abuse enables society to develop greater understanding of the nature of child sexual abuse. Openness and societal conversation might be the most vital aspect of creating a more accurate picture of the real levels of sexual abuse victimisation of young people in contemporary Britain.

Saabirah Osman, Arden University

FACT 43

More than three-quarters of people sleeping rough have been victims of crime or anti-social behaviour in the past year

Daniel McCulloch

The claim in the title of this discussion is that more than three-quarters of people sleeping rough have been victims of crime or anti-social behaviour in the past year. To be precise, the claim actually refers to research by the homelessness charity Crisis, which stated that of the 458 people sleeping rough they surveyed, 77% reported being victims of crime or anti-social behaviour in the previous year (Sanders and Albanese, 2016) – so this statistic might not apply equally to all people sleeping rough. However, there is plenty of evidence to suggest that people sleeping rough experience crime at a significantly higher rate than housed populations (Ballintyne, 1999; Newburn and Rock, 2005; Huey, 2012).

While many people think of homelessness and rough sleeping as the same, there are differences between the two. Homelessness broadly refers to a person having no accommodation that they can occupy or access, or where it is unreasonable for them to occupy that accommodation. Rough sleeping refers to sleeping or 'bedding down' in the open air, or in places not designed for habitation (for example bus stops, stairwells, car parks, cars or derelict buildings). So, while someone who is sleeping rough is experiencing homelessness, not everyone who experiences homelessness sleeps rough.

Our knowledge about people who are sleeping rough being victims of crime is extremely limited. This is because the victimisation of people sleeping rough is often not captured in official statistics such as crime surveys, as these tend to survey private households. This is the case for the Crime Survey for England and Wales, the Scottish Crime and Justice Survey and the Northern Ireland Crime Survey. Furthermore, people experiencing rough sleeping are unlikely to report their victimisation to the police or any other services, due to: fear of reprisal; a belief that the police will fail to investigate allegations properly; or because of fear for their own arrest (Ballintyne, 1999; Newburn and Rock, 2005; Scurfield et al, 2005; Sanders and Albanese, 2016). Thus, in understanding victimisation of people sleeping rough, there is a 'dark figure' of crime not captured in official data. This is also the case with crime more widely.

Therefore, our knowledge of victimisation of people sleeping rough often relies on small studies. These studies cannot provide an overall picture of the victimisation of all people sleeping rough, but they can highlight the various ways in which people sleeping rough are victimised. Evidence from these studies points to three main types of crime and anti-social behaviour that people sleeping rough encounter:

- physical and sexual violence – such as being kicked or beaten, being threatened with violence, or being sexually assaulted;
- verbal abuse – such as being shouted at or harassed;
- theft and damage to belongings – such as having possessions vandalised or stolen.

Although on occasion such acts are committed by other people who sleep rough, evidence suggests that most of these acts are perpetrated by members of the general public (Sanders and Albanese, 2016). Thus, for people sleeping rough, it is difficult to predict who might be a threat, when, or for what reason – reinforcing a sense of constant vulnerability to crime. Moreover, while sleeping rough, individuals may be experiencing other complications in their lives, such as difficulties with finding stable employment, strained relationships with family and friends, and physical and mental health difficulties. Such stressful situations can make dealing with experiences of victimisation even more difficult than they might otherwise be.

It is also important to recognise that while crime and anti-social behaviour are experienced widely by people sleeping rough, there are differences in every individual's experiences. Factors such as a person's gender can impact on their experiences of victimisation, with women being more likely to experience sexual violence and men more likely to experience physical violence (Scurfield et al, 2005: 3). Additionally, an individual's experiences of trauma prior to homelessness can affect the impact that victimisation has on them; and victimisation while sleeping rough can reinforce previous trauma. Thus, although people's stories may appear to share similar patterns or trajectories, the unique details of each person's life play an important role in shaping their experiences of victimisation while homeless.

Despite these differences, many people sleeping rough shared by a sense of vulnerability to different forms of victimisation.: 'Dangerousness exists as a constant issue in their lives' (Newburn and Rock, 2005: 13). This vulnerability is reinforced by the need to continuously contend with conditions of discomfort, stigma and embarrassment, which can all contribute to a sense of being vulnerable because of their homelessness. Consequently, people sleeping rough may use extreme techniques to reduce their vulnerability, such as sleeping in industrial bins (which can result in death) or carrying a weapon (which can lead to trouble with the police). Although people sleeping rough are not directly victimised in this way, this is an indirect form of victimisation – with individuals being victimised in other ways, because of their attempts to deal with their vulnerability to crime and anti-social behaviour.

While the victimisation of people sleeping rough is unlikely to appear in official statistics, they are often prosecuted for low-level crimes and nuisances, such as petty theft, begging and drinking in the street. Thus, they are likely to appear in official data as perpetrators of crime. However, many of the acts committed by people sleeping rough are insignificant when compared with the 'invisible' victimisation they may encounter on a daily basis (Huey, 2012). This encourages us to view people sleeping rough as threatening security and 'good order' – supported by 'objective' data, which often records their crimes while overlooking their victimisation. However, it is not just official data that supports such a view. Government policies and media representations also often depict people sleeping rough as being involved in committing crime and anti-social behaviour.

Furthermore, these official accounts reinforce a mythical divide between a supposedly 'deserving' poor, who are good but have fallen on hard times, and an 'undeserving' poor, whose homelessness has allegedly been caused by their own choices. In this scenario, we are encouraged to feel sorry for the 'deserving' victim, who has been unable to control their situation, while feeling less sympathy for the 'undeserving' individual, whose victimisation is supposedly linked to their own 'feckless' behaviour.

Therefore, many people sleeping rough are likely to be victims of crime and anti-social behaviour, and certainly more likely than housed populations to be victimised. However, the experience of sleeping rough is also fundamentally marked by constant feelings of vulnerability. Such feelings are inescapable while sleeping rough, and in trying to manage their own vulnerability, people sleeping rough often encounter other difficulties. Yet, we more often think of people sleeping rough as a threat to security and 'good order', not least because official data and policies focus on these individuals as perpetrators of crime and anti-social behaviour, while overlooking their victimisation. Further still, for those deemed 'undeserving' of our sympathy, even when they are the victimised, this is presented as a consequence of their 'poor choices'. Thus, people sleeping rough are faced with being viewed as blameworthy for their own victimisation, while simultaneously being portrayed as a threat to others.

Dr Daniel McCulloch, The Open University

FACT 44

In 2015/16, the NHS treated over 9,000 cases of female genital mutilation

Dionne Taylor

Female genital mutilation (FGM) is the deliberate cutting, injuring or adapting of the female genitals for non-medical purposes. Startlingly, at least one case of FGM is discovered and/or treated by medical professionals every hour in the UK. Otherwise referred to as 'female circumcision' or 'cutting' (among many other names), FGM is usually carried out on young women and girls from birth up until the age of 15 (Al Hussani, 2003 as cited in Paliwal et al, 2012). Generally taking place before the onset of puberty, FGM often occurs against a girl's willing and informed consent. This is in direct violation of the rights of the child (WHO, 2008). In many cases of FGM, young women and girls are forcibly restrained.

There are three named types of FGM:

- a full removal of all of the clitoris (clitoridectomy);
- partial removal/all of the clitoris, including the inner labia, and/or the removal of the labia (excision);
- a narrowing of the vaginal opening, made through the creation of a seal, formed by cutting and moving the labia (infibulation).

Additional measures consist of pricking, piercing, cutting, scraping and/or burning the female genital area. FGM is not a medical procedure. It is customarily performed by traditional circumcisers or cutters, who often do not have professional medical training or qualifications (Paliwal et al, 2012). Not only can FGM cause extreme pain and distress to those who undergo this traumatic experience, but it can also lead to serious and long-term health implications for the young women and girls. According to the NHS Choices website (2016) 'there are no health benefits ... it can cause long term problems with sex, childbirth and mental health'.

FGM in the UK is an illegal, non-medical procedure, which can take place without pain relief, and tools such as razors and blades are often used (Al Hussani, 2003; El Shawarby and Rymer, 2008 as cited in Paliwal et al, 2012). As a consequence, there is a wide and complex array of physical, social and psychological effects that this has on victims who are subjected to such a procedure.

FGM is a criminal offence under the Female Genital Mutilation Act 2003. The illegality includes:

- taking a child abroad for the procedure;
- helping a girl perform FGM on herself in or outside of the UK;
- helping anyone perform FGM in the UK or from outside the UK even on a UK or resident;
- failing to protect from FGM a girl whom an individual is responsible for.

In 2015/16, it was reported that the NHS attended to over 9,000 cases of FGM (NHS Digital, 2017b). The cases presented were women and girls of varying ages. According to Paliwal et al (2012), 'it is a custom rooted in the cultures of various ethnic groups in at least 28 countries mainly in sub-Saharan Africa' (WHO, 2008).

Further estimates suggest that there are over 90 million females on the African continent – aged nine years old and above – who have experienced some form of FGM (Yoder and Khan, 2008 as cited in Paliwal et al, 2012). FGM is performed in over 25 countries in Africa, parts of the Middle East (for example, Yemen), South East Asia (for example, Malaysia), Europe, North/South America and other countries where migrants from FGM-affected communities live. FGM is also practised in the UK on girls from FGM-affected communities – that is, girls who are born in the UK or have a residential status here, but whose families originate from FGM-practising communities.

FGM was made a criminal act in the UK in 1985, although this was later strengthened under the Female Genital Mutilation Act 2003. However, to date, there has only ever been one FGM prosecution, in which the defendant, who was a qualified and practising NHS doctor, was acquitted in 2015. In this case, it was classed as a reinfibulation, as the woman on whom the procedure was performed had given birth and had previously had FGM. Therefore, it was considered a reinstitution of FGM. It is important to note that the woman at the centre of this case did not support this prosecution and refused to give a statement to the police. Court documentation at the time of the proceedings described the woman as being of Somalian heritage, who had the initial FGM procedure around the age of 7. It is reported that the woman expressed her unease and anxieties for both herself and her family at being labelled as the women involved in the first FGM prosecution in the UK.

FGM remains a controversial phenomenon, laden with cultural, religious and ethnic associations. According to Dorkenoo et al (2007), FGM can be practised by specific ethnic groups, although the rationale for the practice varies between each group. In relation to FGM being a cultural practice, Dorkenoo et al (2007) explain that it 'is embedded in coming of age rituals which are considered necessary for girls to become adults and responsible members of society' (Dorkenoo et al, (2007: 12). There are disagreements on whether FGM is a religious requirement. Dorkenoo et al (2007), for example, explain that it is not mentioned in the Quran or the Bible, yet it is considered a societal norm in the FGM-practising countries. As a practice, FGM can be considered more of a cultural than a religious requirement (Dorkenoo et al, 2007).

The penalty for anyone found to fail to prevent and protect girls from an FGM procedure in England and Wales can be imprisonment for up to seven years. In 2014, the NSPCC launched a national campaign entitled 'Ending FGM'. Alongside a high-profile poster campaign, there was a video that included both survivors and victims of FGM. The women spoke about their lack of knowledge regarding the procedure. One women explained: "I had no idea it was going to happen". Another woman describes her legs being forcibly spread apart and her underwear removed, and explained that a "cloth was placed in my mouth so I couldn't scream". Joy Clarke, a health professional who also appears on the video, states: "FGM has lifelong effects on women". Some of the effects include social, psychological, physical and emotional implications. For example, one woman in the video described "still feeling the blade going through my skin" and having "flashbacks" of the procedure, which took place 25 years ago.

As awareness of the legislation surrounding FGM is raised, it is anticipated that this will have a positive impact, by increasing consciousness of the importance of protecting those who are at risk of experiencing it. So too it is anticipated that it will bring about more prosecutions. According to Kam Thandi, who appears on the NSPCC video:, "FGM is a form of child abuse and it needs to stop".

This point has been further advocated in Townley and Bewley (2017), which suggests that the UK could introduce a Child Genital Mutilation Act, which would effectively make any non-medical genital modifications illegal. This would continue to bring about more awareness of FGM, and more successful prosecutions.

Dr Dionne Taylor, Birmingham City University

FACT 45

Two women are killed each week by a current or former partner in England and Wales

Morag Kennedy

The shocking statistic that two women a week are killed by a partner or former partner is taken from figures from the Office for National Statistics (2016a) and its Compendium on Homicide, based on 10 years of data. It is widely cited by domestic violence charities. The ONS also claims that in the year ending March 2016, some 1.2 million women reported experiences of domestic abuse in England and Wales.

However, while many people perceive domestic abuse solely as physical attacks, the term is much broader and incorporates a range of physical, psychological, emotional, sexual and financial forms of abuse (Home Office, 2013; Strickland and Allen, 2017). Women's Aid (2015) defines domestic abuse as 'an incident or pattern of incidents of controlling, coercive, threatening, degrading and violent behaviour'. This can be perpetrated by intimate partners (for example, boyfriends and girlfriends) or may be carried out by family members, irrespective of gender, age or sexuality. This chapter also focuses on physical and emotional abuse that form a backdrop to how two women are killed each week by a current or former partner.

Physical abuse, on the one hand, consists of controlled or impulsive physical attacks on the victim (Sanderson, 2008). This may involve, but is not limited to, pinching, hair pulling, scalding, burning or stabbing (Kenney, 2012). Some of these assaults may be considered minor in comparison to others. The physical attacks may be directed to a particular part of the body that is not normally visible to others, as a way of concealing cuts and bruises (Sanderson, 2008). However, other abusers may use different forms of physical abuse, which leave no indication of physical injury. This may include administering ice-cold baths or asphyxiation (Sanderson, 2008). Furthermore, some abusers may use physical neglect as a way of controlling the victim, by neglecting the victim's basic needs such as food and shelter. Typically, a woman is assaulted 35 times before her first call to the police (Jaffe and Burris, 1982). This shows that a 'victim's level of fear derives as much from her perception of what *could* happen based on past experiences as from the immediate threat by the perpetrator' (Stark, 2007: 94).

Psychological and/or emotional abuse, on the other hand, involves verbal and non-verbal abuse that is critical in establishing coercive control. These two terms – 'psychological abuse' and 'emotional abuse' – tend to be used interchangeably: 'psychological abuse' influences the mind, including mental health; whereas 'emotional abuse' influences the victim's emotions and sense of wellbeing (Women's Aid, 2015). Psychological/emotional abuse encompasses: rejection; humiliation; degradation; threats and/or terrorisation; exploitation and/or use of 'male privilege' to obtain services; and isolation (Walker, 1984; Tolman, 1989; Follingstad and DeHart, 2000). Walker (1979) states that emotional maltreatment, specified verbal battering, social humiliation and economic deprivation are considered key factors of psychological abuse. Psychological or, indeed, emotional abuse has also been compared to torture by Amnesty International (NiCarthy, 1986). Likewise, similar techniques used within coercive control have also been used in concentration camps, on hostages, on prisoners and on prisoners of war (Stark, 2007). Furthermore, Marshall (1994) has inferred that physical abuse may be used as an attempt to dominate a victim, when other psychological forms of domination have failed.

Emotional domestic abuse and, indeed, coercive control appears to be at the forefront of reform campaigns in the UK, given the new legislation that came into effect in 2015:

> Controlling or coercive behaviour is defined under section 76 of the Serious Crime Act 2015 as causing someone to fear that violence will be used against them on at least two occasions, or generating serious alarm or distress that has a substantial effect on their usual day-to-day activities (Bowcott, 2015: 1).

This clearly resonates with Levy's (2008) discussion of domestic abuse, in that the main component of domestic abuse is to exert and maintain control by micro-regulating the victim's everyday life. Often this involves exerting control over behaviours that are associated with stereotypical female roles, such as cooking, cleaning and sexual performance (Levy, 2008).

In terms of the incidence of domestic abuse, the Crime Survey for England and Wales reports that approximately 7% of women and 4% of men experienced some form of domestic abuse in 2015/16, which equates to around 1.2 million female and 651,000 male victims (Strickland and Allen, 2017). Furthermore, it was estimated that 26% of women and 13% of men have experienced any form domestic abuse since the age of 16; this amounts to 4.3 million female victims of domestic abuse and 2.2 million male victims between the ages of 16 and 59 (Strickland and Allen, 2017). In fact, domestic abuse has a higher rate of repeat victimisation than any other crime (Home Office, 2003). However, it is important to note that the Crime Survey for England and Wales does not account for unreported crime, nor does it explain why the crime has been committed.

One example of physical and psychological/emotional abuse is the case of Fakhara Karim. Her abuse was carried out over a number of years. Karim was victimised by her husband, Mustafa Bashir, for wearing Western clothing. She was also verbally abused by her husband when she went out with her female friends. Bashir referred to his wife as a 'slag' on these occasions. During her abuse, Karim was also forced to drink bleach and take tablets to kill herself (Sabur, 2017). Moreover, Karim was beaten with a cricket bat, while her husband was reported as saying: "if I hit you with this bat with my full power then you would be dead" (Sabur, 2017). In this case, Mustafa Bashir was spared a prison sentence, after falsely claiming that it would be detrimental to his career as a Leicestershire county cricketer. Instead, Bashir was ordered to attend a behavioural workshop, pay £1,000 costs and banned from contacting Fakhara Karim (Sabur, 2017). The judge also suggested that he was unconvinced of Karim's vulnerability, as she was an intelligent woman with a wealth of education. As if being beaten repeatedly with a cricket bat was not enough to endure, Karim was also not believed by the system put in place to protect her from such abuse.

This is one of the problems facing victims of domestic abuse today. Without a physical injury, many victims are unable to provide proof of abuse; and even with physical injuries, some victims are dismissed. This lowers their status further in a society that treats them with as much contempt as do their abusers.

As such, it is important that we, as a society, recognise the varying types of domestic abuse. Evidently, it is not as clear-cut as some may think. Loring (1994) goes so far as to ascribe a cyclical pattern to domestic abuse. However, it must be noted that this notion may not fit with psychological abuse, which is more linear in nature. As there is still this idea that abuse equates to physical harm, many victims may be unaware that they are experiencing abuse, thereby leaving them unable to protect themselves from this type of harm (Loring, 1994; Marshall, 1994). These more subtle forms of abuse are more likely to enable a perpetrator to control the victim in comparison to physical assaults, whereby 'covert abuse juxtaposed with loving behavior may increase the victim's uncertainty about herself and her perceptions' (Follingstad and DeHart, 2000: 895).

Morag Kennedy, Birmingham City University

FACT 46

Almost 50% of stalkers present themselves at their victim's workplace

Craig Jackson

Stalking is a specific form of criminal offence and a recognised social problem. According to the British Crime Survey (2010), approximately 20% of females and 10% of males receive unwanted stalking behaviours over their lifetime, and this figure continues to increase annually.

Stalking is any unwanted and unwarranted continued attention and contact from the perpetrator to a victim, which results in distress or fear. This can often occur when the perpetrator is obsessed or fixated with a victim. Perpetrators may not always be aware of the distress they cause and, in some cases, because of their delusional beliefs or lack of empathy and understanding of other people's perspectives, they believe they are helping a victim or making them feel important. Mostly, however, stalkers are acutely aware of the damage caused and the impact they make.

Stalking can have a huge impact on victims, especially if the stalking occurs in both domestic and workplace spheres. It can lead to feelings of fear and anxiety, and develop into physical health problems, depression and even post-traumatic stress disorder (PTSD). This can also have an impact on a victim's domestic life and family members. Research generally shows that 90% of stalkers are male and about 80% of victims are female (Logan, 2010), and that females are significantly most likely to be stalked by a current or former partner. Most victims are females who are harassed by men wishing to establish or re-establish a relationship, for example ex-husbands/partners, who will not accept the ending of a relationship and who may also seek revenge for 'rejection' often constitute the largest single group of stalkers (approximately 40%).

Initially, many victims do not report early-stage stalking incidents to managers, friends or even the police, for fear they may be judged as being somehow responsible and because they do not want to appear to cause a 'fuss'. However, as the cumulative impact of stalking progresses, behavioural and psychological changes in a victim may make their situation more noticeable, for example poor time-keeping, irritability, nervousness, reduced social functioning, increased number of sickness absence spells, poor concentration or performance at work, and increased GP/healthcare appointments. Recognising such behavioural difficulties may assist others in their duty to help a victim as soon as possible. This is especially important given that almost half of all stalkers at some point present themselves at the victim's place of work.

The link between workplaces and stalking is only now being understood. Many stalking relationships develop from workplace interactions. Some stalkers are colleagues of the victim, or even customers/clients who have come into some form of contact. A smaller number of stalkers choose victims in particular workplaces or professions, because the victim's job may give them easy access with little challenge, such as telephonists or receptionists, or other customer-facing roles. As around half of all stalkers target their victims in workplaces, they are a risk not only for the victims but also for other colleagues who may interact with the stalker, as well as other members of the public who may legitimately be at the premises. Many stalking victims leave employment as a consequence of stalker activities, not just because of health-related problems brought about because of the distress, but also as a final way of trying to avoid being stalked altogether.

Current understanding of stalkers suggests that not all workplace stalkers have the same psychopathology or motivational factors, and there is some evidence to suggest that there can be a classification – or typology – of stalking as such (Mohandie et al, 2006).

- *Rejected stalkers*: these arise from the breakdown of a relationship. They are usually a former (sexual) partner of a victim and this appears to be the biggest single typology.
- *Resentful stalkers*: these arise from a perceived mistreatment or humiliation, with the stalker's control and power over a victim itself seen as 'settling the score'. This type of stalker often presents themselves as the victim.
- *Intimacy-seeking stalkers*: these arise from a lack of close relationships and intimacy – the victims become 'fantasy' figures, and these desires and fantasies can be the result of some severe mental health problems or psychosis (for example erotomanic delusions).
- *Incompetent suitor stalkers*: these arise from loneliness, but the stalker does not seek intimate relationships, merely short-term sexual relationships. There can be occasional overlap with mild learning disability or cognitive impairments held by the stalker.
- *Predatory stalkers*: these arise in the context of deviant sexual practices and interest in the victim. The stalking can be gratifying and instrumental at the same time, and the stalking activity itself may become the way of gaining pleasure (for example, voyeurism), and can also help the stalker to garner information about a victim, which they see as valuable and rewarding.

There are dozens of different actions that stalkers take to unnerve a victim, ranging from personal visits to workplaces through to virtual contact via social media, and through a proxy (for example, by ordering products to be delivered to the victim). These can include:

- blackmail (including so-called 'revenge porn')

- computer hacking/account hacking
- criminal damage (home/work/vehicle)
- excessive contact (letter writing/emails/text messages), often over short periods of time
- false complaints to employers
- false legal claims
- following or giving the impression a victim has been followed
- physical assault
- retrieving personal information/details (physically or online)
- rumour-spreading and defamation
- sending unsolicited gifts
- sexual assault
- signing a victim up for services they do not want
- social network abuse
- telephone calls (silent calls or pleading/angry/threatening conversations)
- threats
- time-wasting
- watching/monitoring
- visiting the workplace

Being stalked may impact upon a victim's ability to work in a variety of ways, as well as their wider social functioning (Jackson, 2015). Initially, stalking behaviours can often severely directly interfere with a victim's ability to leave their home and get to work regularly (extreme methods include frightening a victim to stay home through threatening emails, messages or phone calls, through to vandalising vehicles or making the commute difficult). Second, stalkers can make the workplace appear to be unsafe for a victim, by targeting their messages/interactions to the workplace rather than solely a victim's home. By (the threat of) appearing at the workplace unannounced, stalkers may give the workplace an additional air of unpredictability and threat. Third, the psychological impacts upon a stalking victim reduce their overall 'workability', making them more anxious, forgetful, unable to concentrate, and possibly disorganised – which may clearly impact upon their employability.

As stalking behaviours often evolve and change as a result of technology developments, there is limited research on the impact that stalking makes to an individual's ability to function, but it is evident that victims suffer from many emotional symptoms, including depression, anxiety and PTSD. They may also suffer from self-loathing, blame, shame, guilt, embarrassment, low self-esteem, and feel severe isolation from others. Such symptoms would no doubt be worsened if employment were also lost as a consequence of being stalked. Understanding the potential consequences of stalking means more can be done to ably assist victims, and to potentially minimise any short-term and long-term harm inflicted on them.

Because the relationship between workplaces and stalking can often be crucial (Jackson, 2015), there are measures that should focus on victims' places of occupation. Stalking policies should be in place: to minimise risks to all those who could potentially be involved; to keep the victim working while being stalked if they so wish; and to support the victim if they need time off work (due to the effects outlined earlier, as well as for legal matters). Such policies should also make it clear that employees who engage in stalking behaviours themselves will be investigated, and disciplinary action will be taken against any such employee, if criminal procedures are initiated.

Policies should take the a priori position that a victim is not to be blamed for being stalked; acknowledge factors that can make a victim more or less vulnerable; and implement actions that can help to make a victim increase their resilience. Management should take a discreet approach and try to ascertain details with an open-ended, non-judgemental and non-threatening approach. Assuring a victim that they will be believed and taken seriously is important, as it is the fear of this not happening that prevents many victims from reporting the stalking.

Professor Craig Jackson, Birmingham City University

Part Ten
Crime and technology

FACT 47

Around one in six of all estimated crimes in England and Wales in the year to September 2016 were fraud committed online, according to the Office for National Statistics

Keith Spiller

The fact quoted above in the title here (Office for National Statistics, 2017b) is an example of the media headlines often associated with cybercrime. Other examples include: 'UK fraud hits record £1.1bn as cybercrime soars' (Guardian, 2017); and '1 in 10 people in England and Wales have been the victim of cybercrime' (Telegraph, 2016). What these headlines and many others indicate is the growing impact of cybercrime in the UK.

For criminologists, this is a burgeoning area of interest, particularly in gaining greater insight into how we can begin to understand the growing levels of this crime – how it is done, the impact of cybercrime and, importantly, how it is being combated by law enforcement. Presently, cybercrime is the fastest-growing area of crime in the UK and is predicted to have the highest level of offences in the coming decade, so it is of significant interest to criminologists (Yar, 2013).

Indeed, you may have been a victim of cybercrime yourself. Perhaps you have received an email from the 'representative' of some well-positioned person who has fallen on hard times and needs your bank account to lodge some money. Or you may have been contacted via social media by a friend who has lost money on holiday and needs funds to get home. Or you have received a call from a computer 'support' centre, informing you that your computer has developed a problem and the kind person on the line will take over your computer in order to help you.

These strategies are relatively well known, and with the growing awareness of scams or the methods used, cybercriminals tend to apply short-lived strategies. Cybercrime is a fast-moving field that requires innovation and ingenuity to stay ahead of the police and to play on the naivety of those who cybercriminals wish to steal from or defraud. Deception is a key element to cybercrime; when this advantage is lost, committing the crime becomes more difficult (MacEwan, 2013).

For criminals, this is a relatively convenient crime to initiate compared to other criminal activities.– It can be conducted from their home, an office or anywhere with an internet connection. Rarely does the culprit put themselves in physical danger – as a burglar or car thief might. Equally, the rewards from cybercrime can be extremely high. FElsewhere in media it has been claimed that the average loss per UK resident is £210 per year to cybercrime (Office for National Statistics, 2017b).

However, we must also acknowledge that cybercrimes do not always involve theft or the pursuit of financial gain. Cybercrime is a criminal act that includes the use of digital formats to commit crime. The range of acts can include:

- cyberterror
- cyberwar
- identity theft
- e-fraud
- piracy
- malicious software
- harassment
- bullying
- stalking
- child pornography

Policing cybercrime is difficult, and is often complicated because there is a geographical spread across jurisdictions. Crime can originate from countries outside of where the crime is committed – hence apprehending individuals requires cross-border cooperation and can prove problematic. Equally, complicating the policing of cybercrimes is the fact that there are low levels of reporting on cybercrime. Moreover, offences can multiply quickly – just think of how an offensive tweet may be shared and spread. It is these complications that formulate how cybercrime is impacting on society – and indeed how police forces are attempting to combat this area of criminal activity.

Some recent examples demonstrate how rapidly the crime can impact on UK systems – and indeed in more global settings.

- In May 2017, the NHS computer system was paralysed by the malware 'WannaCry'. This was a ransomware that was unintentionally downloaded, possibly from an email, onto the NHS system. It then infected the system and prevented users from accessing their data. In this case, a ransom was demanded to unlock the system. Over 16 health trusts in the UK were infected, causing major disruptions to the NHS computer system.
- In the US, the hacking of email accounts related to the Democratic nominee for the Presidential election in 2016 continues to cause fallout. An aide to Hillary Clinton had their email account hacked, and sensitive information was obtained. This information – and the fact that a supposedly secure email account was hacked and used for political gain in the election – has raised many calls for explanation and security tightening (*New York Times*, 2017).
- Elsewhere, Kim DotCom (operating from Queenstown, New Zealand) is accused of infringing piracy laws; his company Megaupload enables users to share digital media, for example film and music. This counters copyright laws where it is illegal to share downloads. He is currently facing extradition to the US to face these charges.

These are just some of the more high-profile examples of recent cybercrime, but we must also be aware of vulnerabilities to cybercrime. This is something that at times we have to entrust to the systems we use, because few of us are cybersecurity experts. However, even in situations where you would expect high levels of security, it can be compromised. One interesting example illustrates the point. Perhaps not everyone has to worry about the security of their superyacht – however, a number of yachts have had their systems hacked and taken over, and the information found has been used for blackmail and extortion. In most cases, it appears that the yacht's wi-fi was the weak point that allowed attackers to gain access.

Policing these systems is difficult. UK police forces have been proactive in highlighting the levels of cybercrime in the UK and in providing strategies and methods for how we can protect ourselves online. New laws have been introduced to enable prosecutions. One such law is the Abusive Behaviour and Sexual Harm Act 2016, which has been used in incidences of revenge porn (a criminal act where explicit images are loaded onto the internet without the consent of the person in the image). One could also add the Computer Misuse Act 1990, which now includes a number of amendments as to how cybercrime is being confronted.

Nevertheless, as the Office for National Statistics states (Office for National Statistics, 2017b), there is clear evidence that cybercrime is growing exponentially in the UK, and our laws and means of policing this area of crime are under pressure. We can assume that cybercrime will become a more central component of the discipline of criminology.

Dr Keith Spiller, Birmingham City University

FACT 48

The number of alleged crimes involving social media such as Facebook and Twitter have increased nearly eightfold between 2008 and 2012

Elizabeth Yardley

In recent years, we have seen multiple reports of an increase in reported crimes involving social media. In December 2012, *BBC News* reported that 'The number of alleged crimes involving Facebook and Twitter has increased nearly eight-fold in four years' and that 4,908 offences had been reported to police in the previous year (BBC, 2012). Then in June 2015, it was claimed that more than 16,000 alleged crimes involving Facebook or Twitter were reported to the police (Evans, 2015). So less than three years on from the 2012 figures, the number of reports appeared to have more than tripled.

These figures encompassed a range of offending behaviours, including abuse, harassment and threats. This raises a range of criminological questions. We have to deal with these statistics themselves and cast a critical eye on their emergence. We must also look more broadly at the role of social media in our everyday lives and the implications for criminality and victimisation.

The statistics quoted here were obtained via a Freedom of Information request by the Press Association. As such, the topic of social media in crime is one that has been constructed by the news media; they have identified this as an issue and have sought out information about it. The very fact that the question is being asked implies that there is a story in this, and there is an expectation about what the response is likely to be. Is it likely that this would have been reported on, if the figures had shown that the number of alleged crimes involving social media was on the decline? Perhaps not. The language used in the reporting is also revealing: the title of the BBC article is 'Huge rise in social media "crimes"', while Evans's article is entitled 'Police facing rising tide of social media crimes'. This is presented as a new threat, a worrying trend, one that is out of control and has the makings of a contemporary social problem. As such, this is a potentially newsworthy topic (Jewkes, 2015).

We also need to be clear about *how* an incident comes to be recorded by police. No matter what type of crime we are talking about, there is a clear path to how it becomes (or does not become) a crime statistic. First, when a suspected crime takes place, someone needs to notice that it has happened. That person, or another individual, then needs to report it to the police. The police then need to agree that this is indeed a crime, and record it as such, before commencing an investigation. At several points along this path, the crime – or alleged crime – could fall off the radar. If we are talking about threats made on Twitter, for instance, the person at whom the threat is aimed might not see it. If they do see it, or are alerted to it by someone else, they might just brush it off and see it as not worth reporting to the police. If they do report it to the police, it might not reach the necessary threshold to be considered a crime. We need to bear in mind that many incidents on social media that would be considered a breach of the law will never be recognised in crime statistics, and will remain part of the dark figure of crime. This term is utilised to describe a plethora of criminal offences that go undetected by the police and/or are not reported by the public. When we see crime statistics reported in the news media, we should always treat them as a representation rather than a reality.

Dealing with reports of increases or decreases in particular crimes should also be approached with caution. Why might there be an increase in the number of reported incidents involving social media? Maybe this type of crime really is on the increase? Or could it be that people are becoming more aware of the fact that many online communications are subject to the same laws as face-to-face interactions? Perhaps they are better informed about how to report these incidents to the police?

The role of third-sector organisations and victim advocates has been an important part of educating the public about online victimisation in recent years. For example, TellMAMA (Measuring Anti-Muslim Attacks) is an organisation that engages in raising awareness about anti-Muslim abuse, records such incidents and supports victims via referrals to partner agencies. These organisations have been critical in breaking down the distinctions between 'online' and 'offline' abuse. As the public become more aware that what happens online has real-life, embodied consequences – and that abuse is abuse, wherever it is experienced – the likelihood of incidents being reported to the authorities increases.

We need to remember that social media is a relatively new aspect of our lives. Facebook was founded in 2004, Twitter in 2006. While such technologies became part of the fabric of everyday life very rapidly, the way in which we give them meaning and develop practices around them takes longer. We are still developing norms, values and attitudes that shape our use of social media. This includes our own informal rules that help us to distinguish between what is *socially acceptable* and what is not. These frameworks will not be the same for everyone. There is a plurality of digital cultures – what might be seen as acceptable in one group might be viewed as highly offensive and rude in another. Questions of what is *legally acceptable* exist alongside concerns about social acceptability. However, the law is always playing catch-up in this regard. It was only in 2016 that the Crown Prosecution Service in England and Wales developed guidance setting out the range of offences for which social media users could face prosecution.

The way in which these figures have been reported serves to create the impression that crimes committed using social media are distinct and different, almost as if they are in a category of their own. This is problematic and muddies the waters. People have always harassed, threatened and been abusive towards others. Social media has not created this behaviour, but it does represent a new tool that offenders can use to perpetrate this type of harm. The crimes being discussed are what Wall (2007) would categorise as computer-assisted crimes – crimes that existed prior to the existence of the internet, but which take on a new lease of life in the social media age. As social media has become part and parcel of everyday life, it has become part and parcel of everyday crime as well.

The nature and the extent of the potential harm can, however, be amplified as these crimes develop an online element. Take the example of revenge porn. In the past, if an individual wanted to shame, embarrass and humiliate their former partner, they could photocopy an intimate picture and post it through all the letterboxes on the street and/or send it to members of their family or employer. Today, that same image might be uploaded to a website or social media platform. More people will see the image and it is difficult to control its subsequent distribution. To use a contemporary adage: – the internet never forgets.

However, discussing social media as a digital tool inflicting old harms in new ways is not where criminological analysis should end. We need to understand better how social media is meaningful to different people for different reasons. We need to explore why particular individuals use it in harmful and criminal ways. We need to look at people's *experiences* of social media, what they are doing with it and why, and how this forms part of their social identities in a networked society (Yardley, 2017). We must consider digital/online (criminal) activities as a process rather than an outcome (Ferrell et al, 2015).

Social media has not changed the world in any fundamental sense, but it has changed our sense of *being* in the world. As such, it introduces new questions about the *doing* of harm.

Elizabeth Yardley, Birmingham City University

FACT 49
There is estimated to be one CCTV camera for every 14 people in the UK
Pravanjot Kapil Singh Uppal

When discussing closed-circuit television (CCTV), it is hard to ignore the totalitarian state created in George Orwell's *Nineteen Eighty-Four*. The very notion that one will conform unquestionably to the powers above through a dictatorship regime or, in Orwell's case, fear of continual surveillance, is synonymous with both modern life and the literary world created by the author.

These concepts were first put forth by Orwell in 1948 and have evolved as society and technology continue to develop. With new laws, such as the Investigatory Powers Act 2016 (nicknamed the 'Snoopers' Charter'), allowing even more access to UK citizens' use of technology without a warrant, it could be argued that we are not far away from the gaze of the Orwellian 'Big Brother'.

In exploring the topic of surveillance in the 21st century, it is important to consider the work of utilitarian Jeremy Bentham (whom staunchly believed that the criminal justice system should serve to benefit the majority at the detriment of the few) along with French philosopher Michel Foucault.

Jeremy Bentham was an 18th-century philosopher, known for his development of the idea of the 'panopticon' (even though it was his brother Samuel Bentham who originally conceived of it). The 'panopticon' was a conceptual prison, designed with a central watch tower and surrounded on multiple levels by the inmates cells. This notion was to rehabilitate the criminal not through physical punishment, but through mending the body and soul. The panopticon was to allow a single watchman to observe all inmates of an institution, without the inmates being able to identify whether they are being watched. According to Bentham, the concept could be applied to any large institution, such as schools and workhouses, in the hope that the peril of continual surveillance would deter disobedience, along with the visibility of inmates/labourers being maximised through their spatial separation (Hubbard et al, 2002).

Building on this concept is Foucault (1977), whose philosophy was based on relationships: first between the systems of social control (government) and those within a disciplinary setting (prisoners); and second the convergence of power and knowledge attained via observing others. Foucault felt that greater knowledge and understanding were created by the emergence of a disciplinary power, resulting in suitable behaviour through a panoptic discipline (as opposed to total surveillance).

From both of these criminological standpoints, we can see how the original concept of being surveyed has evolved to become a part of contemporary society.

In the 1960s, a visit from the royal family of Thailand to London meant that the Metropolitan Police introduced two temporary cameras into Trafalgar Square to help monitor crowds. As this was viewed as a success, CCTV was primarily owned by the government and used solely as a surveillance tool for the police force to monitor the transgressions of the public.

There were some attempts at this time to expand the use of cameras. For example, CCTV was added to train lines across London and Liverpool, in the hope of bolstering the security of the areas against primarily acquisitive crime. However, due to the expensive nature of the newly built technology, it took time to expand out into the public domain.

Through the 1970s, advancements in technology allowed for recording of video footage for later inspection, meaning that video surveillance would now be used on football matches (during the hooliganism era of the 1970s and 1980s) and to monitor traffic. But the poorly produced black-and-white image was often useless. However, the spread of CCTV continued with the refinement of technology. By March 1999, the then Home Secretary, Jack Straw, pledged £170 million for up to 20,000 more CCTV systems (Duffy, 1999). This shifted CCTV from town centres to residential areas, schools, parks and shopping centres (to name but a few), displaying how those initial thoughts of Bentham and Foucault were now emerging into reality. As a society, we were now being watched and monitored in an ever greater number of public areas, in order to deter unwanted behaviour.

In 2013, the British Security Industry Association estimated (in a report entitled *The picture is not clear* (British Security Industry Association, 2013)) that there were around 6 million CCTV cameras in the UK, with 750,000 in sensitive areas such as schools and hospitals. With this estimate, it is said that there is a camera for every 14 citizens in the UK. Compare this with the two installed in the 1960s, along with the fact that CCTV was not commonplace in residential areas until the late 1990s, and a clear picture emerges of how fast the government has moved to implement this new form of technology.

In the modern day surveillance has extended much further than the traditional remit of CCTV. Transgressing the fixed point of the public arena it is now also within the phone you use every day, the tablet you stream Netflix on, and the PC you use to navigate the internet.

With this next phase there are new questions regarding the balance between liberty and security, and whether you truly need one in order to have the other. It also arguably creates new opportunities for victimisation, such as webcam sex video scams. With the proliferation of cameras and the rise of cyberspace, we must ask ourselves how much we value our right to privacy, lest we find ourselves in a world not too dissimilar to that of Orwell's *Nineteen Eighty-Four*.

However, while CCTV is often at the forefront of surveillance and the detection of crime, and debate continues to play out about the value and efficacy of camera monitoring, the mass proliferation of digital media/recording devices into social life is transforming profoundly how crime is planned, organised, perpetrated, experienced, represented, witnessed, detected and controlled. Moreover, the extensive daily use of these technologies, by institutions and individuals alike, produces immense quantities of data that mediate social events, actions and experiences in significant, if sometimes subtle, ways. For example, the rise of consumer-oriented payment systems is an increasingly common feature of the retail environment. While these systems have mechanisms for monitoring, up to a third of customers regularly steal when using self-service checkouts in supermarkets (Taylor, 2016).

Debates concerning monitoring have to transcend the normal and traditional right to privacy, reflecting the way that monitoring has now gone way beyond surveillance of the body only. The rise of big data – and its links to means of communication, knowledge and entertainment, as well as resources for analytical and criminal manipulation and community mobilisation are intrinsic to this. While you might be watched on CCTV in the UK more than in any other country on earth, you are also being surveyed much more than you might think by a wide array of stakeholders apart from the state.

Pravanjot Kapil Singh Uppal, Swansea University

FACT 50

There are currently some 11,000 offenders subject to 'tagging' on any day in England and Wales, and the UK is one of Europe's keenest adopters of electronic monitoring of offenders

Adam Lynes

In the 1990s, England and Wales led the way as the only European jurisdiction to have experimented with electronic monitoring of offenders – or 'tagging' – but it is now becoming a more common practice, as technology advances. Today in England on any given day there will be some 11,000 offenders subject to tagging. This rapid growth, it shows the way that new technologies can quickly become part of the penal landscape.

'Tagging' traces its roots back to US Judge Jack Love in New Mexico, who devised an early scheme having been inspired by a *Spiderman* comic strip (Mair and Nee, 1990: 4). The first person recorded as being tagged was in the US in April 1983. The US National Institute of Justice was satisfied with the equipment and reported that home confinement was an acceptable proposition.

The growth of tagging has been rapid. In the 1980s and 1990s, the UK government first experimented with tagging, but it did not become an established part of the criminal justice system until the late 1990s. Earlier that decade, three experimental schemes, ostensibly targeted at remand prisoners, were followed by a government White Paper, *Crime, Justice and Protecting the Public* (Home Office, 1990), that promoted the idea of 'tagging' offenders, suggesting that this work be undertaken by a private agency rather than the probation service (Nellis, 2004).

Previously in Great Britain, the writer Tom Stacey took a proposal to the Home Office in 1981 for the electronic tagging of offenders to track their movements. Stacey proposed a system of home curfew, using cellular radio telephone technology. Stacey himself had been briefly imprisoned abroad in his former role as a foreign correspondent, and for several years had served as a 'prison visitor' in England. He was alarmed by the growing prison population. In a letter to *The Times* on 6 October 1982, he outlined the proposal and immediately founded the Offender's Tag Association, composed of electronic scientists, penologists and prominent citizens. The term 'tagging' thus entered the lexicon in the English criminal justice context. From the outset, there was a clear economic consideration in adopting electronic monitoring, as it quickly became apparent that 90 days in custody could cost five times more than the equivalent level of electronic monitoring.

The Criminal Justice Act 1991 paved the way for a second trial. It introduced the curfew order, with electronic monitoring as a community sentence. However, it was not until legislation in the Criminal Justice and Public Order Act 1994 that the curfew with electronic monitoring properly came into existence. The Home Detention Curfew scheme, which allowed prisoners to be released from custody early, became widely used in 1999 following the Crime and Disorder Act 1998. Certain prisoners serving sentences of between three months and four years can be considered for the scheme, which can grant early release between 10 days and 135 days earlier than the halfway point of the sentence.

Electronic monitoring of a curfew has become an integral part of the criminal justice system in the UK. It is used at various stages of criminal cases to monitor compliance with a curfew, to remain at their home residence for a specified number of hours a day (or evening) or to be excluded from specified areas at specific times (such as football stadiums or retail environments) . Those subject to electronic monitoring may be given curfews as part of bail conditions, when they are sentenced under the Criminal Justice Act 2003 in England and Wales (with separate legislation applying in Scotland). Additionally, the growth in electronic monitoring was seen with curfew given under the Terrorism Prevention and Investigation Measures Act 2011 (previously known as a Control Order under the Prevention of Terrorism Act 2005).

Today, electronic monitoring is an accepted aspect of the criminal justice system. In particular, in recent years, as technology has advanced and the possibility of electronic monitoring via satellite tracking has become a reality, the government has shown a commitment to the use of electronic monitoring in criminal justice.

However, it is not free from controversy. Its controversial position is at least in part due to the involvement of the private sector in its delivery. In 2013, the Serious Fraud Office was called in by the then Justice Secretary Christopher Grayling to investigate the private security company G4S for overcharging tens of millions of pounds on electronic tagging contracts for offenders. This led to an investigation into the activities of Serco and G4S, who retrospectively agreed to repay £68.5 million (Serco) and £109 million (G4S) back to the taxpayer. The companies were subsequently stripped of their contract, with another private company – Capita – taking over responsibility.

In 2017, another criminal investigation saw the police make several arrests in relation to allegations that released criminals on tag had paid corrupt Capita employees to have loose tags fitted, allowing them to remove them and break the terms of their release without detection.

However, despite such controversies, the use of electronic monitoring continues to be widespread. In Scotland, those convicted of a serious sexual or violent crime, and who are judged to pose a danger to the community, are to be given a sentence known as an Order for Lifelong Restriction. This means that the offender will be detained indefinitely, until the Parole Board for Scotland determines that they no longer pose a risk to the safety of others. If the offender is released on parole, he or she is to be electronically tagged and kept under close supervision by the Scottish Parole Board for the remainder of the offender's life.

However, while electronic monitoring looks likely to form part of the criminal justice system for several years, debates about its efficacy continue. A symposium held before the House of Commons Public Accounts Committee for the Centre for Crime and Justice Studies in January 2018 published a damning assessment of the government's failed attempt to introduce a new generation of GPS-enabled tags. It, concludeding that the 'overly ambitious, overly complicated and ... poorly delivered' programme had been 'a catastrophic waste of public money' (Travis, 2018).

However, beyond the cost-efficacy of GPS tracking as a sanction, more generally rapid identification systems, computerisation and technological control mean that there may be much more important debates in the future. How criminal justice, surveillance and monitoring, punishment and exclusion may interconnect, and the morality and ethics of such policy, will be the big debate in criminal justice in Britain and beyond in the coming years.

Dr Adam Lynes, Birmingham City University

References

Aebi, M., Tiago, M. and Burkhardt, C. (2015) *Council of Europe Annual Penal Statistics, Survey 2014*. Strasbourg: Council of Europe.

AIM (2005) *Faking it: Why Counterfeiting Matters. Briefing Paper April 2005*. Brussels: Association des Industries de Marque (European Brands Association).

Alcohol and Crime Commission (2014) *The Alcohol and Crime Commission Report*. London: Alcohol and Crime Commission. https://www.thersa.org/globalassets/pdfs/blogs/alcohol___crime_commission_report_1.pdf

Alcohol Policy UK (2015) *53% of violent incidents alcohol-related: British Crime Survey 2013/14*. https://www.alcoholpolicy.net/2015/02/53-of-violent-incidents-alcohol-related-british-crime-survey-201314.html

Allen, W. (2007) The reporting and underreporting of rape. *Southern Economic Journal*, 73, 623-641.

Allnock, D. and Miller, P. (2013) *No one noticed, no one heard*. London: NSPCC.

Andresen, A. M. (2012) Homicide in Lithuania, in A. Liem and W. Pridemore (eds) *Handbook of European Homicide Research: Patterns, Explanations and Country Studies*. New York: Springer Science + Business Media, pp. 437-51.

Antjoule, N. (2016) *The Hate Crime Report 2016: Homophobic, Biphobia and Transphobia in the UK*. London: Galop.

Appleton, C. (2010) *Life after life imprisonment.* Oxford: Clarendon.

Appleton, C. and Grøver, B. (2007) The Pros and Cons of Life Without Parole. *British Journal of Criminology,* 47(4), 597–615.

Awan, I. and Zempi, I. (2016) The affinity between online and offline anti-Muslim hate crime: Dynamics and impacts. *Aggression and Violent Behavior,* 27, 1–8.

Baldwin, J. (1993) Police interview techniques – establishing truth or proof? *British Journal of Criminology,* 33, 325–351.

Baldwin, L. and Epstein, R. (2017) *Short but not sweet: A study of the impact of short custodial sentences on mothers & their children.* https://www.dora.dmu.ac.uk/bitstream/handle/2086/14301/Final3ResearchreportLBRE.doc?sequence=3&isAllowed=y

Bales, K. et al (2009) *Modern Slavery.* Oneworld Publications.

Ballintyne, S. (1999) *Unsafe Streets: Street Homelessness and Crime.* London: The Institute for Public Policy Research.

Banton, M. (1964) *The Policeman in the Community.* London: Tavistock Publications.

Barker, M. (2013) Consent is a grey area? A comparison of understandings of consent in fifty shades of grey and on the BDSM blogosphere. *Sexualities,* 16(3), 896–914.

Barry, M. and Leonardsen, D. (2012) Inequality and punitivism in late modern societies: Scandinavian exceptionalism revisited. *European Journal of Probation,* 4(2), 46–61.

Basel Convention on the Control of Transboundary Movements of Hazardous Wastes and their Disposal (1989). www.basel.int/TheConvention/Overview/TextoftheConvention/tabid/1275/Default.aspx

Baskin, D. and Sommers, I. (2012) The influence of forensic evidence on the case outcomes of assault and robbery incidents. *Criminal Justice Policy and Review,* 2(2), 186–210.

Batt, J. (2005) *Stolen Innocence: A Mother's Fight for Justice*. London: Ebury Press.

BBC (2012) Huge rise in social media 'crimes'. *BBC News*, 27 December. www.bbc.co.uk/news/uk-20851797

BBC (2013) *Independent Commission on Mental Health and Policing Report*. http://news.bbc.co.uk/1/shared/bsp/hi/pdfs/10_05_13_report.pdf

BBC (2016) Black Lives Matter protesters close London City Airport runway. *BBC News*, 6 September. www.bbc.co.uk/news/uk-england-london-37283869

BBC (2018) Community prisons for women plan shelved by ministers. *BBC News*, 27th June. https://www.bbc.co.uk/news/uk-44622498

Bean, P. (2014) *Drugs and Crime*. Uffculme: Willan Publishing.

Beck, A. and Hopkins, M. (2016) Scan and rob! Convenience shopping, crime opportunity and corporate social responsibility in a mobile world. *The Security Journal*. Advance online publication. doi:10.1057/sj.2016.6

Becker, R. F. and Dutelle, A. (2013) *Criminal Investigation* (4th edn). Burlington, MA: Jones and Bartlett.

Behlmer, G. (1982) *Child Abuse and Moral Reform in England 1870-1908*. Stanford, CA: Stanford University Press.

Bentley, H., O'Hagan, O., Brown, A., Vasco, N., Lynch, C., Peppiate, J., Webber, M., Ball, R., Miller, P., Byrne, A., Hafizi, M. and Letendrie, F. (2017) *How safe are our children? The most comprehensive overview of child protection in the UK 2017*. London: NSPCC.

Berlins, M. (2009) Knock it on the head, BBC. Judges don't use gavels. *The Guardian*, 23rd November. https://www.theguardian.com/uk/2009/nov/23/writ-large-courtroom-drama-bbc

Berman, G. and Feinblatt, J. (2005) *Good Courts: The case for problem solving justice*. New Orleans, LO: Quid Pro Quo.

Bertram, E., Blachman, M., Sharpe, K. and Andreas, P. (1996) *Drug War Politics: The Price of Denial*. London: University of California Press.

Best, D., Quigley, A. and Bailey, A. (2004) Police shooting as a method of self-harming: A review of the evidence for 'suicide by cop' in England and Wales between 1998 and 2001. *International Journal of the Sociology of Law*, 32(4), 349-361.

Beynon, C., McVeigh, C., McVeigh, J., Leavey, C. and Bellis, M. (2008) The Involvement of Drugs and Alcohol in Drug-Facilitated Sexual Assault. *Trauma, Violence, & Abuse*, 9(3), 178-188. doi:10.1177/1524838008320221

Binder, R. (1981) Why women don't report sexual assault. *The Journal of Clinical Psychiatry*, 42(11), 437-438.

Bittner, E. (1990) *Aspects of Police Work*. Boston, MA: Northeastern University Press.

Black, M. (2017) Judge accuses ice hockey of operating in a 'legal vacuum'. *The Telegraph & Argus*, 7 November. www.thetelegraphandargus.co.uk/sport/15646385. Judge_accuses_ice_hockey_of_operating_in__legal_ vacuum__as_player_claims_violent_attack_was__what_ happens__in_the_sport/

Bletchly, R. (2017) After London terror attack - should all police be armed? Arguments for and against. *Mirror*, 23 March. www.mirror.co.uk/news/uk-news/after-london-terror-attack-should-10087838

Borum, R. (2003) Understanding the terrorist mindset. *FBI Law Enforcement Bulletin*, 72(7), 7-10.

Bottoms, A. (2012) Developing Socio-Spatial criminology, in M. Maguire, R. Morgan and R. Reiner (eds) *The Oxford Handbook of Criminology* (5th edn). Oxford: Oxford University Press, 450-489.

Bowcott, O. (2015) Controlling or coercive domestic abuse to risk five-year prison term. *The Guardian*, 29 December. https://www.theguardian.com/society/2015/dec/29/domestic-abuse-law-controlling-coercive-behaviour

Bowen, P. and Whitehead, S. (2013) *Better courts: Cutting crime through court innovation*. London: New Economics Foundation and Centre for Justice Innovation.

Braithwaite, J. (2011) The Regulatory State, in R. E. Goodwin (ed.) *The Oxford Handbook of Political Science*. Oxford: Oxford University Press, 217-240.

Brett, A. (2004) 'Kindling theory' in arson: How dangerous are fire setters? *Australian and New Zealand Journal of Psychiatry*, 38, 419-425.

Brewer, P. R. and Ley, B. L. (2010) Media use and public perceptions of DNA evidence. *Science Communication*, 32 (1) 93-117.

Bridges, L. (2012) Four days in August: the UK riots. *Race & Class*, 54(1), 1-12.

British Retail Consortium (2016) *Cost of theft for retailers at highest level since records began*. https://brc.org.uk/news/2016/cost-of-theft-for-retailers-at-highest-level-since-records-began

British Security Industry Association (2013) *The picture is not clear. How Many CCTV surveillance cameras in the UK*. Report by the British Security Industry Association. https://www.bsia.co.uk/Portals/4/Publications/195-cctv-stats-preview-copy.pdf

Brown, G. (2016) The Danger of Not Following Police Orders When Approached. *The ABNF Journal*, 27(4), 81-82.

Brown, G. R. (2016a) The Blue Line on Thin Ice: Police Use of Force Modifications in the Era of Cameraphones and YouTube. *British Journal of Criminology*, 56, 293-312.

Brown, R. (2016b) Vehicle crime prevention and the co-evolutionary arms race: recent offender countermoves using immobiliser bypass technology. *The Security Journal*, 30(1), 60-73.

Brown, C. (1997) Hurd takes on prison reform trust. *Independent*, 15th January. https://www.independent.co.uk/news/hurd-takes-on-prison-reform-trust-1283200.html

Brown, R. and Thomas, N. (2003) Aging vehicles: Evidence of the effectiveness of new car security from the home office car theft index. *Security Journal*, 16(3), 45-53.

Brown, R., Walters, M. and Paterson, J. (2017) Examining the Impacts of Hate Crimes Against Lesbian, Gay, Bisexual and Transgender People. *International Network for Hate Studies*, 17 May. www.internationalhatestudies.com/psychological-perspectives-on-hate-crimes-against-lesbian-gay-bisexual-and-transgender-people/

Bullock, K. and Tilley, N. (2002) *Shootings, Gangs and Violent Incidents in Manchester: Developing a Crime Reduction Strategy – Crime Reduction Research Series Paper No. 13*. London: Home Office.

Buxton, J. (2013) *The Political Economy of Narcotics* (2nd edn). London: Zed Books.

Bye, K. E. (2012) Alcohol and Homicide in Europe, in A. Liem and W. Pridemore (eds) *Handbook of European Homicide Research: Patterns, Explanations and Country Studies*. New York: Springer Science + Business Media.

Caless, B. (2007) 'Numties in Yellow Jackets': The Nature of Hostility Towards the Police Community Support Officer in Neighbourhood Policing Teams. *Policing*, 1(2), 187-195.

Canton, R. (2017) *Why Punish? An Introduction to the Philosophy of Punishment*. London: Palgrave.

Carrabine, E., Cox, P., Lee, M., Plummer, K. and South, N. (2009) *Criminology: A sociological introduction* (2nd edn). New York: Routledge.

Carrabine, E., Iganski, P., Lee, M., Plummer, K. and South, N. (2014) *Criminology: A Sociological Introduction*. London: Routledge.

Casciani, D. (2017) Manchester attack: The bewildering complexity of a terror inquiry. *BBC News*, 25 May. www.bbc.co.uk/news/uk-england-manchester-40050549

Centre for Social Justice (2009) *Dying to Belong: An In-depth Review of Street Gangs in Britain*. London: The Centre for Social Justice.

Chakraborti, N., Garland, J. and Hardy, S. (2014) *The Leicester Hate Crime Project: Findings and conclusions*. Leicester: University of Leicester.

Chan, J. (1996) Changing police culture. *British Journal of Criminology*, 36(1), 109-134.

Christmann, K. and Wong, K. (2010) Hate Crime Victims and Hate Crime Reporting: Some Impertinent Questions, in N. Chakraborti (ed.) *Hate Crime: Concepts, Policy, Future Directions*. London: Routledge, 194-208.

Clark, F. (2015) Rise in online pharmacies sees counterfeit drugs go global. *The Lancet*, 3 October. www.thelancet.com/journals/lancet/article/PIIS0140-6736(15)00394-3/fulltext

Clarke, R. (1997) *Situational Crime Prevention: Successful Case Studies*. New York: Harrow and Heston.

Cockcroft, T. (2013) *Police Culture: Themes and Concepts*. Abingdon: Routledge.

Coffey, S. (2006) *No Glass Slipper: Surviving and Conquering Painful Life Experience*. New York: iUniverse.

Colburn, K. (1986) Deviance and legitimacy in ice hockey: A micro-structural theory of violence. *The Sociological Quarterly*, 27: 63–74.

College of Policing (2014) *Hate Crime Operational Guidance*. Coventry: College of Policing.

College of Policing (2015) *College of Policing Analysis: Estimating Demand on the Police Service.* www.college. police.uk/News/College-news/Documents/Demand%20 Report%2023_1_15_noBleed.pdf

College of Policing (2017) *Policing Education Qualifications Framework (PEQF).* https://www.college.police.uk/What-we-do/Learning/Policing-Education-Qualifications-Framework/Pages/Policing-Education-Qualifications-Framework.aspx

Collins, R. (2009) *Violence: A micro-sociological theory.* Princeton University Press.

Commentaries on the laws of England (1893) J.B. Lippincott Co: Philadelphia.

Connell, R. W. (2005) *Masculinities.* Cambridge: Polity.

Cook, T. and Tattersall, A. (2008) *Senior Investigating Officers Handbook.* Oxford: Oxford University Press.

Cope, N. (2004) 'Intelligence led policing or policing led intelligence?' Integrating volume crime analysis into policing. *British Journal of Criminology,* 44(2), 188-203.

Cops, D. and Pleysier, S. (2014) Usual suspects, ideal victims and vice versa: The relationship between youth offending and victimization and the mediating influence of risky lifestyles. *European Journal of Criminology,* 11(3), 361-378.

Corcoran, H. and Smith, K. (2016) Hate Crimes, England and Wales, 2015/16, *Home Office Statistical Bulletin 11/16.* London: Home Office.

Cornwall, J. (2016) The boys who killed James Bulger. *The Sydney Morning Herald,* 21 July. www.smh.com.au/ lifestyle/life-and-relationships/real-life/the-boys-who-killed-james-bulger-20130208-2e2nd.html

Corston, J. (2007) *The Corston Report: A report of a review of women with particular vulnerabilities in the criminal justice system.* London: Home Office.

Corston, J. (2011) *Women in the penal system: Second report on women with particular vulnerabilities in the criminal justice system.* http://howardleague.org/wp-content/uploads/2016/04/Women-in-the-penal-system.pdf

Cree, V.E. (2008) Confronting sex trafficking: lessons from history. *International Social Work*, 51(6), 763-76.

Cullen, E. and Newell, T. (1999) *Murderers and Life Imprisonment: Containment, Treatment, Safety and Risk.* Winchester: Waterside Press.

Daily Mirror (1993) Freaks of Nature. *Daily Mirror*, 25th November.

Davenport, J. (2017) Number of deaths from police chases highest in a decade, new statistics reveal. *Evening Standard*, 25th July. https://www.standard.co.uk/news/crime/number-of-deaths-from-police-chases-highest-in-a-decade-new-statistics-reveal-a3595391.html

Davies, M., Croall, H. and Tyrer, J. (2015) *Criminal Justice* (3rd edn/4th edn). Essex: Pearson Education.

Dean, W. (2015) Gavel bashing: why banging in court on TV is a serious factual offence. *The Guardian*, 18th August. https://www.theguardian.com/tv-and-radio/shortcuts/2015/aug/18/gavels-television-court-scenes-judges-scandalous-lady-w

Deering, J. and Feilzer, M. (2015) Probation officers feel betrayed by 'shambolic' part-privatisation. *The Guardian*, 7 July. https://www.theguardian.com/public-leaders-network/2015/jul/07/probation-officers-betrayed-part-privatisation-service

Defence Analytical Services and Advice (2010) *Estimating the proportion of offenders supervised by Probation trusts in England and Wales who are ex-Armed Forces.* London: Ministry of Defence.

DEFRA (2016a) *Fixed penalty notices: issuing and enforcement by councils.* Department of Environment, Food and Rural Affairs (9 May). https://www.gov.uk/guidance/fixed-penalty-notices-issuing-and-enforcement-by-councils

DEFRA (2016b) *UK Statistics on Waste.* DEFRA/Government Statistical Service (15 December) https://www.gov.uk/government/uploads/system/uploads/attachment_data/file/593040/UK_statsonwaste_statsnotice_Dec2016_FINALv2_2.pdf

DEFRA (2017) *Fly-tipping statistics for England, 2016/17.* DEFRA/Government Statistical Service 19 October). https://www.gov.uk/government/uploads/system/uploads/attachment_data/file/652958/Flytipping_201617_statistical_release_FINAL.pdf

Department for Communities and Local Government (2011) *The Economic Cost of Fire: Fire Research Reports 3/2011.* London: DCLG.

Deuze, M. (2012) *Media Life.* Cambridge: Polity Press.

Devereaux, S. (2013) England's 'Bloody Code' in Crisis and Transition: Executions at the Old Bailey 1760–1837. *Journal of the Canadian Historical Association,* 24(2), 71-113.

Di Nicola, A. (2005) Trafficking in human beings and smuggling of migrants. In Reichel P (ed) *Handbook of Transnational Crime & Justice.* California: Sage, pp181-203.

Dodd, V. and Gayle, D. (2016) Police satisfied with stop and search reform despite racial inequality. *The Guardian,* 27th October. https://www.theguardian.com/uk-news/2016/oct/27/police-satisfied-with-stop-and-search-reform-despite-racial-inequality

Doley, R. M., Dickens, G. L. and Gannon, T. A. (2016) *The Psychology of Arson.* London: Routledge.

Donald, C. (2017) *To be armed or not be armed, that was the question.* Police Federation. www.polfed.org/newsroom/Blogs.aspx?item=129

Donoghue, J. (2014) *Transforming Criminal Justice?: Problem-Solving and Court Specialisation.* London: Routledge.

Dorkenoo, E., Morison, L. and Macfarlane, A. (2007) *A statistical study to estimate the prevalence of female genital mutilation in England and Wales. Summary report.* London: FORWARD.

Dorling, D. (2004) Prime Suspect: Homicide in Britain, in P. Hillyard, C. Pantazis, S. Tombs and D. Gordon (eds) *Beyond Criminology.* London: Pluto.

Duffy, J. (1999) Something to watch over us. http://news.bbc.co.uk/1/hi/uk/334853.stm

Dunning, E. (1999) *Sport matters: Sociological studies of sport, violence, and civilization.* London: Psychology Press.

Edwards, T. (2006) *Cultures of Masculinity.* London: Routledge.

Eldredge, D. C. (1998) *Ending the War on Drugs: A Solution for America.* New York: Bridge Works Publishing

Elias, N. (1978) The civilizing process, Vol. I. *The history of manners, 310.*

Ellis, A. (2016) *Men, Masculinities and Violence: An Ethnographic Study.* London: Routledge.

Ellis, A., Winlow, S. and Hall, S. (2017) 'Throughout my life I've had people walk all over me': trauma in the biographies of violent men. *Sociological Review,* 1-15.

Emsley, C. (2013) *Soldier, Sailor, Beggarman, Thief: Crime and the British Armed Services.* Oxford: Oxford University Press.

Ending Gangs and Youth Violence (EGYV) (2011) *Ending gang and youth violence: cross-government report.* London: HM Government.

English Collective of Prostitutes (2016) *Decriminalisation of Prostitution: The Evidence* Report *of Parliamentary Symposium.* London: House of Commons.

Environment Agency (2016) *Leeds businessman receives record jail sentence over £2.2m recycling fraud*. Environment Agency press release (18 July). https://www.gov.uk/government/news/leeds-businessman-receives-record-jail-sentence-over-22m-recycling-fraud

Environment Agency (2017) *Environment agency takes a stand on illegal waste*. Environment Agency press release (4 April). https://www.gov.uk/government/news/environment-agency-takes-a-stand-on-illegal-waste

Environmental Services Association Education Trust (2017) *Rethinking Waste Crime*. ESAET (May 2017). http://www.esauk.org/application/files/7515/3589/6448/20170502_Rethinking_Waste_Crime.pdf

Epstein, R. (2014) *Mothers in Prison: the sentencing of mothers and the rights of the child*. London: Howard League.

Ericson, R. V. (2005) The police as reproducers as order, in T. Newburn (ed.) *Policing: Key Reading*. London: Routledge, 215-246.

European Commission (2010) *Europe in figures: Eurostat yearbook 2010*. Luxembourg: Publications Office of the European Union.

Evans, M. (2015) Police face rising tide of social media crimes. *The Telegraph*, 5 June.

Evans, M. (2017) Car theft soars as criminals learn how to beat security devices. *The Telegraph*, 27 September. www.telegraph.co.uk/news/2017/09/27/car-theft-soars-criminals-learn-beat-security-devices/

Falk, O., Wallinius, M., Lundström, S., Frisell, T., Anckarsäter, H. and Kerekes, N. (2014) The 1 % of the population accountable for 63 % of all violent crime convictions, *Social Psychiatry and Psychiatric Epidemiology*, 49(4), 559-71.

Falconer, C. (2018) British justice is in flames. The MoJ's fiddling is criminal. *The Guardian* [online], 6th February. https://www.theguardian.com/commentisfree/2018/feb/06/british-justice-collapse-moj-prisons-probation-legal-aid-lord-chancellor-charles-falconer

Federal Bureau of Investigation (2017) *Crime in the United States.* https://ucr.fbi.gov/crime-in-the-u.s/2017/crime-in-the-u.s.-2017

Ferguson, C. J., White, D. E., Cherry, S., Lorenz, M. and Bhimani, Z. (2003) Defining and classifying serial murder in the context of perpetrator motivation. *Journal of Criminal Justice*, 31, 287-329.

Ferrell, J. (1999) Cultural criminology. *Annual Review of Sociology*, 25(1), 395-418.

Ferrell, J. (2004) Boredom, crime and criminology. *Theoretical Criminology*, 8(3), 287-302.

Ferrell, J., Hayward, K. and Young, J. (2015) *Cultural Criminology*. London: Sage.

Fielding, N. (1994) Cop Canteen Culture, in T. Newburn and E. A. Stanko (eds) *Just Boys Doing Business? Men, Masculinities and Crime*. London: Routledge.

Finkelhor, D. (1984) *Child sexual abuse*. New York: Macmillan.

Finkelhor, D., Ormrod, R.K. and Turner, H.A. (2007) Poly-victimization: A neglected component in child victimization. *Child Abuse & Neglect*, 31(1), 7-26.

Finkelson, L. and Oswalt, R. (1995) College Date Rape: Incidence and Reporting. *Psychological Reports*, 77(2), 526-526. doi:10.2466/pr0.1995.77.2.526

Finlay, B. D. (2011) Counterfeit Drugs and National Security, *Stimson*, February. https://www.files.ethz.ch/isn/127562/Counterfeit_Drugs_and_National_Security.pdf

Fiore, K. (2014) Bodybuilders Bulk Up Using ... Cancer Drugs? *Medpage Today*, 16 January. https://www.medpagetoday.com/primarycare/exercisefitness/43839

Follingstad, D. R. and DeHart, D. D. (2000) Defining psychological abuse of husbands toward wives: Contexts, behaviors, and typologies. *Journal of Interpersonal Violence*, 15(9), 891–920.

Ford, M., Mills, H. and Grimshaw, R. (2016) *Profile of the Provision for armed forces veterans under probation supervision*. London: Forces in Mind Trust.

Forster, S. (2017) *Operation Jasper*. National Trading Standards eCrime Team. www.tradingstandardsecrime.org.uk/products-worth-millions-seized-in-counterfeiting-crackdown/

Foster, J., Souhami, A. and Newburn, T. (2005) Assessing the Impact of the Stephen Lawrence Inquiry. *Home Office Research Study, No. 294*. London: Home Office.

Foucault, M. (1977) *Discipline and Punishment: The Birth of the Prison*. London: Penguin.

Freudenberg, N. (2014) *Lethal But Legal: Corporations*. New York: Oxford University Press.

Friesendorf, C. (2007) Pathologies of security governance: efforts against human trafficking in Europe. *Security Dialogue*, 38(3), 379–402.

Gallagher, J. (2015) Record 'fake drugs' haul worth £16m by UK agency. *BBC News*, 18 June. www.bbc.co.UK/news/health-33183330

Gannon, T. A. and Barrowcliffe, E. (2010) Firesetting in the general population: The development and validation of the Fire Setting and Fire Proclivity Scales. *Legal and Criminological Psychology*, 17(1), 105–122.

Gannon, T. A., Ó Ciardha, C., Barnoux, M., Tyler, N., Mozova, K. and Alleyne, E. (2013) Male imprisoned firesetters have different characteristics than other imprisoned offenders and require specialist treatment. *Psychiatry*, 76(4), 349–364.

Gannon, T. A., Ó Ciardha, C., Doley, R. M. and Alleyne, E. (2012) The Multi-Trajectory Theory of Adult Firesetting (M-TTAF). *Aggression and Violent Behavior*, 17(2), 107–121.

Garland, D. (2001) *The Culture of Control: Crime and Social Order in Contemporary Society*. Oxford: Oxford University Press.

Genge, N.E. (2004) *The Forensic Casebook*. London: Ebury Press.

Gilbert, K.L. and Rashawn, R. (2016) Why police kill black males with impunity: Applying public health critical race praxis (PHCRP) to address the determinants of policing behaviors and "justifiable" homicides in the USA. *Journal of Urban Health*, 93 (Suppl 1), 122-140.

Gilligan, J. (2000) *Violence: Reflections on our Deadliest Epidemic*. London: Jessica Kingsley.

Global Drugs Survey (2017) *Key Findings & Report, Global Drugs Survey 2017*. https://www.globaldrugsurvey.com/wp-content/themes/globaldrugsurvey/results/GDS2017_key-findings-report_final.pdf

Glyn-Jones, A. (2000) *Holding up a Mirror: How Civilizations Decline* (2nd edn), Exeter: Imprint Academic.

Godfrey, B. S., Farrall, S. and Cox, D. J. (2007) *Criminal Lives: Family Life, Employment, and Offending*. Oxford: Oxford University Press.

Goffman, E. (1990 [1963]) *Stigma: Notes on the Management of Spoiled Identity*. London. Penguin Books.

Goldhill, O. (2010) The Innocence of Youth?, *The Harvard Crimson*, 10 May. www.thecrimson.com/article/2010/5/10/venabless-crime-trial-venables/

Goldsmith, A. (2010) Policing's New Visibility. *British Journal of Criminology*, 50, 914-934.

Grana, S. J., Ollenburger, J. C., and Nicholas, M. (2002) *The Social Context of Law* (2nd edn). Upper Saddle River: Prentice-Hall.

Green, D. A. (2008) Suitable vehicles: Framing blame and justice when children kill a child. *Crime Media Culture*, 4(2), 197-220.

Grewcock, M. (1996) System Which Neglects the Child, in P. Cavadino (ed.) *From Children Who Kill*. Winchester: Waterside Press, 55-66.

Groombridge, N. (2016) *Sports criminology: A critical criminology of sport and games*. London: Policy Press.

Guardian (2011) Man jailed for record tyre dumps. *The Guardian*, 8 November. https://www.theguardian.com/environment/2011/nov/08/man-jailed-tyre-dump

Guardian (2017) UK fraud hits record £1.1bn as cybercrime soars. *The Guardian*, 24 January. https://www.theguardian.com/uk-news/2017/jan/24/uk-fraud-record-cybercrime-kpmg

Guillory, R. (2014) *Criminal Behaviour*. Glasgow: Freight Books.

Haggerty, K. D. and Sandhu, A. (2014) The Police Crisis of Visibility. *IEEE Technology and Society Magazine*, Summer, 9-12.

Hall, S (2007) The emergence and breakdown of the pseudo-pacification process. In Watson, K. (ed) *Assaulting the Past: Placing Violence in Historical Context*. Cambridge: Cambridge Scholars Press.

Hall, A. and Antonopoulos, G. A. (2016) *Fake meds online: the internet and the transnational market in illicit pharmaceuticals*. Basingstoke: Palgrave.

Hall, N. (2013) *Hate Crime* (2nd edn). London: Routledge.

Hall, S. (2002) Daubing the drudges of fury: Men, violence and the piety of the 'hegemonic masculinity' thesis. *Theoretical Criminology*, 6(1), 35-61.

Hall, S. (2012) *Theorizing Crime and Deviance: A New Perspective*. London: Sage.

Hall, S. and Winlow, S. (2015) *Revitalizing criminological theory: Towards a new ultra-realism*. London: Routledge.

Hallsworth, S. and Young, T. (2008), Gang Talk and Gang Talkers: A Critique. *Crime Media and Culture*, 4, 175-95.

Hardy, S. and Chakraborti, N. (2016) *Healing the Harms: Identifying How Best to Support Hate Crime Victims.* Leicester: University of Leicester.

Hardy, S. and Chakraborti, N. (2017a) *A Postcode Lottery? Mapping Support Services,* Leicester: University of Leicester.

Hardy, S. and Chakraborti, N. (2017b) *Hate Crime: Identifying and Dismantling Barriers to Justice,* Leicester: University of Leicester.

Heidensohn, F. (1992) *Women in Control: The Role of Women in Law Enforcement.* Oxford: Oxford University Press.

Heinonen, J. A., Holt, T. J. and Wilson, J. M. (2012) Product Counterfeits in the Online Environment: An Empirical Assessment of Victimization and Reporting Characteristics. *International Criminal Justice Review*, 22(4), 353-371.

Hendrick, H. (1994) *Child Welfare. England 1872–1989.* London: Routledge.

Hickey, E. (1997) *Serial murderers and their victims* (2nd edn). Belmont: Wadsworth.

Hickey, E. (2006) *Serial murderers and their victims* (4th edn). London: Thomson Higher Education.

Hillyard, P. (1993) *Suspect Community - People's Experience of the Prevention of Terrorism Acts in Britain.* London: Pluto Press.

HM Chief Inspector of Prisons for England and Wales (2015) *Annual report.* London: HMSO.

HM Chief Inspector of Prisons for England and Wales (2016) *Annual report.* London: HMSO.

HM Government (2015) *Working together to safeguard children: a guide to inter-agency working to safeguard and promote the welfare of children.* https://www.gov.uk/government/uploads/system/uploads/attachment_data/file/592101/Working_Together_to_Safeguard_Children_20170213.pdf

HM Government (2017) *Proven Reoffending Statistics Quarterly Bulletin, April 2014 to March 2015*. https://www.gov.uk/government/uploads/system/uploads/attachment_data/file/585908/proven-reoffending-quarterly-bulletin.pdf

HM Inspectorate of Probation for England and Wales (2017) *2017 Annual Report*. Manchester: Civil Justice Centre.

HMIP (2017) *Prison Conditions*. London: HMSO.

HMRC (2016) *HMRC Tax and NIC Receipts: Monthly and annual historical record*. London. https://assets.publishing.service.gov.uk/government/uploads/system/uploads/attachment_data/file/539194/Jun16_Receipts_NS_Bulletin_Final.pdf

Hollin, C. R., Davies, S. D., Duggan, C., Huband, N., McCarthy, L. and Clarke, M. (2013) Patients with a history of arson admitted to medium security: Characteristics on admission and follow-up post discharge. *Medicine, Science and the Law*, 53(3), 154–160.

Home Office (2001a) *Policing a New Century; A Blueprint for Reform*, London: HMSO.

Home Office (2001b) *Criminal Justice: The Way Ahead*. Cm 5074. London: Home Office.

Home Office (2003) Crime in England and Wales 2002/2003, Statistical Bulletin. London: Crown Copyright. http://webarchive.nationalarchives.gov.uk/20110218141841/http://rds.homeoffice.gov.uk/rds/pdfs2/hosb703.pdf

Home Office (2004c) *Confident Communities in a Secure Britain: The Home Office Strategic Plan 2004-08*. Cm 6287. London: Home Office.

Home Office (2012) *A minimum unit price for Alcohol Impact Assessment*. London: Home Office, 5.

Home Office (2013) *Domestic Violence and Abuse*. www.gov.uk/guidence/domestic-violence-and-abuse#history

Home Office (2015) *Gangs and Youth Crime*. London: House of Commons.

Home Office (2016) Proscribed Terrorist Organisations. London: Home Office.

Home Office (2018) *Stop and Search*. London: House of Commons.

Hopkins, M. (2016a) Business, victimisation and victimology: Reflections on contemporary patterns of commercial victimisation and the concept of businesses as 'ideal victims'. *International Review of Victimology*, 22(2), 161-179.

Hopkins, M. (2016b) The crime drop and the changing face of commercial victimisation: Reflections on the 'commercial crime drop' in the United Kingdom and the implications for future research. *Criminology and Criminal Justice*, 16(4), 410-431.

Hopkins, M. and Gill, M. (2017) Business, crime and crime prevention: emerging debates and future challenges, in N. Tilley and A. Sidebottom (eds) *Handbook of Crime Prevention and Community Safety* (2nd edn). London: Routledge, 373-394.

Horsley, M. (2015) *The Dark Side of Prosperity: Late Capitalism's Culture of Indebtedness*. Farnham: Ashgate.

Horsley, M. (2017) Beg, Borrow or Steal: Addiction, Payment Means and Monetary Resources. Paper presented to British Society of Criminology Annual Conference, Sheffield Hallam University, 7 July.

Horsley, M., Kotze, J. and Hall, S. (2015) The Maintenance of Orderly Disorder: Modernity, Markets and the Pseudo-Pacification Process. *Journal on European History of Law*, 6(1), 18-29.

Horvath, M. and Brown, J. (2007) Alcohol as drug of choice; Is drug-assisted rape a misnomer? *Psychology, Crime & Law*, 13(5), 417-429.

House of Commons (1810) *Parliamentary Debates (Hansard)*. 9th February 1810, col. 366-374.

House of Commons (2015) *Gangs and youth crime.* https://publications.parliament.uk/pa/cm201415/cmselect/cmhaff/199/19904.htm

House of Commons (2017) *UK Prison Population Statistics.* House of Commons Library. http://researchbriefings.parliament.uk/Research Briefing/Summary/SN04334

House of Commons Home Affairs Committee (2016) *Prostitution: Third Report of Session 2016–17 HC26.* London: House of Commons.

House of Lords (1997) *Judgments – Reg. v. Secretary of State for the Home Department, Ex parte V. and Reg. v. Secretary of State for the Home Department, Ex parte T.* https://publications.parliament.uk/pa/ld199798/ldjudgmt/jd970612/vandt01.htm

Houses of Parliament (2016) *Digital Forensics and Crime*, 20th March. London: Parliamentary Office of Science and Technology,

Howard League (2011) *Report of the Inquiry into Former Armed Service Personnel in Prison.* https://howardleague.org/publications/report-of-the-inquiry-into-former-armed-service-personnel-in-prison-2/

Howard League (2016a) *Faint Hope: What to do about long sentences.* London: Howard League for Penal Reform.

Howard League (2016b) *The Voice of a Child.* http://howardleague.org/wp-content/uploads/2016/05/The-Voice-of-a-Child-Howard-League-UN-CRC-DGD-submission-August-2011.pdf

Hubbard, P., Kitchin, R., Bartley, B., Fuller, D. (2002) *Thinking Geographically: Space, theory and contemporary human geography.* London: Continuum.

Hudson, K. (2005) *Offending Identities: Sex offenders' Perspectives on their Treatment and Management.* Cullompton: Willan Publishing.

Huey, L. (2012) *Invisible Victims: Homelessness and the Growing Security Gap.* Toronto: University of Toronto Press.

Hulonce, L. (2017) Workhouse Children, in J. Turner, P. Taylor, K. Corteen and S. Morley (eds) *A Companion to the History of Crime and Criminal Justice*. Bristol: Policy Press, 286-288.

Humphreys, L. (1975) *Tearoom Trade: Impersonal Sex in Public Places* (enlarged edn). London: Routledge.

Hutto, S., Jonathan, W. and Green, R. D. (2016) Social Movements Against Racist Police Brutality and Department of Justice Intervention in Prince George's County, Maryland. *Journal of Urban Health: Bulletin of the New York Academy of Medicine*, 93(1), 89.

Iganski, P. and Lagou, S. (2015) The Personal Injuries of 'Hate Crime', in N. Hall, A. Corb, P. Giannasi and J. Grieve (eds) *The Routledge International Handbook on Hate Crime*. London: Routledge, 34-46.

Independent (1993) James Bulger: The death of innocence. *The Independent*, 28th November. https://www.independent.co.uk/news/uk/crime/james-bulger-the-death-of-innocence-739586.html

IPCG (2007) *Intellectual property crime report*. Intellectual Property Crime Group. UK Intellectual Property Office. www.ipo.gov.uk/ipcreport07.pdf

IPCG (2010) *Intellectual Property Crime Report 2009–2010*. Intellectual Property Crime Group. UK Intellectual Property Office. www.ipo.gov.uk/ipcreport09.pdf

IPCG (2014) Intellectual Property Crime Report 2013/14. Intellectual Property Crime Group. UK Intellectual Property Office. https://assets.publishing.service.gov.uk/government/uploads/system/uploads/attachment_data/file/374283/ipcreport13.PDF

Jackman, M. R. (2002) Violence in Social Life. *Annual Review of Sociology*, 28(1), 387-415.

Jackson, C. A. (2015) *Managing the Effects of Workplace Stalking and Harassment*. Management of Health Risks Special Report.

Jackson, G., Patel, S. and Khan, S. (2011) Assessing the problem of counterfeit medications in the United Kingdom. *International Journal of Clinical Practice*, 66(3), 241-250.

Jackson, L. (2000) *Child Sexual Abuse in Victorian England*. London: Routledge.

Jackson, G., Patel, S. and Khan, S. (2012) Assessing the problem of counterfeit medications in the United Kingdom. *International Journal of Clinical Practice*, 66(3), 241-50.

Jaffe, P. and Burris, C. A. (1982) *An integrated response to wife battering: A community model*. Ottawa: Research Report of the Solicitor General of Canada.

James, A. and Raine, J. (1998) *The new politics of criminal justice*. London: Longman Publishing.

Jay, A. (2014) *Independent Inquiry into Child Sexual Exploitation in Rotherham 1997–2013*. Rotherham: Metropolitan Borough Council.

Jayaraman, A. and Frazer, J. (2006) Arson: A Growing Inferno. *Medicine, Science and the Law*, 46(4), 295-300.

Jenkins, P. (1988) Serial Murder in England, 1940-1985. *Journal of Criminal Justice*, 16, 1-15.

Jewkes, Y. (2015) *Media and Crime* (3rd edn). London: Sage.

Jones, O. (2016) Not all men commit abuse against women. But all must condemn it. *The Guardian*, 8 September. https://www.theguardian.com/commentisfree/2016/sep/08/men-abuse-women-condemn-male-violence-masculine

Jones, R. (2017) Sharp rise in county court judgments against consumers. *The Guardian*, 6th February. https://www.theguardian.com/money/2017/feb/06/sharp-rise-in-county-court-judgments-against-consumers

Keeling, N. (2014) Bitter Pill as Viagra Fraudster is jailed, *Manchester Evening News*, 3 October. https://www.questia.com/newspaper/1P2-38087438/bitter-pill-as-viagra-fraudster-is-jailed-pounds

Kemshall, H. (2001) *Risk Assessment and Management of Known Sexual and Violent Offenders: A Review of Current Issues*. Police Research Series, Paper 140 .London: Home Office.

Kemshall, H. (2008) *Understanding the community management of high risk offenders*. Maidenhead: Open University Press.

Kenney, K. L. (2012) *Domestic Violence*. Edina, MN: ABDO Publishing Company.

Kennison, P. and Loumansky, A. (2007) Shoot to kill – understanding police use of force in combatting suicide terrorism. *Crime, Law and Social Change*, 47(3), 151-168.

Kentish, B. (2017) Manchester bombing: Sharp rise in number of UK terror plots foiled since March, say officials. *The Independent*, 25 May 2017. www.independent.co.uk/news/uk/home-news/manchester-bombing-uk-terror-plots-foiled-rise-number-security-services-officials-a7755471.html

Khomami, N. (2018) Alleged neo-Nazi admits plotting murder of MP Rosie Cooper. *The Guardian*, 12th June. https://www.theguardian.com/uk-news/2018/jun/12/man-pleads-guilty-to-plot-to-labour-mp-rosie-cooper

King, P. and Ward, R. (2015) Rethinking the Bloody Code in Eighteenth-Century Britain: Capital Punishment at the Centre and on the Periphery. *Past & Present*, 228(1), 159-205.

Kinnell, H. (2008) *Violence and Sex Work in Britain*. Cullompton, Devon: Willan Publishing.

Kinsey, R., Lea, J. and Young, J. (1986) *Losing the Fight against Crime*. Basil Blackwell.

Kitchen, T. and Schneider, R. (2007) *Crime Prevention and the Build Environment*. Abingdon: Routledge.

Kreft, H. (2017a) Three men are charged with drugs offences after large-scale operation in Burton. *Burton Mail*, 30 June. www.burtonmail.co.uk/news/burton-news/three-men-charged-drugs-offences-154567

Kreft, H. (2017b) Four people charged in Burton following county-wide drugs operation, *Burton Mail*, 25 July. www.burtonmail.co.uk/news/burton-news/four-people-charged-burton-following-233984

Kubrin, C., Squires, G., Graves, S. and Ousey, G. (2011) Does Fringe Banking Exacerbate Neighbourhood Crime Rates? *Criminology & Public Policy*, 10(2), 437-66.

Lacasse, A. and Mendelson, M. (2007) Sexual Coercion Among Adolescents. *Journal of Interpersonal Violence*, 22(4), 424-437. doi:10.1177/0886260506297027

Lambie, I. and Randell, I. (2011) Creating a firestorm: A review of children who deliberately light fires. *Evaluation and Program Planning*, 35, 445-452.

Lampard, K. and Marsden, E. (2015) *Themes and lessons learned from NHS investigations into matters relating to Jimmy Savile.* Independent report for the Secretary of State for Health.

Lantern Project (2012) *Statistics on child sexual abuse.* www.lanternproject.org.uk/statistics-on-child-sexual-abuse/

Laquer, W. (2003) No end to war: terrorism in the twenty-first century. New York: Continuum.

Large, J. (2015) 'Get Real Don't Buy Fakes'. Fashion Fakes and Flawed Policy: The Problem with Taking a Consumer-Responsibility Approach to Reducing the Problem of Counterfeiting. *Criminology and Criminal Justice*, 15(2), 169-185.

Laurance, J. (2009) The Big Question: Is Methadone Being Over-prescribed as a treatment for drug addiction? *The Independent*, 10 December. www.independent.co.uk/life-style/health-and-families/health-news/the-big-question-is-methadone-being-over-prescribed-as-a-treatment-for-drug-addiction-1837156.html

Lavin-Morris, F. (2016) *UK Drugs Policy an embarrassment, we must modernise and legalise*. Adam Smith Institute. https://www.adamsmith.org/news/uk-drugs-policy-an-embarrassment-we-must-modernise-and-legalise

Lavorgna, A. (2014) The online trade in counterfeit pharmaceuticals: new criminal opportunities, trends and challenges. *European Journal of Criminology*. First published online on 5 November 2014 as doi: 10.1177/1477370814554722

Levine, H. G. (1978) The discovery of addiction. Changing conceptions of habitual drunkenness in America. *Journal of Studies of Alcohol*, 39(1), 143-74.

Levy, B. (2008) *Women and Violence*. Berkeley, CA: Seal Press.

Lewis, P. (2010) Police surveillance of Muslims set up with 'no regard for law. *The Guardian*, 30 September.

Lewis, P. (2012) Police face racism scandal after black man records abuse. *The Guardian*, 30 March. https://www.theguardian.com/uk/2012/mar/30/police-racism-black-man-abuse

Liebling, A., Maruna, S. and Mcara, L. (2017) *The Oxford Handbook of Criminology* (6th edn). Oxford: Oxford University Press.

Lindberg, N., Holi, M. M., Tani, P. and Virkkunen, M. (2005) Looking for pyromania: Characteristics of a consecutive sample of Finnish male criminals with histories of recidivist fire setting between 1973 and 1993. *BMC Psychiatry*, 47(5): 1-5.

Lijphart, A. (1999) *Patterns of democracy*. New Haven: Yale University Press.

Llewelyn-Thomas, S. and Prior, G. (2007) *North Liverpool Community Justice Centre: Surveys of Local Residents*. London: Ministry of Justice.

Lobasz, J.K. (2009) Beyond border security: Feminist approaches to human trafficking. *Security Studies*, 18, 319-44.

Logan, T. (2010) *Research on partner stalking: Putting the pieces together*. Lexington, KY: University of Kentucky.

Loring, M. T. (1994) *Emotional Abuse*. New York: Lexington Books.

Lowery, W. (2017) *They Can't Kill Us All: The Story of Black Lives Matter*. Harmondsworth: Penguin.

Ludlow, A. (2015) *Privatising Public Prisons Labour Law and the Public Procurement Process*. Oxford: Hart.

Lundrigan, S. and Canter, D. (2008) A Multivariate analysis of Serial Murderers' Disposal Site Location Choice, in D. Canter and D. Youngs (eds) *Applications of Geographical Offender Profiling*. Aldershot: Ashgate Publishing Limited, 25-41.

Lusk, M. and Lucas, F. (2009) The challenge of human trafficking and contemporary slavery. *Journal of Comparative Social Welfare*, 25(1), 49-57.

Lynes, A. (2017) *The Road to Murder: why Driving is the Occupation of Choice for British Serial Killers*. Hook: Waterside Press.

MacAskill, E. (2017) Lone attackers are the biggest challenge for security services. *The Guardian*, 22 March. https://www.theguardian.com/uk-news/2017/mar/22/lone-attackers-are-the-biggest-challenge-for-security-services

MacEwan, N. (2013) A Tricky Situation: Deception in Cyberspace. *The Journal of Criminal Law*, 77(5), 417-432.

MacIntyre, D., Wilson, D., Yardley, E. and Brolan, L. (2014) The British Hitman: 1974-2013. *The Howard Journal of Criminal Justice*, 53(4), 325-340.

MacManus, D., Dean, K., Jones, M., Rona, R. J., Greenberg, N., Hull, L., Fahy, T., Wessley, S. and Fear, N. T. (2013) Violent Offending by UK Military Personnel Deployed to Iraq and Afghanistan: a data linkage cohort study. *The Lancet*, 381, 907-917.

Macpherson, W. (1999) *Steven Lawrence Inquiry, Report of an Inquiry by Sir William Macpherson of Cluny*. London: HMSO.

Mair, G. and Millings, M. (2011) *Doing Justice Locally: The North Liverpool Community Justice Centre*, London: Centre for Crime and Justice Studies.

Mair, G. and Nee, C. (1990) *Electronic Monitoring: The Trials and their Results*. Home Office Research Study 120. London: HMSO.

Manchester Evening News (2010) A terrible crime with two victims. *Manchester Evening News*, 13th August. https://www.manchestereveningnews.co.uk/news/greater-manchester-news/a-terrible-crime-with-two-victims-1047375

Mann, N. (2012) Ageing Child Sex Offenders in Prison: Denial, Manipulation and Community. *The Howard Journal of Criminal Justice*, 51(4), 345-358.

Mann, N. (2014) *Doing Harder Time? The Experiences of an Ageing Male Prison Population in England and Wales*. Aldershot: Ashgate Publishing.

Marshall, H. I. and Summers, L. D. (2012) Contemporary Differences in Rates and Trends of Homicide among European Nations, in A. C. M. Liem and W. A. Pridemore (eds) *Handbook of European Homicide Research: Patterns, Explanations and Country Studies*. New York: Springer Science + Business Media.

Marshall, L. L. (1994) Physical and Psychological Abuse, in W. R. Cupach and B. H. Spitzberg (eds) *The Dark Side of Interpersonal Communication*. Hillsdale, NJ: Erlbaum, 281-311.

Mawby, R. C. and Wright, A. (2012) The Police Organisation, in T. Newburn (ed.) *Handbook of Policing*. London: Routledge, 169-195.

Mayhew, P., Clarke, R., Sturman, A. and Hough, J. (1976) *Crime as Opportunity*. Home Office Research Study No. 34. London: HMSO.

McCall l. P., Nieuwbeerta, P., Engen L. R. and Thames M. K. (2012) Explaining Variation in Homicide Rates Across Eastern and Western European Cities: The Effects of Social, Political and Economic Forces, in A. C. M. Liem and W. A. Pridemore (eds) *Handbook of European Homicide Research: Patterns, Explanations and Country Studies*. New York: Springer Science + Business Media.

McGarry, R. and Walklate, S. (2016) (eds) *The Palgrave Handbook of Criminology and War*. London: Palgrave Macmillan.

McGowen, R. (1994) Civilizing Punishment: The End of the Public Execution in England. *Journal of British Studies*, 33(3), 257-282.

McGregor, A. (2016) Politics, Police Accountability, and Public Health: Civilian Review in Newark, New Jersey. *Journal of Urban Health: Bulletin of the New York Academy of Medicine*, 93(1), 141-153.

McIntosh, M. (1968) The Homosexual Role. *Social Problems*, 16(2), 182-192.

Metropolitan Police (n.d) *How we use stop and search*. https://www.met.police.uk/advice/advice-and-information/st-s/stop-and-search/how-we-use-stop-and-search/

McKillop, N., Brown, S., Johnson, I., Smallbone, S. and Ogilvie, J. M. (2017) Can Systemic Interventions Designed to Reduce Reoffending by Youth also Reduce Their Victimization? *Journal of Child & Adolescent Trauma*, 10(1), 41-50.

McLaughlin, E. (2006) *The New Policing*. London: Sage Publications.

McLaughlin, K. (2015) Advocacy research and social policy. *The International Journal of Sociology and Social Policy*, 35(3), 239-51.

McSweeney, T., Turnball, P. J. and Hough, M. (2008) *Tackling drug markets & distribution networks in the UK*, 4(11). London: UK Drug Policy Commission. http://www.ukdpc.org.uk/wp-content/uploads/Policy%20report%20-%20Tackling%20drug%20markets%20and%20distribution%20networks%20in%20the%20UK.pdf

Mills, H., Skodbo, S. and Blyth, P. (2013) *Understanding organised crime: estimating the scale and the social and economic costs*. Research Report 73. London: Home Office.

Ministry of Defence (2016) *New £10m Covenant fund awarded to 176 Armed Forces projects*. Ministry of Defence, 22nd March. https://www.gov.uk/government/news/new-10m-covenant-fund-awarded-to-176-armed-forces-projects

Ministry of Justice (2017a) *Criminal Justice Statistics- Quarterly Update March 2017*, London: Ministry of Justice.

Ministry of Justice (2017b) *Offender Management Statistics*. London: Ministry of Justice.

Ministry of Justice (2017c) *Prison Reform Trust Representation to the Autumn Budget 2017*. Prison Reform Trust. http://www.prisonreformtrust.org.uk/Portals/0/Documents/Consultation%20responses/Representation%20to%20the%202017%20budget.pdf

Ministry of Justice (2017d) *Multi-Agency Public Protection Arrangements Annual Report 2016/17*. Ministry of Justice, 26th October. https://assets.publishing.service.gov.uk/government/uploads/system/uploads/attachment_data/file/655022/MAPPA-annual-report-2016-17.pdf

Ministry of Justice (2018) *Annual Report and Accounts 2017-18*. House of Commons. https://assets.publishing. service.gov.uk/government/uploads/system/uploads/ attachment_data/file/722536/MoJ_annual_reports_and_ accounts_2017-18__print_.pdf

Minson, S., Nadin, R. and Earle, J. (2015) *Sentencing of mothers: Improving the sentencing process and outcomes for women with dependent children*. London: Prison Reform Trust.

Moffitt, T. E. (1993) Adolescence-limited and life-course-persistent antisocial behavior: a developmental taxonomy. *Psychological Review*, 100(4), 674.

Moghaddam, F. M. (2005) The staircase to terrorism: A psychological exploration. *American Psychologist*, 60(2), 161.

Mohandie, K., Meloy, R., McGowan, M. G. and Williams, J. (2006) The RECON typology of stalking: Reliability and validity based upon a large sample of North American stalkers. *Journal of Forensic Sciences*, 51, 147–55.

Morgan, M., Shaw, O., Feist, A. and Byron, C. (2016) *Reducing Criminal Opportunity: Vehicle Security and Vehicle Crime*. Research Report No. 87. London: HMSO.

Morley, S. (2017) National Society for the Prevention of Cruelty to Children, in J. Turner, P. Taylor, K. Corteen and S. Morley (eds) *A Companion to the History of Crime and Criminal Justice*. Bristol: Policy Press, 149-151.

Mott, J. (1975) The criminal histories of male non-medical opiate users in the United Kingdom. *Bulletin in Narcotics*, 4, 41-48.

Mugellini, G. (2013) *Measuring and analyzing crime against the private sector: International experiences and the Mexican Practice*. Mexico: Instituto Nacional de Estadistica y Geografia.

Murphy, C. (2015) *Sex Workers' Rights are Human Rights*. Amnesty International. https://www.amnesty.org/en/latest/news/2015/08/sex-workers-rights-are-human-rights/

Murray, E. (2014) Veteran offenders in Cheshire: Making sense of the 'noise'. *Probation Journal*, 61(3), 251–264.

Murray, E. (2016) 'The Violent Veteran' A Governmental Problem in England and Wales, in R. McGarry and S. Walklate (eds) *The Palgrave Handbook of Criminology and War*. London: Palgrave Macmillan.

Murray, J. and Farrington, D. P. (2008) The Effects of Parental Imprisonment, in M. Tonry (ed.) *Crime and Justice: A review of research*. Chicago: University of Chicago Press, 133–206.

National Crime Agency (2017a) *Modern slavery and human trafficking*. http://www.nationalcrimeagency.gov.uk/crime-threats/human-trafficking

National Crime Agency (2017b) *Drugs*. www.nationalcrimeagency.gov.uk/crime-threats/drugs

National Police Chiefs' Council (2017) *Latest hate crime figures covering the period of 2017 UK terrorist attacks published*. https://news.npcc.police.uk/releases/latest-hate-crime-figures-covering-the-period-of-2017-uk-terrorist-attacks-published

National Statistics (2016) *Deaths during or following police contact in England and Wales: 2015 to 2016*. https://www.gov.uk/government/statistics/deaths-during-or-following-police-contact-in-england-and-wales-2015-to-2016

NCA (2017) *National Referral Mechanism Statistics – End of Year Summary 2016*. www.nationalcrimeagency.gov.uk

Nellis, M. (2004) 'I Know Where You Live!': Electronic Monitoring and Penal Policy in England and Wales 1999–2003. *British Journal of Community Justice*, 2(3), 33–59.

New York Times (2017) Hillary Clinton says Russia used hacking 'to great effect' in her defeat. *New York Times*, 6 April. https://www.nytimes.com/2017/04/06/nyregion/hillary-clinton-russia-hacking-election-trump.html

New Zealand Government (2008) *Report of the Prostitution Law Review Committee on the Operation of the Prostitution Reform Act 2003*. Crown Copyright, New Zealand.

Newburn, T. (2013) *Criminology* (2nd edn). New York: Routledge.

Newburn, T. (2017) *Criminology* (3rd edn). London: Routledge.

Newburn, T. and Rock, P. (2005) *Living in Fear: Violence and Victimisation in the Lives of Single Homeless People*. London: Crisis.

Newburn, T., Williamson, T. and Wright, A. (2007) *Handbook of Criminal Investigation*. London: Willan Publishing.

Newton, M. (2006) *The Encyclopaedia of Serial Killers*. New York: InfoBase Publishing.

NHS Choices (2016) *Female genital mutilation*. https://www.nhs.uk/conditions/female-genital-mutilation-fgm

NHS Digital (2017a) *Statistics on Drugs Misuse: England, 2017*. http://webarchive.nationalarchives.gov.uk/20180328135520tf_/http://digital.nhs.uk/catalogue/PUB23442

NHS Digital (2017b) *Female Genital Mutilation (FGM) Annual Report 2016/17*. https://files.digital.nhs.uk/publication/g/c/fgm-apr-2016-mar-2017-exp-rep.pdf

NiCarthy, G. (1986) *Getting free: A handbook for women in abusive relationships*. Seattle, WA: Seal Press.

Noblett, S. and Nelson, B. (2001) A psychosocial approach to arson: A case controlled study of female offenders. *Medicine, Science and the Law*, 41, 325–30

NSPCC (2013) *Child sexual abuse; An NSPCC research briefing.* https://www.nspcc.org.uk/globalassets/documents/information-service/research-briefing-child-sexual-abuse.pdf

NSPCC (2017) *Sexual abuse: what is sexual abuse.* https://www.nspcc.org.uk/preventing-abuse/child-abuse-and-neglect/child-sexual-abuse/

OECD (2008) *The Economic Impact of Counterfeiting and Piracy.* Organisation for Economic Co-Operation and Development. www.oecdbookshop.org/oecd/display.asp?lang=EN&sf1=identifiers&st1=9789264045521

OECD and EUIPO (2016) *Global trade in fake goods worth nearly half a trillion dollars a year,* Organisation for Economic Co-Operation and Development and European Union Intellectual Property Office, www.oecd.org/industry/global-trade-in-fake-goods-worth-nearly-half-a-trillion-dollars-a-year.htm

Office for National Statistics (2013) *Police workforce, England and Wales,* 31 March 2013. London: Home Office.

Office for National Statistics (2016a) *Crime in England and Wales: A year ending March 2016.* London: ONS.

Office for National Statistics (2017a) *Crime in England and Wales: year ending June 2017.* https://www.ons.gov.uk/releases/crimeinenglandandwalesyearendingjune2017

Office for National Statistics (2017b) *Crime in England and Wales: A year ending June 2017.* London: ONS.

Office for National Statistics (2018) *Family spending in the UK: financial year ending 2017.* https://www.ons.gov.uk/peoplepopulationandcommunity/personalandhouseholdfinances/expenditure/bulletins/familyspendingintheuk/financialyearending2017

Orwell, G. (2004) *Nineteen Eighty-Four* (Penguin Modern Classics). Harmondsworth: Penguin Classics.

OSCE (2013) *Office of the Special Representative and Co-ordinator for Combating Trafficking in Human Beings, Trafficking in Human Beings for the Purpose of Organ Removal in the OSCE Region: Analysis and Findings, Occasional Paper Series no. 6 (July 2013).*

Overs, C. (2002) *Sex Workers: Part of the Solution.* World Health Organization. www.who.int/hiv/topics/vct/sw_toolkit/115solution.pdf

Paliwal, P., Ali, S., Bradshaw, S., Hughes, A. and Jolly, K. (2013) Management of type III genital mutilation in Birmingham, UK: a retrospective audit. *Midwifery*, 30(3): 282-88.

Palmer, E. J., Hollin, C. R., Hatcher, R. M. and Ayres, T. C. (2010) Arson, in F. Brookman, M. Maguire, H. Pierpoint and T. Bennett (eds) *Handbook on Crime.* Cullompton: Willan Publishing, 380-392.

Parliament (2017) *House of Commons – Radicalisation: the counter-narrative and identifying the tipping point – Home Affairs Committee.* http://publications.parliament.uk/pa/cm201617/cmselect/cmhaff/135/13507.htm

Patton, C. L. and Fremouw, W. J. (2016) Examining 'suicide by cop': A critical review of the literature. *Aggression and Violent Behavior*, 27, 107.

Pells, R. (2016) More students turning to banned 'brain boosting' drug than ever before. *The Independent*, 6 June. www.independent.co.uk/student/student-life/noopept-study-drug-legal-high-banned-brain-boosting-students-record-numbers-a7068071.html

Pendlebury, A. (2006) Perceptions of playing culture in sport: The problem of diverse opinion in the light of Barnes. *The Entertainment and Sports Law Journal*, 4(2), 5.

Phillips, S. (2014) *Former members of the armed forces and the criminal justice system. A review on behalf of the Secretary of State for Justice.* London: Ministry of Justice.

Police Shootings (2017) *Fatal police shootings*. Inquest. https://www.inquest.org.uk/fatal-police-shootings

Posick, C. (2013) The overlap between offending and victimization among adolescents: Results from the second international self-report delinquency study. *Journal of Contemporary Criminal Justice*, 29(1), 106-124.

Potter, G. R. (2008) The growth of cannabis cultivation: Explanations for import substitution in the UK, in D. J. Korf (ed.) *Cannabis in Europe: Dynamics in perception, policy and markets*. Lengerich, Germany: Pabst Science Publishers, 87-105.

Powell, T. (2017) Armed police will no longer be automatically suspended for using their guns. *The Evening Standard*, 7 March. London (UK).

Pozo, A. and Walker, C. (2014) 'UK Armed Forces Charities: An Overview and Analysis', *Directory of Social Change* [online] available at: https://www.dsc.org.uk/wp-content/uploads/2014/09/Sector-Insight-UK-Armed-Forces-Charities.pdf

Precht, T. (2007) *Home grown terrorism and Islamist radicalisation in Europe. From conversion to terrorism.* Danish Ministry of Defence. https://www.scribd.com/document/261299859/Home-Grown-Terrorism-and-Islamist-Radicalisation-in-Europe-An-Assessment-of-Influencing-Factors-2

Prison Reform Trust (2011) *Innocent Until Proven Guilty: Tackling the Overuse of Custodial Remand*. London: Prison Reform Trust.

Prison Reform Trust (2016) *Bromley Briefings Prison Factfile*. London: Prison Reform Trust. http://www.thebromleytrust.org.uk/files/2016factfile.pdf

Prison Reform Trust (2017) *Prison: the facts. Bromley Briefings Summer 2017.*

Prisons and Probation Ombudsman (2013) *Learning from PPO investigations: End of life care, March 2013*. http://www.ppo.gov.uk/app/uploads/2014/07/Learning_from_PPO_investigations_-_End_of_life_care_final_web.pdf

Prisons and Probation Ombudsman (2017) *Learning from PPO investigations: Older Prisoners, June 2017*. http://www.ppo.gov.uk/app/uploads/2017/06/6-3460_PPO_Older-Prisoners_WEB.pdf

Pryce, V. (2013) *Prisonomics*. London: Biteback.

Public Health England (2016a) *Adult substance misuse statistics from the National Drug Treatment Monitoring System (NDTMS)*. London: Public Health England. https://assets.publishing.service.gov.uk/government/uploads/system/uploads/attachment_data/file/658056/Adult-statistics-from-the-national-drug-treatment-monitoring-system-2016-2017.pdf

Public Health England (2016b) *UK Focal Point on Drugs Report*. www.nta.nhs.uk/uploads/2905931ukdrugsituation2016webaccessible.pdf

Public Health England (2017) *Health matters: preventing drug misuse deaths*. https://www.gov.uk/government/publications/health-matters-preventing-drug-misuse-deaths/health-matters-preventing-drug-misuse-deaths

Public Health England (2018) *Alcohol and drug prevention, treatment and recovery: why invest?* https://www.gov.uk/government/publications/alcohol-and-drug-prevention-treatment-and-recovery-why-invest/alcohol-and-drug-prevention-treatment-and-recovery-why-invest

Punch, M. (1979a) *Policing the Inner City*. Amsterdam: Palgrave Macmillan.

Punch, M. (1979b) The Secret Social Service, in S. Holdaway (ed.) *The British Police*. London: Edward Arnold.

R v Angela Bristow, Paul Hayter, Raymond Ryan [2006] EWHC 2674.

Radford, L., Corral, S., Bradley, C., Fisher, H., Bassett, C., Howat, N. and Collishaw, S. (2011) *Child abuse and neglect in the UK today*. London: NSPCC.

Rahman, M. and Lynes, A. (2017) Ride to Die: Understanding Masculine Honour and Collective Identity in the Motorcycle Underworld, *The Howard Journal of Criminal Justice*. Wiley Publications (Under Peer Review).

Raine, A. (2013) *The Anatomy of Violence*. London: Penguin.

Ray, L. (2011) *Violence and Society*. London: Sage.

Reiner, R. (2010) *The Politics of the Police* (4th edn). Oxford: Oxford University Press.

Rentoul, J. (2016) Mea Culpa: Order in court – no gavels. *Independent*, 11th November. https://www.independent.co.uk/voices/mea-culpa-order-in-court-no-gavels-a7411191.html

Rice, M. E. and Harris, G. T. (1991) Firesetters admitted to a maximum security psychiatric institution: offenders and offenses. *Journal of Interpersonal Violence*, 6, 641–75.

Richardson Jr, J. B., St Vil, C. and Cooper, C. (2016) Who Shot Ya? How Emergency Departments Can Collect Reliable Police Shooting Data. *Journal of Urban Health*, 93(S1), 8–31.

Rivito, H. (1987) *The animal estate: the English and other creatures in the Victorian age*. Cambridge, MA: Harvard University Press.

Roberts, J. V. (2008) *Punishing Persistent Offenders: Exploring Community and Offender Perspectives*. Oxford: Oxford University Press.

Robinson, E. (2014) What America's police departments don't want you to know: How many people are killed by police each year? *The Washington Post*, Washington, DC.

Rogers, M. L. and Pridemore, W. A. (2017) Global Patterns and Trends in Homicide, in F. Brookman, E. R. Maguire and M. Maguire (eds) *The Handbook of Homicide*. Chichester, West Sussex: Wiley-Blackwell.

Rojek, C. (2016) Counterfeit commerce; relations of production, distribution and exchange, *Cultural Sociology.* Online First 23 June 2016 doi:10.1177/1749975516650233

Rowe, M. (2006) Following the Leader: Front-Line Narratives on Police Leadership. *Policing: An International Journal of Police Strategies & Management*, 29(4), 757–767.

Rowe, M. (2014) *Introduction to Policing.* London: Sage.

Rowlands, M. (2010a) *UK: New coalition government pledges to 'reverse the substantial erosion of civil liberties and roll-back state intrusion'.* www.statewatch.org/analyses/no–159–coalition-gov-civlibs.pdf

Rowlands, M. (2010b) *Rolling back the authoritarian state? An analysis of the coalition government's commitment to civil liberties.* www.statewatch.org/analyses/no–104–coalition-government-civil-liberties.pdf

Sabur, R. (2017) Abusive husband spared jail amid claims he lied about having a contract as a county cricketer. *The Telegraph*, 27 March. www.telegraph.co.uk/news/2017/03/27/judge-says-wife-forced-drink-bleach-not-vulnerable-has-friends/

Sagan, C. (1980) *Cosmos: A Personal Voyage.* PBS, 28th September.

Salter, M. and Dagistanli, S. (2015) Cultures of abuse: Sex grooming, Organised abuse and race in Rochdale, UK. *International Journal for Crime, Justice and Social Democracy*, 4(2), 50–64.

Sanders, B. and Albanese, F. (2016) *'It's no life at all': Rough sleepers' experiences of violence and abuse on the streets of England and Wales.* London: Crisis.

Sanderson, C. (2008) *Counselling Survivors of Domestic Abuse.* London: Jessica Kingsley Publishers.

Scott, M. (2015) Theresa May wants to ban pleasure. *The Telegraph*, 2 June. www.telegraph.co.uk/news/general-election-2015/politics-blog/11645354/Theresa-May-wants-to-ban-pleasure.html

Scurfield, J., Rees, P. and Norman, P. (2005) Criminal victimisation of the homeless: an investigation of Big Issue vendors in Leeds. *Radical Statistics*, 99, 3-11.

Shalev Greene, K. and Pakes, F. (2013) *Absent: An Exploration of Common Police Procedures for Safeguarding Practices in Cases of Missing Children and Adults*. https://researchportal.port.ac.uk/portal/en/publications/absent(0707093e-d15d-429c-8502-96413427d7b3).html

Shaw, D. (2014) Independent Police Complaints Commission plans overhaul after review. *BBC News*. www.bbc.co.uk/news/uk-26602773

Sidebottom, A., Thornton, A., Tompson, L., Belur, J., Tilley, N. and Bowers, K. (2017) A systematic review of tagging as a method to reduce theft in retail environments. *Crime Science*, 6, 7. DOI: 10.1186/s40163-017-0068-y

Silvestri, M. (2011) *Women in Charge: Policing, Gender and Leadership*. London: Routledge.

Simm, J. (2009) *Punishment and Prisons: Power and the Carceral State*. London: Sage.

Skolnick, J. H. (1975) *Justice Without Trial: Law Enforcement in Democratic Society*. New York: John Wiley & Sons Inc.

Smit, R. P., De Jong, R. R. and Bijleveld, C. J. H. (2012) Homicide Data in Europe: Definitions, Sources, and Statistics, in A. C. M. Liem and W. A. Pridemore (eds) *Handbook of European Homicide Research: Patterns, Explanations and Country Studies*. New York: Springer Science + Business Media.

Smith, R. (2008) Entrepreneurship, Police Leadership, and the Investigation of Crime in Changing Times. *Journal of Investigative Psychology and Offender Profiling*, 5(3), 209-225.

Smithson, H., Ralphs, R. and Williams. P. (2012) Used and Abused: The Problematic Usage of Gang Terminology in the United Kingdom and Its Implications for Ethnic Minority Youth. *British Journal of Criminology*, 53(1), 113-128.

Soothill, K., Ackerley, E. and Francis, B. (2004) The criminal career of arsonists. *Medicine, Science and the Law*, 44, 27-40.

Spalek, B. (2017) (ed.) *Crime Victims: Theory, Policy and Practice*. London: Palgrave Macmillan.

Stanko, S., Gillespie, W. and Crews, G. A. (2004) *Living in Prison: A History of the Correctional System with an Insider's View*. London: Greenwood Press.

Stark, E. (2007) *Coercive Control: How men entrap women in personal life*. New York: Oxford University Press.

Strickland, P. and Allen, G. (2017) *Domestic Violence in England and Wales*, Briefing Paper, June. London: House of Commons Library. http://researchbriefings.files. parliament.uk/documents/SN06337/SN06337.pdf

Summit, R. C. (1983) The child sexual abuse accommodation syndrome. *Child Abuse and Neglect*, 7, 177-193.

Supporting UK Service leavers and their families in the transition to civilian life' (2016) *Rand Europe* [online] available at: https://www.fim-trust.org/wp-content/ uploads/2016/09/Supporting-UK-Service-leavers-and-their-families-in-the-transition-to-civilian-life.pdf

Surette, R. (2015) *Media, Crime, and Criminal Justice*. Stamford: Cengage Learning.

Swaine, J. (2018) Donald Trump's team defends 'alternative facts' after widespread protests. *The Guardian* [online], 23rd January. https://www.theguardian.com/us-news/2017/ jan/22/donald-trump-kellyanne-conway-inauguration-alternative-facts

Swanswell Charitable Trust (2015) *Annual Report 2014–2015*. Coventry: Swanswell Charitable Trust. https:// www.swanswell.org/uploaded_files/1000/images/ Swanswell_annual_report_and_financial_statements_year_ ending_31_March_2015_signed_10_September_2015.pdf

Taylor, E. (2016) Supermarket self-checkouts and retail theft: The curious case of the SWIPERS. *Criminology & Criminal Justice,* 16(5), 552-67.

Taylor, P. and Powell, J. (2017) Corporal Punishment, in J. Turner, P. Taylor, K. Corteen and S. Morley (eds) *A Companion to the History of Crime and Criminal Justice*. Bristol: Policy Press, 43-45.

Telegraph (2014) David Cameron: 'Life should mean life' for prison sentences. *The Telegraph*, 2nd January. https://www.telegraph.co.uk/news/politics/david-cameron/10547103/David-Cameron-Life-should-mean-life-for-prison-sentences.html

Telegraph (2016) Cyber crime: One in 10 people now victim of fraud or online offences, figures show. *The Telegraph*, 21 July. www.telegraph.co.uk/news/2016/07/21/one-in-people-now-victims-of-cyber-crime/

Toshkov, D. (2016) No, Accession to the European Union Does Not Increase the Homicide Rate. *European Sociological Review*, 32(3), 405-410.

Townley. L. and Bewley, S. (2017) *Why the law against female genital mutilation should be scrapped*. London: City University of London. https://www.city.ac.uk/news/2017/november/why-the-law-against-female-genital-mutilation-should-be-scrapped

Transition Mapping Study (2013) *Forces In Mind Trust*. https://www.fim-trust.org/wp-content/uploads/2015/01/20130810-TMS-Report.pdf

Travis, A. (2010) Howard is right: 'prison works' – but this is no way to cut crime. *The Guardian*, 7 December. https://www.theguardian.com/society/2010/dec/07/michael-howard-prison-works-analysis

Travis, A. (2014) Two companies to run more than half of privatised probation services. *The Guardian*, 29 October. https://www.theguardian.com/uk-news/2014/oct/29/justice-probation-contracts-private-companies

Travis, A. (2018) Offender tagging scheme is 'catastrophic waste of public money', *The Guardian*, 24 January. https://www.theguardian.com/society/2018/jan/24/offender-tagging-scheme-is-catastrophic-waste-of-public-money

Treadwell, J. (2012) From the car boot to booting it up? eBay, online counterfeit crime and the transformation of the criminal marketplace. *Criminology and Criminal Justice*, 12(2), 175-192.

Treadwell, J. (2016) The Forces in the Firing Line? Social Policy and the 'Acceptable Face' of Violent Criminality, in R. McGarry and S. Walklate (eds) *The Palgrave Handbook of Criminology and War*. London: Palgrave Macmillan.

Treadwell, J. and Gooch, K. (2015) An ASBO for violent gangsters or just continuing criminalisation of young people? – Thinking about the value of the 'Gangbo'. In *Papers from the British Criminology Conference*, 15, 60-76.

Turner, J. (2012) Ordinary Female Offenders: Stafford Borough, 1880-1905. *Crime, Histoire and Sociétiés / Crime, History and Societies.* 16(2), 55-78.

Tyler, L. and King, L. (2000) Arming a traditionally disarmed police: an examination of police use of CS gas in the UK. *Policing: An International Journal of Police Strategies & Management*, 23(3), 390-400.

UK Drug Policy Commission (2008) *Reducing Drug Use, Reducing Reoffending*. London: UK Drug Policy Commission. www.ukdpc.org.uk/wp-content/uploads/Policy%20report%20-%20Reducing%20drug%20use,%20reducing%20reoffending%20(summary).pdf

Ullman, S. (2003) A critical review of field studies on the link of alcohol and adult sexual assault in women. *Aggression and Violent Behavior*, 8(5), 471-486. doi:10.1016/s1359-1789(03)00032-6

United Nations Office on Drugs and Crime (UNODC) (2009) *Global Report On Trafficking In Persons Executive Summary UNODC. Human Trafficking Indicators.* https://www.unodc.org/pdf/HT_indicators_E_LOWRES.pdf

United Nations Office on Drugs and Crime (UNODC) (2013) *Global Study on Homicide 2013: Trends, Contexts, Data.* https://www.unodc.org/documents/gsh/pdfs/2014_GLOBAL_HOMICIDE_BOOK_web.pdf

United Nations Office on Drugs and Crime (UNODC) (2015) *Homicide Statistics, Crime and Criminal Justice.* http://www.unodc.org/unodc/en/data-and-analysis/statistics.html

United Nations Office on Drugs and Crime (UNODC) (n.d.) *Focus On: The Illicit Trafficking of Counterfeit Goods and Transnational Organised Crime,* United Nations Office on Drugs and Crime. www.unodc.org/documents/counterfeit/FocusSheet/Counterfeit_focussheet_EN_HIRES.pdf

Vagg, J. and Harris, J. (1998) Bad goods: Product counterfeiting and enforcement strategies, in M. Gill (ed.) *Crime at Work Vol. 2: Increasing the Risk for Offenders.* Virginia: Perpetuity.

van Ours, J. and Vollaard, B. (2016) The Engine Immobiliser: A Non-starter for Car Thieves, *The Economic Journal*, 126, 1264-1291. DOI: 10.111/ecoj.12196.

Wacquant, L. (2009) *Punishing the Poor: The Neoliberal Government of Social Insecurity.* Durham, NC: Duke University Press.

Waddington, P. A. (1999a) *Policing Citizens: Authority and Rights.* London: Routledge.

Waddington, P. A. J. (1999b) Police (canteen) sub-culture. An appreciation. *British Journal of Criminology*, 39(2), 287-309.

Waldron, B. (2017) Five arrested during Staffordshire Police operation to crack down on drug abuse. *Burton Mail,* 28 July. www.burtonmail.co.uk/news/local-news/five-arrested-during-staffordshire-police-243378

Walker, C. (2011) *Terrorism and the Law.* Oxford: Oxford University Press.

Walker, L. E. (1979) *The Battered Woman.* New York: Harper & Row, Publishers.

Walker, L. E. (1984) *The Battered Woman Syndrome.* New York: Springer Publishing Company.

Wall, D. (1998) *The Chief Constables of England and Wales: The Socio-Legal History of a Criminal Justice Elite.* Aldershot: Ashgate.

Wall, D. (2007) *Cybercrime.* Cambridge: Polity.

Walters, G. D. (2014) *Drugs, Crime and their Relationships: theory, research, practice and policy.* Burlington, MA: Jones & Bartlett.

Walters, G. D., Knight, R. A., Grann, M. and Dahle, K. P. (2008) Incremental validity of the Psychopathy Checklist facet scores: predicting release outcome in six samples. *Journal of Abnormal Psychology,* 117(2), 396.

Walters, M. and Brown, R. (2016) *Preventing Hate Crime: Emerging Practices and Recommendations for the Improved Management of Criminal Justice Interventions.* Manchester: Equality and Human Rights Commission.

Walters, M. A. (2014) *Hate Crime and Restorative Justice: Exploring Causes, Repairing Harms.* Oxford: Oxford University Press.

Ward, J. (2014) *Are problem-solving courts the way forward for justice?* London: Howard League for Penal Reform.

Ware, S. (2014) A 20th Century Debate About Imprisonment for Debt. *American Journal of Legal History,* 54(3), 351-377.

Weeks, J. (1989) *The Regulation of Sexuality since 1800* (2nd edn). London: Longman Group Ltd.

Weitzer, R. (2002) Incidents of police misconduct and public opinion. *Journal of Criminal Justice*, 30(5), 397–408.

Welsh Government (2017) *Deliberate fires 2015–16: Statistical Bulletin*. Welsh Government. https://gov.wales/docs/statistics/2017/170228-deliberate-fires-2015-16-en.pdf

Werner, R. (2014) Can Banks Individually Create Money out of Nothing? *International Review of Financial Analysis*, 36(1), 1–19.

White, J. (2016) *Mansions of Misery: A Biography of the Marshalsea Debtors' Prison* (Kindle edn). London: Vintage.

Wilkinson, R. and Pickett, K. (2010) *The Spirit Level: Why Equality is Better for Everyone*. London: Penguin.

Williams, M. L. and Tregidga, J. (2013) *All Wales Hate Crime Research Project: Research Overview and Executive Summary*. Cardiff: Race Equality First.

Williams, M. L. and Tregidga, J. (2014) Hate crime victimization in Wales: Psychological and physical impacts across seven hate crime victim types. *British Journal of Criminology*, 54(4), 946–967.

Williams, P. and Clarke, R. (2016) *Dangerous associations: Joint enterprise, gangs and racism*. Centre for Crime and Justice Studies. https://www.crimeandjustice.org.uk/publications/dangerous-associations-joint-enterprise-gangs-and-racism

Williams, P., Kinsella, R. and Crossley, C. (2013) Gang and Youth Violence in Manchester City: revisiting the problem profile. Unpublished report, Manchester City Violent Gangs Board: Office of the Police and Crime Commissioner.

Wilson, D. (2007) *Serial Killers: Hunting Britons and Their Victims 1960-2006*. Winchester: Waterside Press.

Wilson, D. (2009) *A History of British Serial Killing*. London: Sphere.

Wilson, D. and Rahman, M. (2015) Becoming a Hitman. *The Howard Journal of Criminal Justice*. Wiley Publications. 54 (3) 250-264. DOI:10.1111/hojo.12126.

Wilson, D., Yardley, E. and Lynes, A. (2015) *Serial Killers and the Phenomenon of Serial Murder: A Student Textbook.* Hook: Waterside Press.

Wilson, J. M. and Fenoff, R. (2014), Distinguishing Counterfeit from Authentic Product Retailers in the Virtual Marketplace. *International Criminal Justice Review,* 24(1), 39-58.

Wing, N. (2017) The Exhaustive List of Everyone who's died of a Marijuana Overdose. *Huff Post*, 20 April. www.huffingtonpost.co.uk/entry/marijuana-lethal dose_us_58f4ec07e4b0b9e9848d6297

Winlow, S., Hobbs, D., Lister, S. and Hadfield, P. (2001) Get ready to duck. Bouncers and the realities of ethnographic research on violent groups. *British Journal of Criminology*, 41(3), 536-548.

Winstock, A. (2017) Why better quality/higher purity cocaine is not always good for your health, *Global Drugs Survey*, 22 May. https://www.globaldrugsurvey.com/why-better-quality-higher-purity-cocaine-is-not-always-better-for-your-health/

Wiredgov (2013) IPCC refers James Herbert investigation to Crown Prosecution Service.

Wolf, R. V. (2007) *Principles of Problem Solving Justice.* Center for Court Innovation, New York: Bureau of Justice Assistance.

Wolitzky-Taylor, K., Resnick, H., McCauley, J., Amstadter, A., Kilpatrick, D. and Ruggiero, K.G. (2015) *Women's Aid: What is domestic abuse?* https://www.ncbi.nlm.nih.gov/pubmed/20522886

Women's Aid (2015) *Annual Survey 2015.* London: Women's Aid, https://1q7dqy2unor827bqjls0c4rn-wpengine.netdna-ssl.com/wp-content/uploads/2015/08/Womens-Aid-Annual-Survey-2015-public-report-F.pdf

Woolmingt. n v DPP (1935) *UKHL 1,* 23rd May, House of Lords from BAILII.

World Heath Organisation (2008) *Eliminating Female Genital Mutilation: An Interagency Statement.* Switzerland: World Health Organisation.

Yakowicz, W. (2017) Illegal Pot Sales Topped $46.4 Billion in 2016, *Inc.* https://www.inc.com/will-yakowicz/marijuana-sales-2016-50-billion.html

Yar, M. (2013) *Cybercrime and society.* London: Sage.

Yardley, E. (2017) *Social Media Homicide Confessions: Stories of killers and their victims.* Bristol: Policy Press.

Yen, I. (2008) Of vice & men: a new approach to eradicating sex trafficking by reducing male demand through educational programs & abolitionist legislation. *Journal of Criminal Law & Criminology.* 98(2), 653–86.

Young, J. (1999) *The Exclusive Society: Social Exclusion, Crime and Difference in Late Modernity.* London: Sage Publications.

Zedner, L. (2000) The Pursuit of Security, in T. Hope and R. Sparks (eds) *Crime, Risk and Insecurity.* London: Routledge.

Index